Effective Teaching
Schools

Chris Kyriacou

Basil Blackwell

Published by Basil Blackwell Ltd
108 Cowley Road
Oxford OX4 1JF
England

British Library Cataloguing in Publication Data

Kyriacou, Chris
    Effective teaching in schools.
    1. Teaching
    I. Title
    371.1'02   LB102S.2

ISBN 0–631–15132–X

Typeset in 10 on 12pt Sabon by Freeman Graphic, Tonbridge
Printed in Great Britain

Contents

For Christine and Helen

Acknowledgements

The author is grateful to the following for permission to include copyright material:
Cambridge University Press for the quotation from Ball (1981) *Beachside Comprehensive*, p. 47. Carfax for the quotation from McNamara's (1980) paper in the *British Educational Research Journal*, vol 6, p. 115. The Controller of Her Majesty's Stationery Office for the quotations from DES (1985) *Better Schools*, p. 55; DES (1985) *Science 5–16*, pp. 8–9; HMI (1979) *Aspects of Secondary Education in England*, pp. 83, 95; HMI (1982) *The New Teacher in School*, pp. 7, 17, 18; HMI (1985) *The Curriculum from 5 to 16*, pp. 22, 40–41 and 49–50; HMI (1985) *Education Observed 3: Good Teachers*, pp. 3, 4; the Cockcroft Report (1982) *Mathematics Counts*, p. 72; the Swann Report (1985) *Education for All*, p. 28; and from the Warnock Report (1978) Special Educational Needs, p. 41. Croom Helm for the quotations from Galloway (1985) *Schools, Pupils and Special Educational Needs*, pp. 98–99 and 104–105. Falmer Press for the quotations from Davies' (1984) paper in Ball (ed) *Comprehensive Schooling: A Reader*, p. 63; and from Grace's (1984) paper in Broadfoot (ed) *Selection, Certification and Control*, p. 110. Heinemann Educational Books for the quotations from Buckley's (1980) paper in Best *et al* (eds) *Perspectives on Pastoral Care*, p. 183 (including author's permission); and from Marland (1975) *The Craft of the Classroom*, p. 18. Holt, Rinehart and Winston for the quotation from Calderhead (1984) *Teachers' Classroom Decision-Making*, p. 74. Lawrence Erlbaum Associates for the quotation from Bennett *et al* (1984) *The Quality of Pupil Learning Experiences*, p. 213. Open Books for the quotation from Rutter *et al* (1979) *Fifteen Thousand Hours*, p. 139 Penguin Books for the quotation from Bernstein's (1970) paper in Rubinstein and Stoneman (eds) *Education for Democracy*, p. 120. Routledge and Kegan Paul for the quotations from Hargreaves (1967) *Social Relations in a Secondary School*, p. 169; and from Hargreaves (1982) *The Challenge for the Comprehensive School*, p. 17.

1 Introduction

This book aims to draw attention to those aspects of teaching and learning in schools which are important for the effectiveness of the educational experience which the teacher provides.

A central task of teacher education is to foster the development of teachers who are able to reflect critically on and evaluate their own teaching. My own teaching within teacher education has been mainly in the area of the psychology of education. What has struck me about the books currently available to those interested in effective teaching is that they largely fall into two camps. Some specifically concern themselves with common-sense observations largely based on the professional experiences of the writers: often termed 'craft knowledge'. Others concern themselves with the presentation and discussion of theories and research which stem from a parent discipline such as psychology or sociology. Such books do not satisfactorily serve the needs of teacher development as described above. The former camp, while often giving good advice, does not provide the necessary framework of understanding which enables teachers to teach effectively. The danger of following advice is that it encourages an attempt to model one's practice upon some envisaged image of teaching – which does little to help one deal with the variety of classroom situations and experiences which occur. Writers in the latter camp tend to cover the theories and research in a way which appears to meet the needs of other theorists and researchers, or those following academically based courses, rather than the needs of those concerned to develop their own teaching effectiveness.

It seems particularly disappointing that the psychology of education has not been able to make as useful a contribution to effective teaching in schools as it might. This is perhaps because writers in this field have not entirely taken on board the need of teachers to develop their effectiveness at the expense of academic concerns. I believe the main contribution which the psychology of education can make to the development of effective teaching is by clarifying how far sound craft knowledge is actually based on aspects of the psychology of teaching and learning. However, it needs to do this not by introducing the theoretical and research base of such psychology; but rather by emphasising the basic underlying psychological principles and considerations involved – at a level of discussion appropriate to the ways in which teachers think about their own teaching, from which craft knowledge is deduced.

The central need is to sharpen craft knowledge through clarification of the psychological considerations involved, but to do this in a way that *strengthens* craft knowledge rather than attempts to undermine it. One cannot expect teachers to be continually switching from craft knowledge to psychological considerations which are different in kind. Rather, a sound craft knowledge should incorporate only those psychological considerations which directly contribute to it, considerations which teachers bring to bear on thinking about their teaching as they teach, or on their planning.

This book thus explicitly attempts to bridge the gap between craft knowledge and discipline based considerations (often discussed as the gap between theory and practice). It aims to contribute to the development of effective teaching by identifying the considerations, and their inter-relationships, which are utilised by teachers in establishing and maintaining the effectiveness of an educational experience. To achieve this aim, it is important to make clear the considerations and practices which appear to be the essence of effective teaching. Much of what is considered here is derived from craft knowledge. Likewise much is derived from discipline based perspectives, most notably psychology. However, it is the attempt to link these considerations together in a way that informs the teacher's own reflection on teaching that is the paramount theme of this book.

The last few years have seen an increasing amount of discussion about effective teaching among teachers, teacher educators and researchers. The debate among teachers has been largely in response to moves by the Department of Education and Science (DES) towards requiring the regular and systematic appraisal of classroom teaching, coupled with a series of publications by the DES and HMI concerning curriculum developments which call for changes in traditional teaching methods and learning experiences. Such developments go beyond simply requiring teachers to take stock of their current practices. Rather, they are pointers to the kind of changes the DES regards as desirable. Some of these are clearly embodied in a number of recent curriculum developments.

The debate among teacher educators has focused upon the attempt to identify those essential teaching skills or competencies that should be fostered during initial teacher training and later in-service courses. Such discussion has been in part derived from widespread developments along these lines in the United States.

The debate among researchers has largely reflected a quickening of interest in effective teaching since the late 1960s. This stems from understanding gained by close observation of the classroom and from an awareness of the need to consider the perceptions of both teachers and pupils regarding classroom tasks and interactions. Research into effective teaching now largely focuses on exploring the inter-relationships between three main elements:

1   Teacher perceptions and strategies
2   Pupil perceptions and strategies
3   Characteristics of the learning task, activities and experience.

In research on effective teaching based on a psychological perspective, prominence is now widely given to the notion of matching the learning experience to the pupil's psychological state (notably in terms of previous understanding and motivation) at the time.

These three parallel debates (among teachers, teacher educators and researchers) make this a particularly exciting time at which to explore the basis of effective teaching in schools, and these debates will surface periodically throughout this book.

In choosing the theme for each chapter, I have been very conscious of the extent to which each theme seems to relate to and touch upon considerations explored in other sections. Such is inevitably the nature of effective teaching: a complex inter-relationship of a number of different concerns each impinging on each other to greater or lesser extents. Nevertheless, I have attempted to focus on themes which appear to me to be the most crucial ones in achieving the aims outlined above.

Chapter 2 *Ways of thinking about effective teaching* considers the three main approaches to looking at effective teaching. The first approach focuses on two central concepts: 'active learning time' and 'quality of instruction'. The former is concerned with the amount of time pupils spend during a lesson (or while at school) actively engaged in learning experiences related to the educational outcomes intended. The latter refers to characteristics of the teaching related to the educational outcomes intended. These two concepts have dominated research on effective teaching in the United States for the last two decades. A large number of studies have attempted to itemise all those aspects of a teacher's classroom behaviour which appear to be associated with maximising pupils' active learning time, or with gains in the educational outcomes intended.

The second approach focuses on teaching as an essentially managerial activity, and has sought to identify central teaching skills or competencies which underlie effective teaching.

The third approach focuses on the key psychological concepts, principles and processes which would appear to be involved when effective teaching is taking place. This approach places emphasis on the pupil's psychological state and how it relates to the success or failure of an educational activity.

In chapter 3 *How pupils learn* the nature of pupil learning itself is explored, and particular attention is paid to those psychological factors involved which were introduced in the previous chapter. Some of what is discussed here has been drawn from attempts to develop a psychology of instruction. This chapter focuses on three aspects which appear to be crucial for learning: the pupil must be *attending* to the learning experience, the pupil must be *receptive* to the learning experience, and the learning experience must be *appropriate* for the desired learning to take place.

In chapter 4 *Setting up the learning experience* the different ways in which teachers can set up educational experiences are considered. One of the things that has most impressed me about teaching and learning in schools has been the large number of teachers who have employed a diversity of approaches to make a learning experience as educationally successful as possible. Too many books on effective teaching have taken a narrow view of proper classroom-based activities in considering relative effectiveness. Much of the most inspiring teaching involves approaches which place emphasis on the pupil being more active and having greater control over the learning experience. Such approaches include experiential learning based on role play or simulation, or collaborative learning based on pupils working together without the direct involvement of the teacher. Such developments can also play an important part in making the more traditional approaches to teaching as successful as possible.

Chapter 5 *Taking account of pupil differences* discusses the implications for effective teaching of the variety of differences between pupils that have a bearing on teaching and learning. The list of such differences could be very long indeed. However, I have chosen what would appear to be the most important ones: ability; motivation; social class; gender; race; and special educational needs. In considering differences between pupils, it is interesting to note the inter-relationships between such categorisations. More importantly, in attempting to consider the implications for particular categories of pupils, it very often becomes apparent that the issues and strategies raised are relevant and appropriate for *all* pupils. For example, when considering the specialised needs of 'gifted children' the central problem appears to be how to keep such pupils interested and stretched by the learning activities provided. In meeting their needs, it is clear that the same needs, and the possible response to them by teachers, could be relevant to all the pupils in the school.

The first half of chapter 6 *Key classroom teaching qualities and tasks* attempts to identify the essential qualities of effective teaching. The discussion here stems from the work of others who have sought to identify key teaching skills or competencies, and from recent studies of my own in this area. It is often claimed that it is easy to recognise good teaching when you see it, but few would claim that it is equally easy to break down such a global assessment into its constituent parts. This problem largely results from the fact that different observers actually mean different things by the notion of good teaching. Moreover, what a particular observer has in mind can usually be achieved in a number of different ways. Nevertheless, when one looks at the discussion of such qualities within the context of teacher education, the essential qualities appear to rest on a fair degree of consensus. Thus the agenda of such qualities seems to be fairly clear, but it has been obscured by differences in preferred headings and the relative weight of emphasis advocated by different writers. The issues raised however, appear to be more common than such differences would indicate.

In the second half of chapter 6, attention moves towards considering the key tasks underpinning effective teaching in the classroom. These tasks can best be considered under three main headings: *Planning, Presentation and monitoring* and *Reflection and evaluation*. These three areas cover aspects of effective teaching based on sound decision-making before, during and after the lesson. The first area deals with questions borne in mind by a teacher when considering the basic format of a learning activity and its content; the second deals with the way the teacher needs to monitor the progress of a lesson and to decide upon the actions necessary to establish and maintain its effectiveness; the third deals with the need to evaluate the success of a lesson and reflect on the implications for future teaching.

Teacher decision-making has recently become an area of attention in its own right as a result of the importance now attached to considering teachers' aims, perceptions and strategies during a lesson. What is often unnerving for student teachers is the number of questions which teachers appear to have to bear in mind while a lesson is in progress, as well as the moment-to-moment decisions they need to make. In a sense, the act of teaching is rather like that of conducting an orchestra where one needs to keep all the separate trains of music in synchrony. Such sensitivity by a teacher to the progress of a lesson would appear to be one of the most crucial aspects of effective teaching.

In chapter 7 *Relationships with pupils* it is argued that a sound relationship between teacher and pupils needs to be based on two qualities: the pupils' acceptance of the teacher's authority, and the establishment of mutual respect and rapport between the teacher and pupils. The development of these two qualities is discussed in the first half of the chapter. The discussion of the teacher's authority looks at the ways in which a teacher establishes and maintains the necessary order and discipline required for effective learning activities to take place. Much has been written and said about discipline in schools, and the need to establish classroom order is seen by many to be the first task of effective teaching, particularly by student teachers. I would argue here, however, that discipline is not something established separate from or in parallel with effective teaching. Rather, good discipline should be a natural consequence of effective teaching. The first task of effective teaching is good presentation of the appropriate learning activity. Pupil misbehaviour should initially point towards a diagnosis of teaching rather than of disciplinary techniques. In essence, the key to establishing authority lies in successfully keeping control over pupils' behaviour during the lesson by maintaining their engagement in the academic demands made upon them. The techniques involved are based on an assumption that the teacher's authority should be taken for granted rather than existing in the exercise of power by recourse to reprimands and punishments. Establishing this type of authority is inextricably bound up with establishing mutual respect and rapport with pupils. The importance of this cannot be over-estimated if a sound teacher–pupil relationship conducive to pupil learning is to be sustained.

In the second half of this chapter, two aspects of effective teaching which underpin sound teacher–pupil relationships are considered. The first of these is the classroom climate. This concerns the emotional tone established in the classroom. Particular attention here is paid to the way teachers and pupils use language in the classroom and respond to each other's use of language. In recent years it has become increasingly clear how the teacher's use of language conveys much more than the simple content of what is said. The teacher's language conveys – through the types of phrases used, its tone, and how and when it is used – a whole range of messages to pupils about the teacher's perceptions and expectations regarding teaching and learning. What is now apparent is that pupils pick up such messages with great sophistication, and often with consequences that the teacher may be unaware of and not intend.

This increasing awareness of the subtleties of teacher–pupil communication has followed in the wake of studies which involved close classroom observation. All learning situations have an important emotional aspect for pupils which can facilitate or hinder learning. To see the success of a learning activity as being solely dependent on its intellectual demands would be entirely mistaken and even dangerous.

The intensity of the emotional reaction of pupils to failure has been well documented. At the heart of effective teaching must be the ability of the teacher to create the right emotional climate and tone for the lesson, which will enable pupils to engage appropriately in the mental attitude required for learning to take place satisfactorily. Such concerns are implicitly linked to pastoral care, and as such, a discussion of the teacher's pastoral care responsibilities forms the second aspect of effective teaching, underpinning sound teacher–pupil relationships, that completes the chapter.

Chapter 8 *Dealing with pupil misbehaviour* explicitly focuses attention on the major strategies and techniques which may be employed to deal effectively with pupil misbehaviour. After considering the nature and causes of pupil misbehaviour and the strategies which can be used to preempt its occurrence, it goes on to examine the use of reprimands and punishments, and the qualities which will increase the likelihood of their being effective. Two particular issues are then considered: how to deal effectively with confrontations; and the role of pastoral care and school policy in relation to exercising discipline. Finally, the behaviour modification approach to dealing with pupil misbehaviour is outlined and the benefits derived from considering this approach are discussed.

In chapter 9 *Three professional concerns* three major professional concerns facing teachers are discussed: the curriculum, teacher appraisal, and teacher stress. Each of these concerns warrants attention in a proper consideration of effective teaching. In considering the curriculum, there is a clear need for teachers to step back somewhat from the immediate tasks of teaching, and to address some wider considerations. All too often effective teaching is characterised as the competence to achieve one's desired educational outcomes. Such a narrow viewpoint can easily lead one to take the teacher's intentions for a lesson as a given and acceptable starting point for the analysis of effectiveness. By stepping back somewhat, it is possible to consider whether the aims, content, learning activities, methods of assessment and feedback employed are actually in line with the most important educational outcomes advocated by a wider audience.

In looking at teacher appraisal I consider current developments in this area, with particular emphasis on the appraisal of classroom teaching. While self-appraisal is an important aspect of teachers' ability to continue to develop and improve their classroom teaching, the introduction of formal and systematic schemes of appraisal involves a number of dangers. To the extent that such schemes can foster and support the professional development of teachers' classroom performance, then they can make an important contribution to effective teaching in schools. However, if such schemes become explicitly assessment-oriented and inspectorial in tone, they could easily do more harm than good.

In considering teacher stress, I discuss the sources of stress facing teachers and the ways in which teachers can cope with stress. Since the mid-1970s, when I first started conducting research into stress among schoolteachers, there has been a marked increase in general awareness and public debate concerning this aspect of teaching. There are a number of aspects of the teacher's professional responsibilities which make occasional stress almost inevitable for the vast majority of teachers: dealing with difficult pupils and colleagues; time pressures; attempting to maintain standards; difficult working conditions ... For some teachers experiencing high levels of stress is a major problem. Experiencing extreme stress over a prolonged period is likely to have a damaging effect on teachers' commitment and enthusiasm towards teaching and may well, in consequence, undermine aspects of their effectiveness. Much stress however, can be dealt with – or at least mitigated in its effects – by the use of appropriate coping actions by teachers. The school can also do much to help, through the support offered by colleagues and by the organisational and management practices it adopts.

The final chapter *Conclusions* reflects on the various themes that have been developed and an attempt is made to consider where the future priorities lie in fostering effective teaching in schools.

2 Ways of thinking about effective teaching

Effective teaching is essentially concerned with how best to bring about the desired pupil learning by some educational activity. Over the years, thinking about effective teaching has been approached in a number of different ways.

Until the 1960s research on effective teaching was largely dominated by attempts to identify attributes of teachers, such as personality traits, sex, age, knowledge and training, which might have a bearing on their effectiveness. As long ago as 1931, for example, Cattell asked 254 people, including directors of education, teacher trainers, schoolteachers and pupils, to 'write down the ten most important traits of the good mature teacher, the ten most important qualities of the good young teacher, and the qualities which normally distinguish the young male from the young female teacher'. Overall, he found that the five qualities of the good teacher most frequently reported were (in order of frequency): 'personality and will', 'intelligence', 'sympathy and tact', 'open-mindedness' and a 'sense of humour'.

Studies which attempted to relate such teacher attributes to educational outcomes have been labelled 'black-box' research (McNamara, 1980) – the metaphor of the black box being applied to the classroom. The point being made was that such research on effective teaching almost completely ignored what might be going on in the classroom.

Since the 1960s, however, research on effective teaching has focused fairly and squarely on activities in the classroom; in particular on the interaction between teacher and pupils. As a result, in thinking about effective teaching there is now a reasonable consensus about a basic framework, within which we can usefully distinguish between three classes of variables (Figure 1).

Context variables refer to all those characteristics of the context of the learning activity, usually a classroom-based lesson, which may have some bearing on the success of the learning activity. Such variables may cover teacher characteristics (eg age, experience); pupil characteristics (eg age, ability); class characteristics (eg size, social class mix); subject characteristics (eg subject matter, level of difficulty); school characteristics (eg ethos, facilities); community characteristics (eg affluence, population density); and characteristics of the occasion (eg time of day, preceding lesson).

Figure 1 A basic framework for thinking about effective teaching

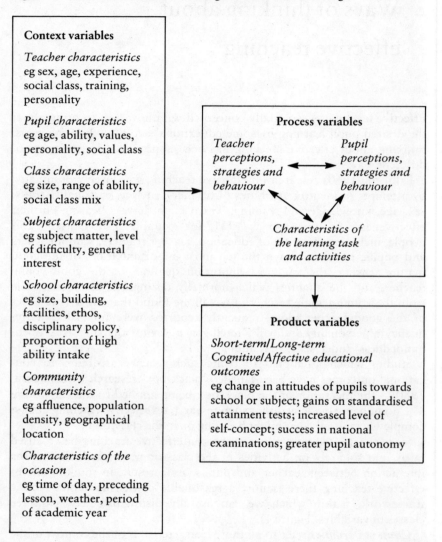

Process variables refer to all those characteristics of teacher and pupil behaviour and of the learning task and activities which take place in the classroom and which may have some bearing on the success of the learning activity. Such variables include teacher's enthusiasm; clarity; use of questions; use of praise and criticism; use of non-verbal communication; management strategies; disciplinary techniques; classroom climate;

organisation of the lesson; suitability of learning tasks; type of feedback pupils receive; pupil involvement in the lesson; pupil-initiated interaction with the teacher; and pupils' strategies for learning. This list is by no means exhaustive!

Product variables refer to all those educational outcomes which are desired by teachers and which have formed the basis of either teachers' planning of the learning activities and/or of objectives or criteria which can be used to consider and monitor effectiveness. The most important educational outcomes would appear to be increased knowledge and skills; increased interest in the subject or topic; increased intellectual motivation; increased academic self-confidence and self-esteem; increased development of pupil autonomy; and increased social development. Many of these outcomes can be translated into variables based on tests, such as external national examinations and attitude tests; other variables are based on more subjective forms of assessment, such as a teacher's opinion.

Conceptual and research problems

This overall framework of *Context–Process–Product* has provided the basis for almost all research on effective teaching reported over the last few decades, although it has been elaborated in a number of different ways (see Bennett, 1976, 1978; Centra and Potter, 1980; Haertel *et al.*, 1983; Kyriacou, 1985; Kyriacou and Newson, 1982; Rutter *et al.*, 1979; Winne and Marx, 1977). Such research has raised a number of very important points concerning both our understanding of these three classes of variables and how research can obtain some evidence of the contribution made to effectiveness by different aspects of the teaching situation (eg Child, 1986).

In considering context variables, it is clear that there are a vast number of aspects to the context of a teaching situation which may have a bearing on its success. The variety of ways in which these aspects can be combined to define a particular context in detail is enormous.

The context for teaching in schools can range from a lesson based on topic work for a mixed ability class in a small rural primary school to a lesson in chemistry for a top set group of fifth-year pupils in a large urban comprehensive school. A major task facing a teacher is in deciding which aspects of the context need to be taken into account when considering the appropriate learning activity. Clearly this variety of teaching contexts creates problems for research: not only does it mean that each study undertaken can only take account of a few aspects of the context at any one time; but also evidence has been generated indicating that one aspect of a context can have a different influence on effectiveness, depending on which other aspects of the context are also present. Thus, for example, size of school may have a different effect within an affluent community than within a community containing much poverty.

In considering process variables, again it is clear that there are a large number of aspects of classroom activities which may be related to effectiveness. In addition, a number of problems have been posed for researchers in considering how best to identify, monitor and record the various aspects of teacher and pupil behaviour and the learning activities. The use of questionnaires, interviews and classroom observation (whether using recording schedules or using participant observation techniques) all have research problems (Kyriacou and Newson, 1982). Nevertheless, since the 1960s, studies of effective teaching do seem to have clarified the basic nature of the many process variables involved in teaching, ranging from very discrete observable behaviours (such as frequency of teacher–pupil eye-contact, and proportion of time spent by teachers talking to the class as a whole) to more global and more subjectively assessed qualities (such as teacher clarity, and classroom ethos).

Recent research has emphasised the importance of looking at the *meaning* of classroom activities for pupils and teachers. Attention has been focused on looking at teachers' and pupils' perceptions and strategies, in order to explore the importance of teacher and pupil behaviour and the classroom activities for effectiveness. Thus, in looking at process variables, we need to keep in mind the important distinction between these three main aspects of the teaching situation: 'teacher perceptions, strategies and behaviour', 'pupil perceptions, strategies and behaviour' and 'characteristics of the learning task and activities' (see Figure 1). This is an important point: to understand the influence of various process variables for effectiveness, we need to consider and take account of how these three main aspects of the teaching situation influence each other and not attempt to see each process variable as one which somehow acts in isolation from everything else going on in the classroom. This consideration will be clarified later in this chapter; in many respects it is one of the most important implicit themes which runs through the whole book.

In considering product variables, one comes to the 64 000 dollar question: what is meant by effective teaching? At the outset of this chapter I stated that effective teaching is essentially concerned with how best to bring about the desired pupil learning by some educational activity. The problem which follows, however, is that there is very little consensus concerning the relative importance of the different educational outcomes which are taken to be the goals of effective teaching, some of which were listed earlier. These goals may emphasise *cognitive* (intellectual) aspects of learning or *affective* (social and emotional) aspects of learning; they may emphasise short-term goals (achievable by the end of the lesson) or long-term goals (achievable at the end of a course or even later); they may be amenable to objective monitoring and assessment or they may involve subjective monitoring and assessment – if assessment be possible at all (see Figure 1).

In listing what appear to be the most important educational outcomes as I did earlier in this chapter, there is a further difficulty. We must take into account the fact that teachers almost invariably appear to teach with a combination of outcomes in mind. This combination of outcomes may vary in importance to the teacher from lesson to lesson, or vary in importance within a lesson. It may also vary in importance when the teacher considers one pupil or group of pupils rather than another pupil or group of pupils. At any moment during a lesson, the teacher is thus attempting to take account of a whole range of goals, with a different emphasis placed on each of them. For example, in dealing with one pupil's answer to a question, the teacher may take into account that particular pupil's lack of self-confidence, and thus the teacher may well behave towards that pupil quite differently than towards another answering the same question. Such teacher behaviour may even appear to an observer to be out of keeping with the apparent emphasis on other outcomes in the lesson when it is assessed as a whole.

Such variation in emphasis is also compounded by the lack of consensus among teachers (not to mention others with an interest in the proceedings such as pupils, parents, educationists, and policy makers) on the aims of education and schooling and the relative emphasis that should be placed on the different educational outcomes deemed to be of importance.

Bennett (1976) for example, in his much publicised study which compared the relative effectiveness of 'formal' and 'informal' teaching styles in the primary school, used a postal questionnaire survey to obtain responses from nearly 800 primary school teachers regarding nine teaching aims. The teachers were asked to rate each aim on a five-point scale of importance which ranged from 'not important' to 'essential'. One aim, 'the acquisition of basic skills in reading and number work', received markedly more ratings as 'essential' (81 per cent of the sample) than the other eight; this was followed by 'the acceptance of normal standards of behaviour' (46 per cent), 'helping pupils to cooperate with each other' (34 per cent), 'an understanding of the world in which pupils live' (32 per cent) and 'the enjoyment of school' (31 per cent). Interestingly, there was a noticeable divergence of opinion regarding the aim 'preparation for academic work in secondary school', with 10 per cent rating this 'essential' and 7 per cent rating this 'not important' (with the remaining 83 per cent spread across the other three response categories). It is also interesting to note that the aim with the lowest rating as 'essential' was 'the promotion of a high level of academic attainment' (4 per cent). This would seem to be surprising, given that skills in reading and number work received the highest rating. Bennett, however, interprets this as indicating that while teachers stress the need for basic skills, the general emphasis is on social and moral, rather than intellectual, development. In looking at these teaching aims, it is immediately apparent that some are very difficult to translate into product variables which could be monitored and assessed.

In a recent study (Kyriacou, 1982), I focused attention on 'O' level teaching, in an attempt to clarify the relative importance teachers might attach to different criteria as indicative of effective teaching for a particular level of teaching and academic attainment. The study involved a postal questionnaire which was completed by 142 comprehensive school heads of departments in four subject areas: biology, English, geography and mathematics. The teachers were asked to rate each of five criteria 'as a criterion for the effectiveness of teaching your subject at 'O' level' on a four-point scale labelled from 'not important as a criterion' to 'an extremely important criterion' (scored 1 to 4 respectively). The mean score of the rating for each subject area group is shown in Table 1. As can be seen, there were a number of differences between the four subject area groups. Overall, greatest importance was attached to developing 'understanding' and 'interest', but there were marked extremes of opinion in relation to 'enjoyment of the course' between English and mathematics and in relation to 'taking 'A' level' between mathematics and biology. In addition, underlying the mean score of the ratings for each subject area group was a range of opinion between teachers within a particular subject group on each criterion. The most noticeable example of this was for the mathematics teachers in relation to 'enjoyment of the course' where 12 per cent rated it 'not important' and 18 per cent rated it 'extremely important' (with the remaining 70 per cent spread across the other two response categories). Looking at these criteria, it is apparent here, as it was in relation to Bennett's study, that it would be difficult to translate some of these criteria into product variables which could be monitored and assessed.

The difficulty in translating educational aims into product variables has led research studies to focus on the most easily accessible, reliable and widely respected yardsticks of educational attainment, namely standardised tests of subject attainment and national examinations. Such a development has thus fostered and reinforced the assumption that the most important educational outcomes are those of intellectual attainment as displayed in such tests and examinations. Not only is such an assumption out of keeping with the professed educational objectives of many teachers, but it also offers greater academic credibility to such tests and examinations than they actually deserve. Standardised subject attainment tests, for example, are actually suspect as indicators of effective teaching. They are designed to test progress in a particular subject area (eg mathematics), but since pupils who have not covered test material must not be disadvantaged they tend to emphasise content common to all school work in that subject area (eg percentages, decimals, division etc).

Table 1 Criteria for effectiveness at 'O' level: mean ratings

Criterion for effectiveness	Mean ratings			
	Biology (N=31)	English (N=42)	Geography (N=36)	Mathematics (N=33)
1 The 'O' level grades achieved by the pupils in the subject	2.94	3.02	3.03	3.09
2 The development of an increased interest by pupils in the subject	3.32	3.36	3.17	2.91
3 The proportion of pupils who go on to take an 'A' level in the subject	1.81	2.00	2.00	2.39
4 The proportion of pupils who develop a good understanding of the subject	3.19	3.43	3.36	3.24
5 The proportion of pupils who felt they had enjoyed the course	3.00	3.29	2.83	2.55

The best subject attainment test of effective teaching is one that tests the material learnt in a particular course (but which, as a result, could not be fairly applied to pupils who had taken other courses). Subject attainment tests, therefore, are likely to advantage teaching with content material close to that of the test, and which gives practice in being tested.

National examinations (eg 'O' level and CSE) are also suspect in a number of ways. Such attainment is influenced by school and teacher policies regarding which examination courses are offered and how pupils are selected for courses and examination entry. The examination results are usually restricted to a crude range of grades, for instance, at 'O' level, no matter how outstanding, one can do no better than a grade A; at the other extreme not being entered for CSE can still cover a range of attainment. In addition, there are serious problems concerning the comparability of standards across different subjects and examination boards (see also the discussion of assessment in general, and GCSE in particular, in chapter 9).

Whichever set of product variables are thus employed as the criteria for monitoring effectiveness, there is likely to be disagreement as to whether the correct set was used. One can certainly sympathise with a teacher who has designed a course with the express purpose of fostering a certain set of educational outcomes (for example, a better understanding of the nature of scientific experiments), but whose effectiveness is judged by pupil success at an 'O' level examination which does not give academic credit to such understanding. Teachers thinking about their own effectiveness are frequently constrained to take account of the views of others concerning the desired educational outcomes. There are no clear guidelines regarding the relative weight that should be given to those interested in the proceedings. At the end of the day, each teacher must rely on his or her own professional integrity and judgement in reconciling the different views on the educational outcomes which should be fostered and emphasised.

In considering the relationship between the notion of effective teaching and the product variables which may be derived, it is also important to note that there are a number of similar and overlapping terms in common usage, such as 'the good teacher' (Taylor, 1962), 'the successful teacher' (Start and Laundy, 1973), 'the liked teacher' (Jersild, 1940), and even, more recently, 'the best teacher in the world'! (Wragg and Wood, 1984a). The distinction between what is 'liked', 'preferred', 'successful', 'good' and 'effective', among others, poses a number of problems in attempting to take into account the implications of a study using one such term for an approach which adopts another. The problem is not simply that of trying to conceptualise what each term means, but also of trying to see how that term might have been interpreted in the context of the study being reported.

For example, Taylor (1962) reported a study in which 866 junior school and 513 secondary school pupils were asked to write two short essays on 'a good teacher' and 'a poor teacher'. From this four categories of the teacher's classroom behaviour were derived: teaching, discipline, personal qualities, and organisation. 500 junior school and 397 secondary school pupils were then asked to respond to a number of items derived from the 'good teacher' essay. Overall, the picture which emerged was that the good teacher 'is firm and keeps order in the classroom', 'is fair and just about punishment', 'explains the work you have to do and helps you with it' and 'is friendly with children in and out of school'. Now, one problem with such a study is that it does not adequately distinguish whether these are the characteristics which the pupils themselves feel are attributes of the good teacher, or whether they are attempting to give 'correct answers' regarding a consensus held widely in society. In addition, it is not clear to what extent the pupils might see 'good' as being equated with 'likeable' rather than 'effective', a tendency likely to be stronger for the younger children.

It is interesting to note at this point that in recent years increasing interest has been paid to the views of pupils concerning effective teaching, and some of these findings will be considered later (particularly in chapter 6). However, such research has been plagued by just this confusion of terminology (McKelvey and Kyriacou, 1985).

In considering what is meant by effective teaching rather than 'good' or any other similar notion, it is important to note one implicit aspect of the term effective. It does imply quite strongly a notion of achieving the desired objectives and hence is likely to be wedded to an assessment of the extent to which the teaching is meeting its aims as indicated by some consideration of objectives and outcomes. In contrast terms such as 'good', 'liked' and 'preferred' seem to emphasise how an observer feels about the teaching and usually focus on qualities and characteristics of the teaching without direct reference to outcomes.

In essence, effective teaching implies identifying what actually works as indicated by outcomes. As such, it is not surprising that *effective* teaching rather than *good* teaching or some other similar term has been the one most widely adopted in discussions of teacher appraisal and merit pay since such a development has largely stemmed from the notion of 'payment by results' as culled from other areas (see chapter 9). The term effective teaching also derives largely from a psychological perspective on thinking about teaching, where the implicit emphasis on identifying observable behaviour in the classroom which can be linked with an influence on observable and measureable product variables is in line with the general psychological perspective regarding how to best explore human behaviour.

Conducting research on effective teaching

As was noted earlier, almost all research on effective teaching reported over the last few decades has employed a basic framework of *Context-Process-Product* (Figure 1, p. 10). This section looks at ways in which studies have attempted to explore effective teaching using this framework. In doing so, attention will be paid to the two main research strategies that have been adopted since the 1960s and which characterise the overwhelming bulk of recent research. The first strategy has attempted to relate process variables to product variables (so called 'process-product' studies); the second strategy has relied almost entirely on process variables alone.

A number of types of studies have attempted to explore aspects of effective teaching. The main types are:
- studies based on teachers' opinions regarding effective teaching (usually employing questionnaires or interviews);
- studies based on pupils' opinions regarding effective teaching (usually employing questionnaires or interviews; some interesting studies have sought pupils' opinions about their own teacher's teaching);

- studies based on classroom observation by an outside observer (using either recording schedules, rating scales or participant observation techniques);
- studies based on rated teaching ability based on a mixture of information (usually based on a headteacher's rating);
- studies based on teachers' descriptions of their own teaching practices;
- studies by teachers of their own teaching (which may include keeping detailed notes about their lessons, and getting the reactions of others such as their pupils or a colleague who may be asked to observe some lessons).

Where a study attempts to relate process variables to product variables, it is termed a 'process-product study'; where it relies on looking at process variables alone, it is termed a 'process study'. Some studies, of course, use a mixture of such approaches.

Process-product studies overwhelmingly dominated research on effective teaching in the United States during the 1960s and 1970s. This led to the creation of a massive data base from which many of the characteristics of effective teaching advocated in textbooks aimed at student teachers have been derived (Good and Brophy, 1980). Generally, such studies employ classroom observation to record the frequency of occurrence of various teacher behaviours and aspects of teacher–pupil interaction (the process variables) and then explore their association with the criteria for effectiveness being employed, such as gains in standardised subject attainment tests (the product variables). This association is most commonly explored by simply correlating the process variables with the product variables, with the assumption that the high correlations will pick out aspects of teaching which most strongly contribute to effectiveness.

An example of such a study is that by Good *et al* (1978). They focused attention on two sets of data, one drawn from a relatively affluent school district, and the other drawn from a district serving low income families. In both cases, roughly 40 teachers of fourth grade (9-year-old) pupils were observed teaching mathematics. Pre- and post-achievement data were collected from which it was possible to compute the mean achievement gain for each teacher. The rationale for the study was to explore whether there were differences in the sizes of correlations between the process and product variables in the high social economic status (SES) setting compared with the low SES setting. In fact, the researchers found few such differences between the two settings, the most notable ones being in the use of academically-focused questions, pacing, praise, seatwork and pupil involvement.

Two major problems face such process-product studies. First, they employ a simplistic research design, attempting to focus on small, discrete, observable behaviours which are then associated relatively independently with the product variables. The idea that 'use of praise' or 'repeating questions' can be explored independent of each other and everything else going on during the lesson, for example, and that each will contribute in its own separate and identifiable way to effectiveness, is very suspect and has contributed to a mass of often contradictory data. The second major problem is that such a research design cannot distinguish between those aspects of classroom processes which simply occur when effective teaching is in progress and those aspects which in themselves constitute the effective teaching.

A number of process-product studies have attempted to meet the problem of focusing on too many discrete behaviours by attempting to explore the relative effectiveness of different 'teaching styles', each style being characterised by some consistent use of certain teaching practices.

Bennett (1976) reported a study which compared the relative effectiveness of being taught by 37 primary school teachers allocated to one of three main teaching styles: 'formal', 'mixed' and 'informal'. The findings were based on pupil gains in standardised tests of reading, mathematics and English. They appeared to indicate that teachers representative of the formal teaching style were generally more effective. Subsequent discussion of the study by a number of authors together with a re-analysis of the data by Aitkin *et al* (1981) has suggested that clear findings cannot be unequivocally drawn from this study. First, there seems to be such variation within teaching styles that there is ample room for both effective and ineffective teachers within a given style (see Gray and Satterly, 1981); indeed, Bennett's study included a case study of a particularly effective teacher employing an informal teaching style. Second, and a very important point applicable to all process-product studies, there is great concern among many researchers that we do not have adequate statistical techniques to enable us to draw clear inferences about the relationship between process and product variables in such a way that unequivocal links can be drawn between aspects of classroom teaching and educational outcomes. The debate surrounding two more recent studies (Rutter *et al*, 1979; Steedman, 1980) indicates a similar concern.

Authors who have attempted to review the findings of process-product studies (Anderson *et al*, 1980; Good and Brophy, 1980; Kyriacou, 1983; Rosenshine, 1971; Ryan and Butler, 1982) have all noted many contradictory findings which severely restrict the number of cause and effect-type inferences that can be drawn and generalised about effective teaching. A major problem here is the diversity of teaching situations which exist in terms of specified context and specified educational outcomes desired. What might appear to be most effective for teaching creative writing to junior school pupils, as judged by pupil project work, may be very different from effective teaching to enable secondary pupils to memorise mathematical formulae, as judged by recall tests. In attempting to generalise about effective teaching, one is required to ask: in what particular context and with what educational outcomes are you concerned?

As a result, a number of recent process-product studies have attempted to explore more subject matter specific contexts while also recognising that different product variables may be associated with the process variables in different ways. For example, Eggleston *et al* (1976) studied science teaching, and employed a specially designed classroom observation schedule (the *Science Teaching Observation Schedule*) for use in science lessons. This used categories focusing on intellectual transactions taking place during teacher–pupil interaction. In a study of 94 science 'O' level classes, the schedule was used to identify three science teaching styles: 'problem solvers', 'informers' and 'enquirers'. Using pre- and post-test scores of the pupils on aspects of learning and attitudes, a number of interesting findings emerged, not least that the majority of the biology teachers appeared to be using the least effective teaching style. Of particular importance, however, was the suggestion that the effectiveness of a style appeared to depend on the subject matter, pupil ability, the type of learning monitored, and whether pupils' attitudes are included as a criterion.

Process studies have attempted to explore effective teaching by relating process variables to each other rather than by linking process variables to product variables. Two main approaches have developed within this strategy. The first uses some aspects of pupil behaviour during the lesson as the criteria for effectiveness; the second relies primarily on the opinions and judgements of those involved, either the observer, the pupils or the teacher, as the mechanism for identifying effectiveness.

The first approach has much in common with process-product studies, but substitutes pupil behaviour during the lesson – whether the pupils are working hard; whether they are showing interest; whether they appear to be learning – in place of product variables based on educational outcomes. Many such studies have used recording schedules to generate a measure of 'pupil time on task', which refers to the amount of time spent by a pupil in appropriate learning behaviour, such as being engaged in the learning task or listening and talking to the teacher about academic related matters. Indeed measurement of pupil time on task has been widely used in the United States, and is beginning to compete with process-product studies in popularity (Anderson, 1984). The particular strength of this approach is that it enables the essence of effective teaching (that is, keeping pupils on task) to be explored more easily, by focusing on the link between teaching and learning-related pupil behaviour, such as time on task.

An interesting example of such a study is that reported by Anderson and Scott (1978), who attempted to explore the relative effectiveness of the different teaching methods a teacher may use during the course of a lesson (classroom discourse; audio-visual presentation; lecture; seatwork and groupwork) for high school pupils, by recording the level of pupil involvement based on an observation schedule of pupil on task behaviour. Their findings indicated that classroom discourse was associated mainly with task-relevant pupil behaviour, although there were differences in the apparent effectiveness of the teaching methods used, depending on the particular aptitude and academic self-concept levels of the various 'pupil learning types' involved in the study. As with process-product studies, this approach also seems too simplistic in its attempt to look at teaching methods in isolation, rather than the relationship of the different methods with each other and the lesson as a whole. For example, 'seatwork' can be used in various ways and at various times in a lesson, and one can explore the quality of the seatwork required; thus seatwork as a global category could cover both effective and ineffective teaching.

A major assumption underlying such studies is that certain process variables, such as time on task, are the crucial determinants of pupil learning. Thus whatever teachers do to keep pupils on task is, in essence, effective teaching. While there is some evidence to indicate that time on task is generally an important determinant of attainment at both primary and secondary school (Bennett, 1978; Fitz-Gibbon and Clark, 1982), a number of researchers (eg Denscombe, 1980; Woods, 1979) have warned of the dangers of assuming that teachers who are able to maintain high levels of pupil on task behaviour are in fact more effective. Some teachers may well be achieving high on task behaviour through control techniques where the intellectual engagement of the pupils with the learning activities is actually poor, or through the use of teaching methods which maintain on-taskness but where the educational outcomes desired are not effectively achieved, as for example with the widespread use of project work where the assumed gains in attainment have not accrued in some of the ways expected.

The second main approach to process studies, that of relying on the opinions and judgements of those involved, has produced a number of very important insights into aspects of teacher and pupil behaviour. For a start, it has thrown light on the importance of taking account of teacher and pupil perceptions and strategies and their reaction to each other's behaviour; it also offers detailed descriptions of how pupils respond to the various learning activities and tasks. This approach to process studies covers a variety of research techniques, but they have in common that their contribution to the understanding of effective teaching lies primarily in the quality of the insights and interpretations they offer which are drawn from the data collected.

One widely employed type of study which exemplifies this approach is that where an outside observer or the teacher uses participant observation techniques to clarify some aspect of classroom processes. Such studies make detailed use of the observer's monitoring of classroom activities and behaviour and the teacher's (who may also be the participant observer) and pupils' own understanding and interpretation of events. The approach adopted often attempts to clarify classroom processes by identifying some taken for granted assumptions about classroom activities and behaviour which can be considered worthy of close analysis and to then use the mixture of observation, interviews with pupils and the teacher (if appropriate), and other methods of data collection, in order to develop an account and interpretation of the classroom processes deemed problematic in some way.

For example, Denscombe's (1980) study of comprehensive school classrooms and Pollard's (1980) study of primary school classrooms both highlight the ways in which teachers' thinking about the learning activities they wish to set up is severely constrained by a number of non-educational factors to do with the realities of school life, particularly how teachers may be judged by their colleagues, and the need to actually survive. These two studies make extensive use of quotations from teachers and of classroom observation to substantiate the interpretations presented. Such accounts at their best are very illuminating and have the quality of authenticity in the sense of actually capturing the essence of classroom realities. Some critics, however, have attacked such studies for embedding their findings within a research context and development of theory which make them of little use to teachers:

> If we could be satisfied that classroom observers were interested in providing reasonably dispassionate information about classroom life and the teaching process then we could accommodate the difficulties attendant upon participant observation and draw on this literature when seeking to enhance our understanding of teaching. But this is not the case, the researchers invariably have a message for us; they have discovered situations in the classroom which need to be rectified, they can contribute to our understanding of teaching, their work is relevant to teachers. This might be possible to take if it were not so often coupled with an arrogant or patronising manner and naive view of classrooms and the problems faced by practising teachers. They use their fieldwork experiences to promote their own research goals; they do no service to the teachers who have welcomed them into their classrooms. (McNamara, 1980, p. 115)

Such a criticism would seem to be valid for some studies (although no doubt the development of educational theory would be used as justification). But the criticism cannot be supported in relation to a number of excellent case studies of teaching where the prime aim was to contribute to increased effectiveness. A very informative series of reports on case studies of teaching, based on the comments of observers, teachers and pupils, was generated by the *Ford Teaching Project* in the 1970s (Elliot and Adelman, 1975). What was particularly innovative about this project was that it attempted to enable teachers to adopt a research orientation towards reflection about their own teaching. The project used the term 'classroom action-research' to refer to a research-oriented attempt by teachers to understand and solve practical problems faced in the classroom, and the term has now achieved wide currency as the basis for a number of case studies and programmes aimed at increasing effective teaching. The study involved both primary and secondary school teachers who were attempting to adopt inquiry/discovery teaching, an approach which places emphasis on pupils' self-directed learning. The main aim of the study was to identify the problems faced by teachers using these methods and to explore strategies which may resolve these problems in particular classrooms and thereby increase the effectiveness of the teaching.

A major strand in the study was to look at ways in which teachers' behaviour might impose constraints on pupils' ability to reason independently from their teachers. In order to explore this, a number of hypotheses were generated and investigated, in the context of particular classrooms, by the teachers and observers. Examples of such hypotheses were:

- When the teacher changes the topic being discussed or investigated pupils will fail to contribute their own ideas because they interpret such actions as attempts on the part of the teacher to get them to conform to his/her line of reasoning.
- Many teachers' questions inhibit pupils from feeling free to branch out on new lines of reasoning, because they are interpreted as an attempt to assess what they should already know or understand.

The reports generated by the project were so rich in their detailing of aspects of teaching that it has proved difficult to derive simple conclusions from them. As a result their dissemination has been limited, but the philosophy and approach adopted by the project have been very influential on much subsequent case study research, particularly by practising teachers.

In recent years much greater use has been made of pupils as teacher evaluators, although this has been done in a number of ways. Some studies have simply used questionnaires to survey pupils' opinions regarding aspects of classroom teaching in general. Others have used questionnaires or interviews to obtain the pupils' opinions regarding a particular lesson or set of lessons. Indeed, in a survey of such studies, McKelvey and Kyriacou (1985) noted that the use of pupils' assessment of a lesson often provided teachers with valuable information and insights into their own teaching. The more widespread use of such techniques by teachers seemed to be constrained by a fear of the political and social implications implicit in such an approach, rather than by any methodological difficulties.

Some researchers have noted that in some cases, problems of understanding subject matter are common to pupils being taught by apparently effective teachers and those being taught by less effective teachers. Such studies have indicated that barriers to successful learning may lie in the subject matter itself rather than in general qualities of the teaching or learning activities. This has led to a number of process studies where the main aim has been to detail the problems faced by pupils in attempting to master certain topics in various subject areas. Some particularly insightful research along these lines has been reported by Hart (1981) in relation to mathematics. Her findings serve to remind those looking at effective teaching that they need to consider the problems associated with the subject matter itself.

One final issue of importance is the extent to which effective teaching may contribute to greater levels of educational outcomes than are achieved by less effective teaching. A number of authors have argued that context variables, particularly pupils' ability and social class, are such major determinants of educational attainment, that the differences which may result from pupils having a more rather than a less effective teacher are very slight indeed (Cuttance, 1980). The developing literature on school effectiveness has further identified aspects of the school attended which, in addition to pupil ability and social class, appear to account for some of the differences in attainment between schools (Gray, 1981; Reynolds, 1985).

It has already been acknowledged that the tracing of cause and effect with regard to effective teaching is difficult. However, it is important to bear in mind the distinction between research on 'teacher effects' and research on effective teaching *per se*. The former is primarily concerned with the statistical explanation of *differences* between pupils in educational attainment rather than in the *level* of educational attainment reached by individual pupils. In contrast, research on effective teaching, in attempting to contribute to the understanding of craft knowledge of teaching, is concerned with aspects of teaching which are effective, even if they are largely used by the majority of teachers and thereby fail to account for differences in educational attainment among a large sample of pupils.

The purpose of considering the types of studies undertaken to explore effective teaching, is to enable the reader to be better informed about the nature of the findings and data used which will be considered throughout this book and to indicate why certain claims about or ways of looking at effective teaching need to be treated with caution.

Having considered the conceptual and research problems associated with the notion of effective teaching, and the issues raised by conducting research on effective teaching, we can usefully look at the main ways of thinking about effective teaching which have emerged from research and from teacher education perspectives.

Models for thinking about effective teaching

As already stated, it is important when thinking about effective teaching to take account of the particular characteristics of the context of the learning activity (eg type of school, subject matter and level of pupil attainment) and the particular educational outcomes desired (eg 'O' level attainment and increased pupil academic self-confidence). At its crudest, the question of effective teaching comprises two main elements: given the context and outcomes being considered, first, *what* aspects of the learning experience contribute to effectiveness? Second, *how* do these aspects have the effect they do?

In considering the 'what' and 'how' of effective teaching, three models have emerged which reflect contemporary thinking about effective teaching (Figure 2). These three models are in fact complementary and are in essence consistent with each other. They represent three ways of looking at the same phenomena, but differ in the basic framework each model uses to elaborate on the key elements employed. Each framework has its own developmental history and has its own distinctive contribution to make to the full understanding of effective teaching (Kyriacou, 1985).

Model 1: A surface level of analysis

This model derives primarily from research studies and theorising about effective teaching. Such an approach in recent years has focused on two main complementary constructs which appear to be the crucial determinants of effectiveness (see Anderson, 1984; Corno, 1979; Peterson and Walberg, 1979). The first construct is *Active learning time* (ALT); it refers to the amount of time spent by pupils actively engaged in the learning task and activities designed to bring about the educational outcomes desired. The second construct is the *Quality of instruction* (QI); this refers to the quality of the learning task and activities in terms of their appropriateness and suitability for bringing about the educational outcomes desired. In essence, model 1 equates effective teaching with maximising ALT and QI.

The construct of active learning time has gradually been refined and made more sophisticated. Early research concentrated on the amount of time pupils spent on outcome-related tasks, and indicated that greater time spent on task behaviour was associated with greater gains in educational attainment. This was generally true whether it resulted from teachers allocating more curriculum time to task behaviour (for example, primary school teachers spending more time during lessons on basic number work) or from individual teachers maintaining task behaviour during a lesson for longer than their colleagues.

Such studies often highlighted ways in which time was wasted during what was judged as less effective teaching, for example, lessons where

Figure 2 Three models for thinking about effective teaching

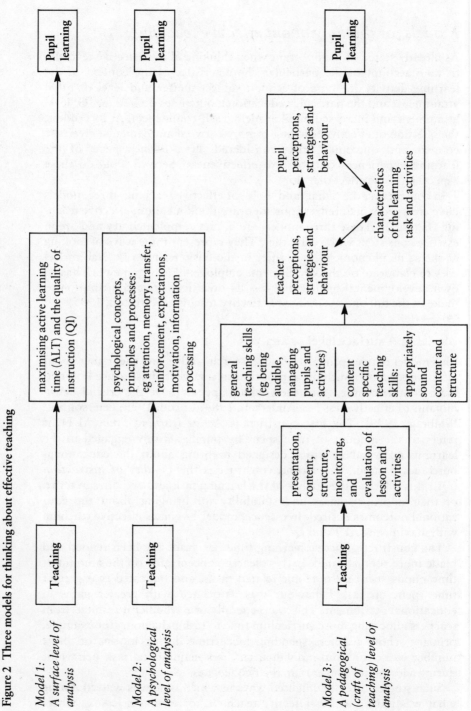

Model 1:
A surface level of analysis

Teaching → maximising active learning time (ALT) and the quality of instruction (QI) → Pupil learning

Model 2:
A psychological level of analysis

Teaching → psychological concepts, principles and processes: eg attention, memory, transfer, reinforcement, expectations, motivation, information processing → Pupil learning

Model 3:
A pedagogical (craft of teaching) level of analysis

Teaching → presentation, content, structure, monitoring, and evaluation of lesson and activities → general teaching skills (eg being audible, managing pupils and activities) / content specific teaching skills: appropriately sound content and structure → teacher perceptions, strategies and behaviour ↔ pupil perceptions, strategies and behaviour ↔ characteristics of the learning task and activities → Pupil learning many pupils had to queue for long periods to see a teacher, or where disciplinary techniques frequently used to reprimand individual pupils disrupted the whole class. The notion of wasting time, however, must be treated with caution given that learning activities designed to foster some educational outcomes (eg pupil autonomy, skills in using practical equipment) may appear costly in time if another educational outcome is substituted by an observer or researcher as the criterion of effectiveness.

More recent studies have attempted to move away from a simple 'amount of time' notion towards attempting to explore the nature of being 'actively engaged'. It is argued that being on task in the sense of listening to a teacher or doing the work demanded does not take account of the nature of that experience. Some pupils appear to be quite capable of doing the task demanded by a teacher without being cognitively or affectively engaged in the fullest sense. Some recent studies have thus sought to employ a notion of active learning time which focuses on the nature of each pupil's active mental engagement in the learning activities (eg Bennett *et al*, 1984). In essence this development is attempting to move away from a 'keeping pupils occupied' view of being on task towards a notion of creating and sustaining the appropriate mental engagement with the learning activities required for effectively bringing about the educational outcomes desired. This development makes the distinction between active learning time and the second main construct, quality of instruction, much harder to sustain than in earlier studies.

The construct of quality of instruction complements active learning time by emphasising that the quality of the teaching and learning activities themselves is important for bringing about the desired educational outcomes. Clearly, a teacher who could sustain a high level of on task behaviour by pupils through, for example, forceful control techniques, but who set up learning experiences which were of poor quality, would not be effective in fostering the desired educational outcomes. Quality of instruction in essence refers to the extent to which the instruction makes it easy for pupils to achieve the intended educational outcomes. Primarily, this involves considering if the learning experience is organised in the most sound and appropriate ways when the characteristics of the pupils (such as ability, prior understanding, and motivation) are taken into account. It covers a number of aspects of the instruction, most notably the teacher's transactions with pupils and the content, structure and organisation of the learning tasks and activities.

A number of writers have attempted to identify those key aspects which characterise a high quality of instruction (Haertel *et al*, 1983). Some have highlighted the psychological aspects of instruction (eg use of reinforcement, directing attention, and promoting transfer of learning); such an approach is elaborated in the second model for thinking about effective teaching outlined below. Other writers have highlighted general qualities (or teaching skills) which appear to be of importance (eg clarity, cognitive matching and pacing); this approach is elaborated in the third model for thinking about effective teaching, which will also be considered below.

However, before turning to considering these other two models, one final point of major importance needs to be made about the relationship between ALT and QI. It has been stressed that these two constructs are complementary. It is important to bear in mind, when thinking about effective teaching, that the vast majority of classroom process variables influence both ALT and QI. This is because the aspects of teaching which maintain high levels of active learning time invariably involve achieving a high level of quality of instruction, and *vice versa*. This inter-relationship between ALT and QI is interestingly apparent in much of the research on classroom management (see Freiberg, 1983; Kounin, 1970; Robertson, 1981), and stems from a recognition that pupils actively engaged in a learning experience represent an interface between ALT and QI. Thus although the distinction between these two constructs is very helpful in thinking about effective teaching, such thinking needs to always bear in mind this inter-relationship and not perceive of these two constructs as operating in an independent fashion.

Model 2: A psychological level of analysis

This second model of thinking about effective teaching derives from attempts to identify the major psychological variables involved. As was noted above, it represents an elaboration of the surface level of analysis from a psychological perspective. Model 1 has been termed a 'surface level' of analysis because reference to the two central constructs of active learning time and quality of instruction indicate the most crucial aspects of effective teaching in terms of the broadest constructs of value. In summary, process variables influence educational outcomes through their influence on ALT and QI. In a sense this represents a 'surface level' explanation of effective teaching. The psychological level of analysis attempts to link the process variables with educational outcomes by explaining this influence in terms of the various psychological concepts, principles and processes involved, and as such can be considered to be in a sense a 'deeper level' explanation of effective teaching.

The psychological level of analysis attempts to make clear the relationship between process variables and educational outcomes by focusing on the relationship between the process variables and the psychological conditions necessary for learning to occur. If certain process variables influence educational outcomes they must be doing so through their influence on each individual pupil in a way that can be traced and explained in terms of the influence on each individual pupil's psychological state and psychological processes. Such an approach is thus concerned to explain how process variables influence educational out-comes by looking at the psychological processes involved in learning.

This model is largely based on the work of teacher educators who have employed a psychological perspective, or psychologists who have felt that knowledge about the nature of learning derived from research could form the basis for developing a psychology of instruction. To date, a vast number of psychological concepts, principles and processes have been identified as underlying aspects of effective teaching. These include attention, memory, transfer, reinforcement, mental set, cueing, feedback, concept discrimination, motivation, identification, ability, information processing, expectations, attitudes and self-concept, to name but a few (these will be discussed in later chapters). The emphasis given to particular psychological concepts, principles and processes, differs across the various theories and frameworks employed as a basis for an 'instructional psychology' (see Good and Brophy, 1980; Haertel *et al*, 1983; Howe, 1984; Tomlinson, 1981). However, it would appear that there are three main aspects of pupil learning which are crucial to a consideration of effective teaching:

1 The pupil must be *attending* to the learning experience.
2 The pupil must be *receptive* to the learning experience (in the sense of being motivated or having a willingness to learn or respond to the experience).
3 The learning experience must be *appropriate* for the desired learning to take place (taking particular account of the pupil's initial knowl-edge and understanding).

These three aspects form the basis of the general conditions required for learning to take place. The analysis of effective teaching from a psychological perspective focuses on these conditions and the factors which facilitate, or hinder, teachers in their efforts to achieve them. This analysis forms the subject of the next chapter, but also relates closely to the discussion in the whole of this book.

Model 3: A pedagogical (craft of teaching) level of analysis

The pedagogical level of analysis has emerged largely from the per-spective of effective teaching employed by teacher educators. It concerns the attempt to describe the craft of teaching in a way that is of value to both student teachers and experienced teachers attending in-service courses. The emphasis within this perspective has been to describe effective teaching in ways which make sense to practitioners and relate to their professional needs and concerns. In this respect, model 3 is based as far as possible on the ways teachers themselves think and talk about their own teaching and the ways teachers attempt to offer advice to student teachers and new entrants to the profession. Unlike the previous two models, this approach has tended to rely on commonsense acceptability to students and established teachers for its validity, rather than on its explicit derivation from research findings. It is interesting that recent research on effective teaching has now adopted this same general approach to thinking about effective teaching, but has attempted to elaborate it through studies focusing on teachers' and pupils' perceptions of teaching.

Most of the early writings within this framework focused on the main aspects of teaching essential for success, namely the content and presentation of the lesson, classroom management and discipline, and relationships with pupils. Such writing tended to be based on the professional teaching experience of the writer and conveyed a tone of advice based on experience. A classic contribution within this approach was Marland's *The Craft of the Classroom* (1975), written by a headteacher and still much in use. Cruder versions of this approach, encapsulated in the phrase 'tips for teachers', can be found in booklets produced by the various teacher unions and aimed at student teachers. While such writings contain much of value, their major shortcoming is that they often fail to provide a basis for understanding from which the advice offered can be interpreted and used to inform a teacher's thinking about his or her own teaching. Attempting to act in a way advised by experienced practitioners does little to foster a teacher's development of increased professional competence beyond the initial stages, although it must be said that sound advice during those early stages certainly alerts student teachers to many pitfalls and to issues of major practical significance.

Such writing formed an early basis for the consideration of the craft knowledge about effective teaching, and had its parallel within teacher training courses, where the theory of teaching was termed 'pedagogy'. Such craft knowledge within teacher training was largely undertaken within 'method courses' which dealt with the method of teaching particular subjects and topics (in contrast to the disciplines of education such as psychology, sociology, philosophy, history and administration). Some enlightened psychology tutors did attempt to consider craft knowledge explicitly and relate such knowledge to a psychological perspective. Unfortunately, in the main, the introduction to the discipline of the psychology of education contained too great an academic emphasis on consideration of the understanding of teaching and learning, rather than examining its contribution to teachers' thinking about their own teaching and its effectiveness.

This approach largely sees teaching as a managerial activity, and seeks to identify the major tasks of teaching and the associated management activities required for effectiveness. It had a major impact on researchers following the appearance of Kounin's (1970) seminal book on classroom management. Kounin drew attention to what appeared to be a number of managerial techniques employed by 'effective' teachers in contrast to less effective teachers, such as 'withitness', 'overlapping', 'smoothness' and 'momentum' (terms which will be dealt with in chapter 6). The particular importance of this study was that it focused attention on aspects of teaching which were subjectively much richer in meaning and significance than the types of process variables being studied at the time. Moreover these aspects quickly established credibility with both the teacher education and the research communities.

Since the publication of Kounin's study, two major strands of development have been pursued. First, there has been an attempt to identify the management activities involved in effective teaching in terms of central 'teaching skills', with an implicit assumption that managerial activities can be broken down into such discrete component skills and that such skills can be fostered and developed within teacher education. This philosophy was clearly exemplified in the work of the *Teacher Education Project* based at the Universities of Nottingham, Exeter and Leicester from 1976 to 1981, and in the resulting publications (eg Wragg, 1984). In considering such skills, it would appear that a useful distinction can be made between *general teaching skills* (such as being audible, and managing pupils and activities) and *content specific teaching skills* (such as the appropriateness of the content, method and structure of the learning activities for the desired educational outcomes) (Figure 2). While these two sets of teaching skills are complementary, the former focuses on general presentation and classroom management skills, whilst the latter focuses on the 'intellectual packaging' of the content and the learning activities. These skills will be elaborated in chapter 6.

The second major strand of development has been an exploration of the significance of the various managerial activities for the teacher and pupils, by taking account of their perceptions. Such an approach is in essence a psychological version of the type of study conducted by sociologists who have attempted to identify the meaning for participants (the teacher and the pupils) of what was happening in the classroom (see Woods, 1980a, 1980b, for examples of this 'ethnographic approach' used by sociologists to explore classroom teaching). This strand of development is at the forefront of current thinking among researchers (eg Bennett *et al*, 1984; Calderhead, 1984; Doyle, 1983, 1984). It involves exploring the inter-relationship between three aspects of classroom processes:

- teacher perceptions, strategies and behaviour;
- pupil perceptions, strategies and behaviour;
- characteristics of the learning task and activities.

Research by Bennett *et al* and Doyle has highlighted how both teachers and pupils have expectations about learning activities and both have strategies for attempting to deal with the demands each makes on the other. In particular, the ways in which pupils attempt to make sense of and react to the purpose of a learning activity and the demands made upon them by the teacher and the learning activity are crucial to the nature of the pupils' engagement in a learning experience and hence to the quality of the actual learning which takes place. The studies by Bennett *et al* and Doyle have indicated that pupils may often respond in ways different from those assumed by the teacher in setting up the activities. Such problems in part stem from the assumptions made by teachers about pupils' levels of motivation, understanding and competence in study skills, and in part from the tendency for pupils to actively identify methods and strategies for meeting the demands of a learning activity which are incorrect or inappropriate (although they may appear to be correct and appropriate in the short-term or in the context of the particular task in hand). To mitigate such problems teachers need to be aware of the pupils' perspective regarding the experience of teaching and learning. This quality of 'social sensitivity' (the ability to see things from another's perspective) has received surprisingly little attention in thinking about effective teaching, although it can be seen to be at the heart of many of the teaching skills frequently considered.

In Figure 2 (model 3) the three boxes intervening between teaching and pupil learning thus represent three major focal points in thinking about effective teaching as a managerial activity, each of which attempts to clarify the nature of the craft of teaching as it relates to effectiveness.

Conclusions

The two major themes developed in this chapter are worth repeating here. First, that in thinking about effective teaching there is a need to take into account the context and the nature of the educational outcomes desired. Second, that there appear to be three main models for thinking about effective teaching. These are complementary but each of them makes a useful and important contribution to the understanding of effective teaching. Many of the issues and points developed in this chapter will be elaborated throughout the book. However, this chapter taken as a whole provides the overall framework for all that will follow.

3 How pupils learn

The essence of effective teaching lies in the ability of the teacher to set up a learning experience which brings about the desired educational outcomes. For this to take place, each pupil must be engaged in the activity of learning. The nature of the psychological state of being engaged in the activity of learning has been the focus of much debate and research by psychologists throughout this century. A number of important psychological concepts, principles and processes involved in both the activity of learning itself and in facilitating the activity have been identified.

This chapter considers those aspects of how pupils learn which have the most practical relevance for effective teaching. Broadly, these fall into four sections. First, a consideration of the psychological nature of the activity of learning as it relates to effective teaching. What psychological state needs to be set up by a teacher for learning to take place? Such a consideration will draw upon the work of those who have attempted to develop a psychological theory of instruction. Second, a consideration of the ways in which the study of human development has thrown important light on the nature of children's learning. Third, a consideration of the mental processes of a cognitive (and intellectual) nature involved in the activity of learning. Fourth, and finally, a consideration of the affective (emotional or particularly motivational) processes involved in the activity of learning.

This chapter thus represents an elaboration of the psychological level of analysis as a model for thinking about effective teaching outlined in the previous chapter. The importance of this approach is that it provides a conceptual framework for teachers in thinking and decision-making about their own teaching and makes explicit why and how pupil learning may or may not be taking place effectively.

The nature of pupil learning

Some writers have considered the nature of pupil learning explicitly within the context of effective teaching. Of these, probably the most influential have been Bruner (1966), Ausubel (1968) and Gagné (1985). Each has explored four major questions concerning the nature of pupil learning:

1   What mental processes are involved when a pupil is engaged in learning?

2   What changes occur in the pupil's cognitive structure which them-
    selves constitute pupil learning?
3   Which psychological factors (concepts, principles and processes)
    facilitate pupil learning?
4   What are the main types of pupil learning?

Although the theorists have elaborated their answers to these four
questions in different ways, there are a number of points of convergence
in their separate approaches. Thus it is possible to establish a degree of
synthesis or consensus on which to build a basic framework for thinking
about the nature of pupil learning, against which the different emphases
of these and other authors may be measured.

The learning process

Pupil learning can be defined as changes in a pupil's behaviour which
take place as a result of being engaged in an educational experience.
Gagné has suggested that there are five main types of pupil learning:

1   *Verbal information*: eg facts, names, principles and generalisations.
2   *Intellectual skills*: 'knowing how' rather than 'knowing that'. These
    can be arranged in increasing order of complexity as 'discriminations',
    'concepts', 'rules' and 'higher-order rules', each of which is seen to
    build upon the less complex skill. Intellectual skills can be demon-
    strated by application to the different examples of the phenomena to
    which they refer.
3   *Cognitive strategies*: ways in which the pupil is able to control and
    manage the mental processes involved in learning, eg strategies for
    attending, thinking and memorising and for dealing with novel
    problems.
4   *Attitudes*: an attitude may be defined as a pupil's feelings towards
    some particular object or class of objects. The fostering of attitudes
    such as those towards ethnic minorities or towards school subjects
    can be identified as an important educational outcome. It is interest-
    ing to note that Gagné emphasises the cognitive and behavioural
    aspects of attitudes as 'preferences which influence personal action',
    rather than placing the more usual emphasis on the emotional aspect
    of an attitude as a 'feeling towards an object'.
5   *Motor skills*: eg playing a musical instrument or operating a type-
    writer.

The most detailed exposition of educational outcomes is Bloom *et al*
(1956) *Taxonomy of Educational Objectives* which attempted to list the
different categories of learning outcomes in each of three domains:
'cognitive', 'affective' and 'psychomotor'. The cognitive domain, for
example, is broken down into six categories of intellectual skills:
knowledge, comprehension, application, analysis, synthesis and evaluation. This approach – identifying in great detail the various categories of
educational outcomes which can form the basis of objectives for teaching
– has had a marked influence on a number of curriculum developments.

Clearly, of prime importance for the teacher's planning and decision-making concerning an educational experience is the need to take account of the intellectual skills that the experience is intended to foster. In addition, the approach has influenced how the stated objectives of a course are assessed, placing emphasis on the importance of matching the content and teaching methods adopted, with the skills that will be assessed. A good example of such a development is the attempt in the *Schools Council 13–16 History Project* to foster the development of a number of historical skills which the traditional teaching of history had not directly addressed (Shemilt, 1980).

Ausubel's treatment of types of learning emphasises two important distinctions in pupil learning. The first is a distinction between reception and discovery learning; the second is a distinction between rote and meaningful learning.

In reception learning the entire content of what is to be learned is presented to the learner in its final form; the learner is required to internalise or incorporate the material presented. By contrast, in discovery learning the content of what is to be learned has first to be discovered by the pupil through some learning activity.

In meaningful learning, the essential characteristic of the learning is that it can be related in a meaningful, non-arbitrary way to what the learner already knows. In rote learning, however, what is learned is characterised by arbitrary associations with the learner's previous knowledge.

These two distinctions, reception versus discovery learning and meaningful versus rote learning, are seen by Ausubel to be independent of each other. Thus reception learning can be either meaningful or rote, and discovery learning may be either meaningful or rote. This is an important observation, since there is a tendency to assume that reception learning is also rote learning, and that discovery learning is also meaningful learning. Meaningful learning has important implications for the notion of teaching for understanding, since it places emphasis on the type of changes in the pupil's cognitive structure that take place during learning, and on the consequent demonstration of learning that the learner can display.

The approaches adopted by Gagné, Ausubel and Bruner are all based on the same essential model of information processing by the learner which must occur for learning to take place. This model is illustrated in Figure 3. There are three main sections to this model. The first section is concerned with the initial reception of sensory information. This involves taking account of the learner's level of attention and the degree to which such attention is directed towards aspects of the whole range of sensory inputs available in the classroom. At the same time, initial reception is also subject to selective perception, which acts as a filter and alerts the

Figure 3   The basic model of information processing which underlies the activity of learning

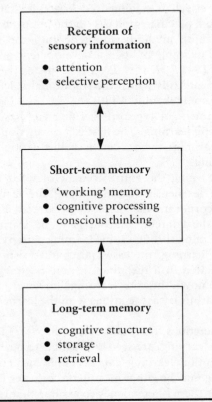

learner to the most significant aspects of the sensory information available. The information processing which takes place here lasts for only a fraction of a second.

The second section is usually termed 'short-term memory' (STM). This is concerned with processing the information which is received through the initial reception. Such processing is in part experienced by the learner as conscious thinking, and involves the application of those cognitive processes outlined by Gagné and Bloom, for example, described above.

The third section is usually termed 'long-term memory' (LTM), and is concerned with the changes which take place in the learner's cognitive structure as a result of the processing of information within short-term memory. Such changes in essence constitute the learning which has taken place, as it is these changes which enable the changes in behaviour resulting from the learning to be demonstrated.

The raw stuff of the activity of learning is thus the interaction between the processing of information in STM and the cognitive structure in LTM. It is important to note that many of the cognitive processes involved in STM are also desired learning outcomes; much education is designed to foster and develop those thinking skills, processes and strategies, which subsequently become part of the mental activity involved in bringing about future, and more sophisticated learning. A very interesting example of the approach to developing such thinking skills is the work of de Bono (1976, 1982), who has designed a number of classroom lessons aimed to foster the perceptual and cognitive strategies involved in thinking.

Ausubel's emphasis on the effectiveness of meaningful learning lies in the view that meaningful learning will involve changes in the cognitive structure of the learner which will be based on 'meaningful associations' (rather than arbitrary ones), and hence contribute to more sophisticated cognitive behaviour (in terms of how such learning can be demonstrated and applied) than does rote learning. Ausubel has also advocated the use of 'advanced organisers'; these refer to the ways in which a teacher can usefully indicate at the start of a lesson how the content and learning activities of the lesson can be organised and related to pupils' previous knowledge and understanding, so that the learning which follows is made meaningful. Ausubel sees the principal function of advanced organisers as bridging the gap between what the learner already knows and what he/she needs to know before he/she can successfully learn the task at hand.

At its crudest, the activity of pupil learning embodied in the model of information processing shown in Figure 3, can be outlined as: *attention + thinking + storage,* where the plus signs denote a two-way direction of influence. This two-way direction of influence is of crucial importance to understanding the processes involved in learning; it draws attention to the fact that at any given time each of the three sections of the model illustrated are subject to influence by the other two sections. It is also important to note that what is stored must also be capable of retrieval, since it is the retrieval of information that is often taken as evidence of learning in schools.

Much has been written about the nature of LTM and the process by which a learner's cognitive structure changes. The work of Piaget, who is primarily a developmental psychologist and whose work will be considered in the next section, has been very influential (Lovell, 1979; Webb, 1980). Piaget (eg Piaget and Inhelder, 1969) has argued that the cognitive structure of LTM essentially consists of *schemas.* Each schema is an organisation of information; they may range from a schema based on coordinating physical actions to one which constitutes conceptual understanding. Cognitive structure involves the acquisition of such schemas and the gradual modification and organisation of existing schemas into more complex ones. This continuous process of the acquisition and modification of schemas is seen to result from the child's interaction with the environment. It involves two basic and complementary cognitive processes used in information processing: *assimilation* and *accommodation*. Assimilation is the process involved when the learner's existing schemas are used to interpret the on-going experience taking place. Accommodation is the process involved when the learner's existing schemas are modified to take account of the new information which stems from the on-going experience taking place. During all information processing, there is continuous involvement of both these processes, but the relative degrees of assimilation and accommodation will depend on the activity. Piaget sees those experiences which involve a balance of assimilation and accommodation as being the ones which have the best educational significance for the learner. It is thus the teacher's task to get this 'cognitive matching' right for each pupil. This task has received much attention in recent studies of effective teaching (eg Bennett *et al,* 1984).

Bruner has attempted to explore the nature of the learner's cognitive structure by considering how children appear to store information in and retrieve information from their cognitive structure. Given that the cognitive structure of the child is in some way an attempt to represent a model of the world, in what ways, Bruner asks, might such a representation be accomplished? He goes on to identify three such modes of representation:

1 *Enactive*: based on knowledge derived from actions concerning physical behaviour (such as learning to ride a bicycle).
2 *Iconic*: based on knowledge derived from forming and organising images, either visually or by some other senses (such as imagining the shortest route between two well-known parts of one's locality).
3 *Symbolic*: based on knowledge derived from the use of language, in terms of words or other symbols (such as discussing philosophically the 'meaning of meaning'!).

Bruner notes that human development appears to run the course of these three systems of representation until all three can be commanded for use. Having considered the basic information-processing framework for the nature of pupil learning, two major concepts need to be related to the operation of this model: *motivation* and *reinforcement*.

What motivates pupil learning? In attempting to answer this question it is important to bear in mind a clear distinction between learning that must take place by an individual as a natural part of interacting with the environment, and the specific learning which is intended by the teacher. Within Piaget's approach, learning is the inevitable consequence of the individual's interaction with the environment; such learning stems from the individual's biologically-based drive towards adapting to the evironment. In that sense, any educational experience which requires pupils to interact in some way with the learning tasks in hand will result in some learning. However, when one asks 'what motivates pupil learning?', one is really asking a question about the ways in which a pupil will make a positive mental effort towards the learning task in hand. If pupils are asked when they felt most motivated towards school learning, their answers will fall into one of two main categories: 'when I was really interested in the work' or 'when I had to'! These two categories represent one of the most important distinctions made in considering pupil learning, that between 'intrinsic motivation' and 'extrinsic motivation' (a distinction recognised by Ausubel, Bruner and Gagné).

Simply speaking, intrinsic motivation stems from a biologically based drive of curiosity. Such motivation involves an interest in the learning task itself and also satisfaction being gained from the task. Intrinsic motivation has been elaborated in a number of ways. Berlyne (1960) has emphasised the way in which individuals seem to have a need to explore and seek out stimulation. He points out that this need can be effectively elicited in any situation which confronts the individual with new information incongruent with that individual's previous understanding. White (1959) has argued that individuals have a basic drive towards competence in which exploration, attention and perception are used to promote an effective and competent interaction with the environment. In Bruner's analysis of the 'will to learn', he adds one more perspective to intrinsic motivation. As well as curiosity and competence, he argues that individuals also have a drive towards joining in with others towards achieving some objective. This drive he terms 'reciprocity', and he argues that it can be effectively elicited where learning is based on group interaction. This idea of 'learning by participating' can be seen to underlie some of the ways of learning that will be considered in the next chapter.

Extrinsic motivation refers to those learning situations where the impetus for the motivation stems from satisfying a personal drive; where the learning task is seen to be a means towards an end which may be in part contingent on the successful completion of the task but is not derived from the task itself. There appear to be two main classes of such drives, those which stem from basic needs (such as hunger and safety) and those which stem from socially acquired needs (such as status and affiliation). The latter are sometimes referred to as 'ego-enhancing' needs (eg Ausubel, 1968). Clearly, success in school learning can satisfy a whole range of needs. One prime motive for school learning appears to be the attempt to earn status, esteem, approval and acceptance (in the eyes of friends, peers, teachers and parents); these may be earned in the short-term by means of obtaining good marks and teacher praise, and in the long-term by entrance to degree courses and professional occupations. Another prime motive for school learning, at least of short-term value, is the avoidance of teacher reprimands and punishments. In both cases such motivation is extrinsic because the end states of such motivation are not particular to the learning task or learning activity.

The view of seeing motivation as deriving from an attempt to satisfy one's needs is very helpful in thinking about pupil learning. A particularly interesting development of this viewpoint is the work of Maslow (1970), who has argued that an individual's basic needs can be arranged in a hierarchy, with those lower in the hierarchy being 'pre-potent' (that is, needing to be satisfied as a matter of greater priority) in relation to needs higher in the hierarchy. Maslow's hierarchy, starting from the lowest level, is as follows:

1 *Physiological needs* (eg need for food and oxygen)
2 *Safety needs* (eg need for security, and freedom from anxiety)
3 *Belongingness and love needs* (the need to feel one belongs, and the need to give and receive love)
4 *Esteem needs* (the need for achievement, competence and mastery, and the need for status and prestige)
5 *Need for self-actualisation* (the need to realise one's potentiality).

As well as basic needs, Maslow also identifies cognitive needs, based on the impulse to satisfy curiosity, to know, to explain and to understand. Maslow sees such cognitive needs as being inter-related with, rather than separate from, the basic needs. Indeed, the cognitive needs involve cognitive capacities (perceptual, intellectual, and learning), which are utilised in part to satisfy the basic needs.

Maslow's hierarchy provides a useful framework for thinking about pupil motivation and needs. In particular, it draws attention to the importance of making sure that those needs lower in the hierarchy (particularly comfort, safety, security, and acceptance) are being met when educational experiences which draw upon the higher needs of esteem and self-actualisation are set up. Maslow's notion of self-actualisation is particularly interesting; in some senses it can be regarded as representing the ultimate goal of education. Maslow has also discussed a related notion of 'peak experiences' which refer to moments of intense delight and ecstasy involved in being 'at one' with experiences involved in self-actualisation. Again, a worthy and important goal for education would be to generate such peak experiences as a result of involvement with aspects of school learning (Maslow, 1968).

The need for achievement has also received a great deal of attention in relation to the motivation of pupils towards school learning. A number of studies have explored the nature and development of both the need for achievement in general and as it is expressed in the context of academic achievement (Weiner, 1980). The need for achievement would appear to involve both intrinsic motivation, in its links with White's notion of competence, and extrinsic motivation, in its links with an individual's need for status and esteem. Recent research on achievement motivation has paid particular attention to how pupils form their aspirations and how they attempt to account to themselves for their expectations of success and failure, referred to as 'attribution theory' (Rogers, 1982; Weiner, 1980).

The notion of 'reinforcement' has played a central role in the development of theories of learning by behavioural psychologists. The work of Skinner (1968) has been particularly influential. Skinner's approach attempts to account for learning (changes in behaviour) by focusing on the consequences for an individual of certain behaviour. He argues that where such behaviour is followed by reinforcement, it is more likely to occur in the same situation on a future occasion. In the absence of reinforcement, such behaviour is less likely to occur. This approach has been termed *operant conditioning*; it seeks to explain learning by identifying pieces of behaviour or actions (operants) and analysing the timing and nature of the subsequent reinforcement. Skinner has focused on two types of reinforcement which *increase* the likelihood of the behaviour occurring: *positive* reinforcement (rewards such as sweets or teacher praise) and *negative* reinforcement (removal of unpleasant consequences, eg opportunity to have a detention cancelled). He defines three types of consequences which *decrease* the likelihood of the behaviour occurring: extinction (absence of reinforcement), punishment (reprimands, detention . . .) and response cost (removal of expected rewards, eg loss of house points or privileges). Control over pupil learning by a teacher is seen to depend upon the teacher arranging the appropriate reinforcement to be contingent upon the desired pupil behaviour. Skinner's work on operant conditioning of animals relied heavily on the process of 'shaping'. This involved reinforcing those behaviours which gradually approximated to the desired behaviour. Thus, if the desired behaviour was to jump up and touch an object, initial rewards would follow any jumping, then only jumping near the object, and finally only jumps which made contact with the object. The great advantage of working with human beings is that one can indicate to pupils in the classroom what the desired behaviours are, and then reinforce their occurrence.

Although this behavioural approach to learning does not deal with the processes involved in acquiring knowledge and understanding, it does have a number of important educational implications. First, it draws attention to the relationship between pupils' behaviour (eg paying attention, disrupting other pupils) and the consequences of the behaviour in terms of its future occurrence. The systematic application of behaviourist principles to shape pupil behaviour, termed 'behaviour modification', has been widely advocated and applied (eg Wheldall, 1983). Second, the research has identified a number of important principles which appear to facilitate learning, for example, quick corrective feedback. Such principles have been used to develop programmed learning packages, characterised by short learning steps and quick corrective feedback. These attempt to ensure a high probability of success on each step, which thus acts as reinforcement (Skinner, 1968).

It is interesting to note at this point that the notion of reinforcement can be usefully linked to the notion of needs as underlying motivation. The link would appear to be that satisfying needs constitutes reinforcement. In the context of the school, the behaviour used by teachers to reinforce pupil behaviour (eg praise, house points, avoidance of sanctions . . .) can be explicitly linked to the needs outlined by Maslow. That success itself at a learning task also acts as a reinforcer can be accounted for by its link with both intrinsic motivation (in terms of eliciting and satisfying curiosity and competence) and extrinsic motivation (particularly the esteem needs and because success may anticipate the satisfaction of other needs). The link between reinforcement and motivation also draws attention to the danger of assuming that certain teacher behaviours are in fact reinforcing or punishing; to avoid this danger a teacher needs to be sensitive to the pupil's motivation and the social context. For example, teacher praise for a pupil in the context of an anti-school ethos in a class may not be reinforcing for that pupil if his need for acceptance by his peers is undermined; another common example is that of a teacher reprimanding a pupil (as punishment) where in fact that pupil is seeking attention or attempting to relieve boredom by stirring things up; in this case, the teacher's reprimands act as reinforcers of the behaviour.

Thus far, we have examined the basic model of information processing which seems to underlie pupil learning, together with some consideration of its operation in relation to the basic nature of learning. Such models and their implications for effective teaching have been conceived and elaborated in a number of ways (Entwistle, 1981; Howe, 1984; Klauer, 1985; Tomlinson, 1981). Overall, though, there appear to be three central and crucial aspects to any consideration of pupil engagement in the activity of learning:

1 *Attentiveness*: the pupil must be attending to the learning experience.
2 *Receptiveness*: the pupil must be receptive to the learning experience, in the sense of being motivated and having a willingness to learn and respond to the experience.
3 *Appropriateness*: the learning experience must be appropriate for the desired learning to take place, taking particular account of the pupil's initial knowledge and understanding.

It is argued here that effective teaching involves getting these three aspects of the learning activities right, and each of these three aspects can be related to particular tasks and qualities of teaching. *Attentiveness* relates to the ways in which teachers can elicit and maintain high levels of pupil attention and concentration (by varying the learning activities, getting pupils actively involved, utilising pupil interests . . .). *Receptiveness* depends in part on the ways in which teachers can make use of the different sources of pupil motivation to facilitate and encourage motivation towards learning (eliciting curiosity, offering the opportunity to be successful, fostering a classroom ethos towards learning . . .). *Appropriateness* refers to the ways in which teachers need to match the learning experience to each pupil's current state of knowledge and understanding, and at the same time ensure that the learning activities actually foster the desired educational outcomes (monitoring of pupils' progress and quick corrective feedback, structuring and presenting activities to facilitate meaningful learning, ensuring that the cognitive processes being fostered and the demonstration of learning required are being appropriately assessed through the type of questioning or tests utilised . . .). These three aspects of pupil learning are clearly inter-related in a number of ways. An elaboration of the main issues related to these three aspects and their implications for effective teaching will now be considered, in relation to developmental, cognitive and affective concerns.

Developmental issues

The work of Piaget, in studying the cognitive development of children, has had a great impact on discussions of teaching and learning in schools. Although Piaget was earlier described as a developmental psychologist, strictly speaking his main concern has not been psychology but rather 'developmental epistemology', the study of how knowledge *per se* develops in children (Piaget, 1972). Piaget's research has focused on a number of important processes, including those of assimilation and accommodation, as noted above. Of these, it is his account of the quality of a child's thinking at different stages of development, and how such stages are characterised and linked, that has had the greatest impact. Although Piaget's writings may be too complex for the lay reader (Gruber and Vonèche, 1977; Piaget, 1976) synopses of the main elements of his approach are widespread, both in texts of educational psychology (eg Tomlinson, 1981) and in subject specific texts (eg mathematics: Bell *et al*, 1983).

In essence, Piaget's theory of cognitive development deals with the gradual refinement of the child's cognitive structure through assimilation and accommodation; this refinement is governed by a combination of the child's interaction with the environment (with an emphasis on active exploration) and the processes of biological maturation of the child's nervous system. The nature of the child's knowledge and the cognitive processes the child displays follow a fixed, cumulative and hierarchical order of development through three main stages: the 'sensori-motor' period (lasting from birth up to, on average, 18 months of age), a period of 'pre-operational and concrete operations' (lasting up to, on average, 11 years of age), and finally a period of 'formal operations'. Each of these stages can be further broken down in tracing the development of particular knowledge and cognitive processes.

By identifying a child's knowledge and cognitive processes at a given time, one can place that child's point of development. For example, young children beginning infant school (at around the age of 5 years) are characterised by being unable to 'decentre' (that is, they focus on one aspect of a situation and on their own perspective) or to 'mentally reverse' operations they have witnessed. Thus they cannot successfully acquire concepts such as the conservation of quantity, and appear to believe that changing an object's shape or appearance (by rolling out a ball of plasticine or stretching out a line of counters) will change its quantity. Piaget sees this as being the result of the child 'centring' on the increase in length and being unable to take into account that the original appearance could be restored. The development of 'decentring' and 'reversibility' plus the development of thinking involving the use of principles (such as the principle of 'invariance': that changes in shape do not change quantity unless something is added or subtracted) paves the way for the development of logical thinking. This normally occurs towards the end of the primary school years, although such logical thinking is limited to concrete examples, and only develops into abstract logical thinking during the secondary school years (on average). It is worth noting that other research has indicated that a number of the tests of a child's cognitive development used by Piaget and his followers can give rise to different interpretations of his findings. Some studies argue that research must take account of what for the child may be an ambiguous use of language in the test (Donaldson, 1978) or an excessive demand on the child's information processing capacities, particularly memory (Bryant, 1974). Such research has often indicated that a child's cognitive development at the time may be more sophisticated than the child is able to demonstrate within the constraints of traditional Piagetian tests.

A number of important implications for effective teaching can be drawn from Piaget's writing and subsequent research within his framework. First and foremost is the notion of 'cognitive matching': the need to pitch the learning experience at the right level for each child. This has two aspects: the learning task needs to foster for the child an experience which can make useful links with what he/she already knows, but which also extends such knowledge and understanding (ie a balance of assimilation and accommodation); the learning task must also take account of the level of biological maturation of the child's nervous system and not overtax the child's capabilities. A related notion is that of 'readiness'. This has been applied in particular to 'readiness for reading' but can actually be applied to all curriculum activities. The notion of readiness involves the teacher looking for signs that a child is ready both in motivation and in cognitive development for the curriculum activity in hand. There is a danger that exposing a child too early to particular curriculum demands may well foster inappropriate learning strategies (eg complete reliance on memorisation) or even painful experiences of failure and inadequacy which could lead to alienation from school learning. Research by Shayer has indicated, alarmingly, that science teaching in secondary schools often makes demands on children at the level of formal operations at an age when many pupils have not attained that level of cognitive development (Shayer, 1978; Shayer and Wylam, 1978). Similar observations have been made in relation to other subjects, such as history (Hallam, 1969). The notion of readiness does not, however, imply that teachers should passively wait for pupils to reach a particular state, but rather that they foster that state at an appropriate time in the child's development.

A second important implication for effective teaching stems from the hierarchical and cumulative nature of cognitive development. This emphasises the need for teachers to structure the curriculum activities in an order which makes intellectual sense in terms of the way knowledge is built up, and for teachers to make use of concrete examples in paving the way for pupils developing principles and relationships at an abstract level.

A third implication stems from Piaget's view of the child as an active learner who is trying to construct an understanding of the world. This places emphasis on teaching activities which actively engage the learner, not in the sense of being physically active, but in the sense of being mentally active in terms of assimilation and accommodation in the learning experience. This would appear to be best fostered by explicitly relating new knowledge to previous knowledge, either through teacher exposition and questioning of pupils, or through demanding that pupils address such connections in their academic tasks. It should be noted, however, that for very young children, physical activities are quite crucial for setting up many educational experiences, and they still have some part to play in later schooling. In addition, physical activity (in contrast to listening) can better sustain attention and provide the learner with the opportunity to control the pace of work and how the learning can be interpreted. The 'Nuffield approach' to the teaching of science, with its greater emphasis on the *activity* of science (particularly experimentation), rather than scientific *knowledge*, represents a development along these lines (Driver, 1983). Recent research on teaching, however, has indicated that the proportion of teacher–pupil interactions devoted to fostering such explicit intellectual connections is very low. For example, Kerry (1982) has noted that teachers overwhelmingly use low-level questions demanding data recall or simple comprehension – usually with one right answer – rather than higher-level questions demanding greater thinking skills such as analysis and evaluation which may have more than one right answer.

Piaget's theory will doubtless be discussed and debated for many years, and his work continues to be elaborated on by others (see, for example,

Brown, 1983; Floyd, 1979). However, the principal themes of his approach, as outlined above, remain of fundamental significance to all those concerned with effective teaching. They have been instrumental in fostering a view of education as concerned mainly to facilitate the development of a child's thinking through activity and experience in learning (a view embodied in the Plowden Report (1967) on primary education) rather than as concerned largely with the accumulation of knowledge.

So far this section has given greatest weight to considering general cognitive development; however a number of other aspects of a child's development have important implications for effective teaching. First, there are particular aspects of cognitive development which require attention, most notably language development and learning to read (Clark, 1983). Both are crucial to a child's capacity to meet the demands of school learning; a major barrier to success for pupils is that their competence in language and reading is over-stretched by many academic demands made on them. In particular, it is important to note that language and reading skills continue to develop throughout the school years. In planning curriculum activities teachers need to take into account pupils' language and reading skills and endeavour to foster the further development of these skills.

Second, during the school years pupils gradually acquire and build up cognitive strategies regarding learning and various study skills. The idea that children need to 'learn how to learn' has still not received sufficient attention, in part because children seem to acquire such skills in an intuitive way – they seem to develop in response to the demands for learning made upon them. Unfortunately, such apparent natural develop- ment may well be masking much wasted effort and time by children not knowing how to direct their mental effort towards the tasks in hand, which may be very discouraging for their experience of learning.

In recent years efforts have been made in both primary and secondary schools to foster study skills, and these have tended to be well received and of benefit to pupils. Such study skills range from information gathering skills (eg how to use the school library to research a topic) to explicit learning activities and strategies (eg problem solving skills such as generating new information from data already given) (Hamblin, 1981; Howe, 1984). What seems to be more obscure is how pupils develop the ability to monitor and direct their own thought processes towards learning during the activity of thinking, termed 'metacognition'. Teachers certainly need to be aware that this capacity to consciously monitor their own thinking may be crucial to pupils' success in learning (Brown, 1983; Kirby, 1984).

Third, it needs to be borne in mind that a child's stage of development appears to place constraints on the capacity for information processing presented in Figure 3. This depends, in part, on biological maturation, which places constraints on the child's span of attention (particularly in terms of how many things a child can simultaneously attend to at 'reception' and in 'STM'). In part also, it reflects the fact that increasing knowledge and understanding, coupled with the development of learning skills, enable older pupils to break up information into meaningful units (which younger children are unable to do for that same information) thereby reducing the demands made on the span of attention (Tomlinson, 1981).

As well as cognitive development, it is important not to overlook the implications of physical and personality development for effective teaching. Interestingly, both are linked at a most important phase during adolescence: the onset of puberty. This has a number of important influences on adolescents' attitudes towards school learning as part of their developing self-concept and on their negotiation of the crisis of adolescence involved in developing a sense of personal identity (Burns, 1982; Lindsay, 1983). Other aspects of such development which may impinge on pupil learning range from social problems which may stem from physical appearance or shortcomings (eg being very short or being clumsy) to difficulties over impulse control which can undermine a pupil's ability to meet both academic and social demands and expectations (Burns, 1982; Laszlo and Bairstow, 1985; Maccoby, 1980).

Finally, important developmental changes are linked to a child's motivation towards learning. It would appear that a child's achievement motivation, in particular his or her motivation towards school learning, is influenced by aspects of the child's home life. Parental child-rearing practices and parent–child relationships have received particular attention. Homes which foster and reinforce a child's motivation towards learning and support achievement-related efforts appear to have significant effects on that child's later attitudes towards school learning (Newson and Newson, 1977; Weiner, 1980). In addition, during the school years there appear to be shifts in children's reliance on particular components of intrinsic and extrinsic motivation which are in part the result of developmental changes in their self-concept and in part the result of their school experiences, although both will be inter-linked (Burns, 1982; Harter, 1981).

Cognitive issues

Perhaps the most important cognitive issues arising from the nature of pupil learning outlined earlier, are those concerning the nature of STM and LTM. These issues concern three main aspects of learning:

1 What is the nature of STM functioning?
2 How is information relayed from STM and stored in LTM?
3 How is previous learning brought to bear in meeting new demands (termed 'transfer of learning')?

The most interesting aspect of STM functioning concerns the conscious mental activity involved in learning. This includes the notion of 'mental effort', which can be conceived of, broadly, as a combination of attention and concentration, and the notion of 'metacognition', as described in the previous section, which concerns the learners' active and conscious direction of their mental activity towards learning. Both are clearly affected by pupils' general motivation and attitudes and by pupils' previous experiences of learning. For example, when faced with a new learning activity, the pupil is engaged in a complex web of decision-making, including such reactions as 'this is boring, I think I'll daydream for a while', 'I don't understand this paragraph, I'd better start it from the beginning again', 'this is an important point which I must memorise by repeating it to myself a few times' and 'how does what the teacher is saying relate to my previous understanding?'. Recent research on pupils' perspectives on learning indicates the richness of such pupil decision-making and how it can be influenced by teachers (Doyle, 1983). Indeed, a major task of effective teaching is to guide such mental activity in the most profitable ways, for example by alerting pupils to particular problems involved in a task or to particular learning strategies they might usefully employ.

The question of how information is processed in STM and then relayed and stored in LTM is one of immense complexity (Howarth and Gillham, 1981). Contemporary thinking is that some of the information processed in STM is not relayed to LTM; however, what is relayed does appear to be permanently stored there, but problems arise in its retrieval. Retrieval failure is most evident in the fact that a pupil may not be able to recall a given piece of information but is readily able to recognise the correct answer if choices are offered. Forgetting can largely be seen to be a failure to retrieve stored information (assuming initial storage did take place). Important learning, however, can be consolidated by practice and revision techniques and by linking the learning to a number of different aspects of the learner's understanding. Learning which is stored but which has very little association with other learning creates major problems for retrieval unless the learning has been 'overlearned' by being well rehearsed and frequently used (eg a particular telephone number) or if a mnemonic device is used (eg use of rhymes such as 'Thirty days hath September . . .', and use of imagery to make strong connections between information to be learnt and another list more readily recalled). As noted earlier, an important advantage of meaningful learning is that of facilitating retrieval. Learning appears to be organised in LTM in terms of a large, complex network of associations within which meaningful links are of paramount importance. Overall, retrieval appears to be dependent upon the strength of initial storage (based on mental effort) and the existence of links (either meaningful or otherwise) which can be used to locate the required information. It is consolidated by subsequent practice and the establishment of further links.

'Transfer of learning' refers to the pupil's ability to make use of previous learning in dealing with new tasks and in new situations. To facilitate such transfer is perhaps one of the most important tasks of effective teaching. One of the major barriers to such transfer is that pupils tend to compartmentalise their learning, using retrieval plans that depend on matching specific characteristics of a learning task to that particular compartment of understanding. This is revealed by an inability to transfer learning from one subject area to another, or from topic to topic within a given subject. This tendency in part arises because the majority of pupils appear to see school learning as involving the ability to produce correct answers in response to particular academic tasks. Hence the learning task primarily becomes one of identifying task attributes and recalling the appropriate behaviour required (Doyle, 1983). This is perhaps most apparent in mathematics, where the techniques used to arrive at the correct answer are often memorised without proper under-standing (Dickson *et al*, 1984), but the tendency will be particularly apparent in all subject areas where understanding is not properly based. Teachers need, therefore, to give pupils practice of such transfer experiences.

Particular attention has been paid recently to attempts to foster transfer from school learning to real-life understanding and applications; it is hoped that making school learning appear more relevant to life outside school may have benefits for pupils' attitudes and motivation. For example in primary schools there has been an increasing use of topic work, which takes advantage of many out-of-school experiences (Gunning *et al*, 1981). In secondary schools, there have been attempts to relate science teaching to real-life applications (for example, looking at the chemical processes involved in the rusting of cars, or the deterioration of building stone) (DES, 1985a) and, in foreign language teaching, to emphasise practical competence (for example, how to book a room in a hotel or order a meal in a foreign country) (Buckby *et al*, 1981).

As was noted earlier, LTM consists of an extremely complex network of associations (this is indicated, interestingly, by 'free association' tests used by psychoanalysts). In the first section of this chapter, the development of such associations was outlined in terms of Piaget's notions of assimilation and accommodation and in terms of Skinner's notions of operant conditioning and reinforcement. In addition to operant con-ditioning (behaviour which is reinforced is more likely to reoccur), a number of associations can be considered in terms of the 'classical conditioning' theory, first developed by Pavlov (1927). This is largely based on associations being built up between stimuli which are paired together, usually within a short time interval, in psychologically signifi-

umstances. Pavlov's most quoted example is that of a dog
to salivate in response to the sound of a bell, the sound having
red with the provision of food on a number of occasions.

ms of effective teaching, classical conditioning theory has two
major implications. First, it draws attention to the way in which
associations can be built up through proximity in time; second, it appears
that such stimuli which come to generate a response, may generalise
to similar stimuli. Thus children may build up associations between
emotional responses, both pleasant and unpleasant, and particular
stimuli. For example, a child may be nervous of a teacher who resembles
a feared father. This explains to some extent how a number of purely
cognitive associations may develop (Gagné, 1985; Good and Brophy,
1980).

Two other important cognitive issues concern *cueing* and *mental set*.
Cueing refers to signals which can be used by teachers to alert pupils in
appropriate ways to various demands. Such signals may be explicit, such
as when a teacher says that a point will be difficult to grasp, or may be
indicated by subtle nuances of a teacher's gestures or tone of voice, for
example, when a teacher pauses for slightly longer than normal to signal
that not everyone is paying attention. Mental set refers to the general
expectations pupils have regarding a particular learning activity, ranging
from its level of interest to which learning strategy is most likely to be
successful. The teacher's use of appropriate cueing throughout a lesson
and his/her ability to induce the appropriate mental set for the tasks in
hand (being interested and attentive, expecting to succeed, and being
ready to apply the appropriate learning strategy) are crucial to establishing and maintaining successful pupil learning.

A further cognitive issue concerns the notion of feedback. As noted
earlier, quick corrective feedback is a great facilitator of learning, both
because of its effects on correcting misunderstanding and because of its
reinforcement and motivational value. However, pupils do appear to be
quite sensitive regarding the type of feedback they prefer. In general,
helpful and supportive feedback is seen to be an important characteristic
of effective teaching, while hostile and deprecating feedback is not
(Kyriacou, 1986a). Feedback is also important in giving information
about the general standard of attainment being achieved, and this has
implications for the ways pupils form their future expectations and
aspirations about school learning.

Stones (1979) argues that concept teaching is the most important skill
involved in effective teaching. In his analysis he identifies three main
phases which can be related to all teaching:

1 *The pre-active phase*: which involves a detailed analysis of the
learning task to be undertaken by pupils in order to achieve the
desired educational objectives; this needs to take account of pupils'
entry competence.

2   *The interactive phase*: which involves the actual teaching being undertaken in the light of appropriate psychological considerations (many of which have been discussed here, although Stones places emphasis on those derived from a behaviourist perspective).

3   *The evaluative phase*: which involves presenting new tasks or demands in order to identify whether the desired learning has taken place.

In discussing concept teaching, Stones focuses on the need to develop concept discrimination by the learner; this refers to the learner being able to distinguish between exemplars of the concepts and non-exemplars. A major pitfall in teaching is that much concept teaching is not explicitly recognised as such, and pupils are left to develop their concepts in ways which are faulty. A common example occurs in mathematics where the tendency to draw a right-angled triangle with the right angle at the base often leads pupils to identify the hypotenuse as the sloping side instead of correctly identifying it as the side opposite the right angle. Stones would argue that explicit identification of exemplars and non-exemplars of the hypotenuse would pre-empt such misunderstanding. Such problems seem to abound in mathematics in particular, and have recently been the focus of much attention (eg Bell *et al*, 1983; Kent, 1979).

Finally, a number of important cognitive issues concern individual differences among pupils. These will be dealt with in chapter 5.

Affective issues

In this context 'affective' issues refer to those emotional and social factors which impinge upon pupils' learning. They include, in particular, issues related to pupil motivation.

Without doubt the most important development in this area over the last decade has been a consideration of the relationship between school learning and the pupil's self-concept. The notion of self-concept has two main aspects. 'Self-image' refers to those general attributes which describe how an individual views himself or herself (fat, clever, an Asian, an adolescent, a pupil, male . . .). 'Self-esteem refers to the sense of worth that an individual feels about himself or herself (ie it is explicitly evaluative about oneself). These two aspects of the self-concept are related to each other and are shaped by an individual's experiences and the attitudes s/he perceives others to have towards him/her (Burns, 1982). It is now well established that for many pupils schooling involves prolonged experience of failure which undermines the development of a healthy ('positive') self-concept in respect of attitudes and motivation towards learning, and contributes to a sense of alienation from school and from what school has to offer. This is particularly marked during the latter years of secondary schooling (among third, fourth and fifth year pupils).

In a discussion of comprehensive schools, Hargreaves (1982), one of the most influential writers on educational issues, has put it thus:

> My argument is that our present secondary-school system, largely through the hidden curriculum, exerts on many pupils, particularly but by no means exclusively from the working-class, a destruction of their dignity which is so massive and pervasive that few subsequently recover from it. To have dignity means to have a sense of being worthy, of possessing creative, inventive and critical capacities, of having the power to achieve personal and social change. When dignity is damaged, one's deepest experience is of being inferior, unable, and powerless. My argument is that our secondary schools inflict such damage, in varying degrees, on many of their pupils. It is not intended by the teachers, the vast majority of whom seek and strive hard to give their pupils dignity as I have defined it. (p. 17)

By 'hidden curriculum' Hargreaves is referring to all the messages conveyed to pupils by their experience of schools – regarding values, attitudes and expectations about themselves and their behaviour. Such messages are often unintended by the teacher, but pupils learn them as readily as the 'formal curriculum' which refers to subjects and subject knowledge. Examples of the messages conveyed to pupils by the hidden curriculum typically involve the notion that 'you have to put up with boring lessons', 'the level of work done by high attaining pupils is more valued by teachers', and 'teachers are in authority and have sole control over what you do in lessons'. The thrust of Hargreaves' analysis is that while schools are intended to foster each pupil's educational development, the teaching method and processes typically adopted together with an examination system based on competition and selection, in fact act as a barrier to such development for many pupils.

Poor motivation towards school learning characterises many secondary school pupils in the senior years and is a major source of stress for their teachers (see chapter 9). It can be seen to be largely an attempt by pupils to preserve their own dignity and sense of worth by opting out of an involvement in academic tasks which have previously resulted in painful consequences, such as low marks, teacher criticism, or appearing to be 'dim' in front of peers. In our society, doing well or not doing well, whatever the activity, matters very much to people, and success and failure are emotionally-charged activities. To foster school learning in a way that does not become an emotionally 'risky' enterprise with a high probability of apparent failure is one of the major challenges facing schools today. To appreciate how some pupils experience schooling, one can think of some activity one is not particularly good at (such as swimming, woodwork, or a particular school subject) and ask oneself how one's own motivation towards learning might have fared had one attended a school where such an activity comprised the majority of the curriculum and was the most important area of success for entry into esteemed professions. Recognition of the emotional aspect of teaching and learning has done much in recent years to foster a better understanding of why pupils may come to lack motivation and often misbehave in apparently senseless ways; from the pupils' perspective such behaviour appears to be a both natural and rational response to their circumstances (Cohen and Manion, 1981; Marsh *et al*, 1978; Salzberger-Wittenberg *et al*, 1983).

Connected with the notion of pupil self-concept is an awareness of the influence of teachers' expectations on pupils' attitudes towards school learning. Studies of teacher expectations became prolific following a widely-publicised study by Rosenthal and Jacobson (1968). In the study, researchers told primary teachers that certain of their pupils had been identified on the basis of a test as likely to make marked gains in academic attainment in the forthcoming school year (in fact, the pupils were randomly chosen). Subsequently, these pupils did indeed make greater gains in their IQ scores than their peers. Subsequent discussion of this study indicates that its findings are suspect in a number of respects, and attempts by other studies to replicate and extend the findings have had a mixed result (Burns, 1982; Rogers, 1982). The 'self-fulfilling prophecy' refers to the idea that teachers' expectations regarding pupils' educational progress are communicated to pupils and have a marked influence on their subsequent attainment. This 'prophecy effect' has not been clearly demonstrated in schools. What does appear to be the case, however, is that teachers' and pupils' expectations regarding each other are of crucial importance, and may serve to reinforce each other. As a result, for a class of low-attaining pupils, the teacher and pupils may come to expect less of each other than both are capable of, a tendency noted with concern by HMI (1984) in their inspections of schools. At the same time, however, it should be noted that holding realistic expectations is crucial to a teacher's ability to make the appropriate level of demands and set up the appropriate type of learning experiences for a particular group of pupils. The type of expectations teachers convey regarding academic tasks and pupil behaviour should attempt to raise standards (rather than reinforce and accept existing ones) and be communicated by carefully setting up the learning tasks and offering supportive and encouraging feedback. Having high expectations which lead to setting work that is too demanding, or attempting to raise standards by hostile and deprecating feedback, is likely to produce the sort of attacks on pupils' self-concept mentioned earlier. This may be just as educationally harmful as having low expectations.

Also connected with the notion of pupil self-concept has been the attempt in recent years to give greater attention to developing pupils' self-confidence, autonomy and initiative with regard to academic tasks (Gammage, 1982). This has revealed considerable differences between pupils: some believe that they have much control or influence over their environment; others feel that their experience of life is largely outside their control, and attributable to luck, fate, or the actions of those with power over them. Studies have indicated that developing a belief in one's own ability to have such control (termed 'locus of control') appears to be an important aspect of developing a positive self-concept, and a critical period for such development appears to be the primary school years. Setting up learning experiences which enable pupils to be more active in planning and conducting academic tasks and activities (with supportive feedback) is thus not only important intellectually but also in fostering a sense of self-confidence and autonomy, in effect a belief in one's own ability. This has a fundamental influence on how pupils approach learning throughout the secondary school years and beyond (Gammage, 1982; Rogers, 1982).

Another important affective issue concerning pupil learning is the psychological process of 'identification': the tendency to identify with, and subsequently model oneself upon and adopt the values of, some other person (Bruner, 1966; Maccoby, 1980). Young children normally identify with their parents, often with one more than the other and not always with the same sex parent. Such identification is seen to be a crucial process in the development of the child's values, attitudes and aspirations, including those towards school learning. In later life, other adults can become the object of identification, most often an individual who is in authority over one and for whom one has developed respect (based on either fear or genuine admiration). During the school years, teachers can often be the objects of identification, and where such identification has taken place it can have a marked influence on the pupil's general behaviour and motivation in that teacher's class. In addition, the process of identification can gradually become more generalised during adolescence so that instead of identifying with an individual one can identify with a group, such as a group of friends who share common values, and where one can as a result experience strong peer group pressure to conform to the group's norms and expectations regarding values and behaviour. Such considerations lie at the heart of understanding the ways in which a pupil's classroom behaviour may be influenced by the social relationships established with the teacher and peers (Cohen and Manion, 1981; Hargreaves, 1975).

A final affective issue worthy of attention concerns the relationship between the pupil's affective state and cognitive processing. A number of such links have already been indicated, and aspects of motivation have been discussed in this context. However one additional link in this respect is the influence of anxiety on pupil's learning. Anxiety is an important source of motivation; it arises whenever academic demands are made and success in meeting those demands is important to the individual. Anxiety is thus a common occurrence during tests and examinations, and during class activities where, for example, the failure to answer a teacher's question may cause embarrassment. Such anxiety can often be elicited intentionally by teachers in order to foster high levels of motivation. Two major dangers, however, are involved in relation to anxiety. The frequent occurrence of anxiety in learning activities may well lead some pupils to reject such activities as of no importance to them (thereby defending themselves from experiencing such anxiety). Furthermore, high levels of anxiety actually place constraints on the breadth and quality of one's cognitive processes, largely because the individual's own awareness of being anxious takes up much of the 'mental space' available for information processing. Indeed, if anxiety levels become too high, an individual literally becomes paralysed. In establishing an effective environment for teaching, the anxiety levels of pupils need to be carefully monitored by teachers to ensure they do not inhibit learning (Tomlinson, 1981).

Conclusions

This chapter has outlined the basic nature of pupil learning together with a consideration of the most important developmental, cognitive and affective issues involved. As it applies to the task of effective teaching, the main value of an understanding of pupil learning is that it enables a teacher to reflect upon an explicit agenda of the major processes and issues involved in such learning. In the framework developed here, the notions of 'attentiveness', 'receptiveness' and 'appropriateness' acted as the focus for thinking about pupil learning. Teachers' thinking about their own teaching comprises much craft knowledge based on experience. The continued development of the quality of teaching stems from teachers thinking critically about their teaching, and the processes and issues raised in this chapter lie at the heart of their consideration of pupil learning itself. In further chapters of this book the major processes and issues identified here will be the basis of the tasks of effective teaching that will be discussed.

4 Setting up the learning experience

This chapter is concerned with the types of learning tasks, activities and experiences which teachers can usefully set up to facilitate pupil learning. One of the things that strikes me most about changes in schools over the last two decades is the increasing diversity in the types of teaching methods used. There has been an increasing recognition by teachers of the importance of 'process' compared with 'product'; that how pupils learn, in terms of the learning experiences offered, is just as important as the content of what is being learnt. This move towards a greater emphasis on process is part of a trend towards making learning a more active experience, not only because this can foster greater understanding, better skills and increased transfer of learning, but also because of its beneficial effects on motivation and attitudes towards learning.

As indicated in the previous chapter, the most important considerations involved in looking at such learning experiences is the degree to which they fulfil three major conditions for pupil learning: attentiveness, receptiveness and appropriateness. In the context of thinking about the ways pupils learn, the basic task of effective teaching is to set up a learning experience which involves pupils engaging in mental activity which brings about changes in the pupil's cognitive structure which constitute the desired learning. Teachers, therefore, need to be sensitive to the ways in which different teaching methods and strategies foster different types of mental activity, and the degree to which the particular mental activity being fostered is the one most appropriate for the desired learning.

Pupils' learning in school can be fostered in two main ways:
1 *Teacher exposition*: listening to teacher exposition, which may include asking or being asked questions, watching a demonstration, and genuine teacher–pupil discussion.
2 *Academic work*: being instructed to undertake or engage in academic tasks and activities, either on one's own or together with other pupils.

Teacher exposition tends to place emphasis on describing and explaining new information to pupils through direct teacher–pupil interaction, and is usually based on teaching the class as a whole. Academic work is much more diverse, and includes the whole range of tasks and activities which pupils are instructed to undertake or engage in. The vast majority of lessons given in classrooms involve a mixture of exposition and academic work. In recent years, however, there has been a move away from exposition-based teaching towards much more academic work; this is based on tasks and activities which are much less teacher-dominated, ranging from independent project work to investigative activities where pupils work together. In considering exposition and academic work, two aspects of the type of learning taking place need to be constantly borne in mind. First, does the learning taking place require pupils simply to memorise, and later recall, new information? Or does it attempt to foster greater understanding by making explicit links and meaningful associations with the pupil's previous knowledge and understanding? Second, what type of educational outcome is primarily being fostered (eg facts, concepts, intellectual skills, problem solving strategies, transfer of learning, attitudes, general learning skills, or consolidation of previous learning)? Taking account of the ways pupils learn is essentially concerned with the need to match as effectively as possible the mental activity being fostered by an educational experience both to the learner and to the desired educational outcomes. The consideration here of teacher exposition and academic work will explore this theme.

Teacher exposition

Teacher exposition is the most central stock-in-trade of teaching and serves a number of functions and purposes, often inter-related (Waterhouse, 1983). The way pupils learn is based on pupils listening and thinking in response to the teacher exposition. Overall, teacher exposition can best be related to pupil learning by looking at its three main uses:
1   making clear the structure and purpose of the learning experience;
2   informing, describing and explaining;
3   using questions and discussion to facilitate and explore pupil learning.

1 Making clear the structure and purpose of the learning experience

One of the most important functions of exposition is to emphasise the essential elements of the learning in hand. This is often characterised in terms of following the maxim: 'tell them what you are going to tell them, tell them, and then tell them what you've told them'. In effect, the teacher needs to brief pupils about the learning tasks and activities which are going to be undertaken. Then, after they have been undertaken, the teacher needs to debrief the pupils about the nature of the learning which should have been accomplished. Unfortunately, there is a tendency for teachers to create well-established routines regarding the structure and organisation of their lessons and to assume that most learning is self-evident in its purpose and nature. This has resulted in a neglect of the briefing and debriefing function on occasions when it would have significantly improved the quality of the pupil learning which took place. This function has been widely advocated by Ausubel in his call for greater use of 'advance organisers' and 'end of lesson reviews' (Good and Brophy, 1980). As well as generally introducing the learning in hand, such exposition also serves to alert pupils to particular points of emphasis that are important if the learning is to be successful. For example, when setting up a practical in science, the teacher may warn pupils in the initial exposition of some early difficulties which may be encountered and how they should be handled.

Another important function of teacher exposition is to induce the appropriate mental set towards the learning in hand, and in particular to elicit pupil motivation by either stimulating interest and curiosity about the topic or activity (intrinsic motivation) and/or emphasising its importance and usefulness and the need for success in the topic or activity in terms of future attainment (extrinsic motivation). A useful way of eliciting intrinsic motivation is not to introduce the topic or activity at the start of the lesson, but rather to indicate the way in which pupils' current knowledge, understanding or skills does not enable them to answer a question, although they may have hunches or ideas. So, for example, pupils might be asked why feathers fall more slowly through air than a penny does, or how to ask a particular type of question in French. The subsequent topic or activity is then introduced to meet the problem posed.

The first main use of teacher exposition is thus concerned with the effective setting up of the learning tasks and activities and with the effective drawing of conclusions following the learning tasks and activities. This use can be extended to the explicit consideration of how a particular lesson may relate to previous and future lessons or indeed activities in other subjects, in order to create a greater sense of coherence for a course as a whole and to foster greater transfer of learning.

2 Informing, describing and explaining

A degree of informing, describing and explaining is clearly involved in the first usage of teacher exposition outlined above. But this second usage can be distinguished from the first usage by being concerned specifically with the 'lesson proper'. That is, it is concerned with the role of teacher exposition either as direct instruction or as complementary to academic tasks and activities being undertaken.

At its extreme, teacher exposition can constitute the only learning activity, as in a lecture. While the use of the lecture mode in schools is much less frequent than in previous decades, it is by no means rare to find such teaching, sometimes in the form of delivering dictated notes, in the senior years of secondary schools. In addition, the lecture mode is sometimes used in short bursts with younger pupils in order to ensure that an accurate and correct piece of writing concerning some topic is recorded. There are two major dangers in the use of such extended exposition. First, pupils are psychologically incapable of attending to such activities for long periods (indeed, many undergraduates seem similarly incapable of such concentration); second, the experience does not in itself constitute meaningful learning, and must be explicitly linked to other learning tasks and activities if it is to be of value.

Another extreme use of teacher exposition is the teacher demonstration of some technique or activity, which pupils are asked to observe, note and copy. The most common example of this occurs in the teaching of mathematics but it also appears to a marked extent in many subject areas, such as science, history and geography (HMI, 1979). The essential characteristics of such a form of teacher exposition is that no pupil need say a word throughout the entire lesson.

The most common form of teaching, in fact, consists of a mixture of teacher exposition and academic tasks and activities, where the teacher exposition takes the form of a mixture of informing, describing, explaining and questioning. In recent years such an emphasis on teacher exposition has been widely criticised. For example, the Cockcroft Report (1982) on the teaching of mathematics in schools argued that:

> Exposition by the teacher has always been a fundamental ingredient of work in the classroom and we believe that this continues to be the case. We wish, though, to stress one aspect of it which seems often to be insufficiently appreciated. Questions and answers should constitute a dialogue. There is a need to take account of, and to respond to, the answers which pupils give to questions asked by the teacher as the exposition develops. Even if an answer is incorrect, or is not the one which the teacher was expecting or hoping to receive, it should not be ignored; exploration of a pupil's incorrect or unexpected response can lead to worthwhile discussion and increased awareness for both teacher and pupil of specific misunderstandings or misinterpretations. (p. 72)

An emphasis on teacher exposition in a lesson tends to go hand in hand with a general approach towards teaching termed 'expository teaching' or 'didactic teaching'. This is usually contrasted with 'discovery learning' or 'exploratory learning' (Heywood, 1982). In expository teaching, the teacher clearly directs the pupils' work and this usually follows the teacher's overview and explanation of the learning. Discovery learning, on the other hand, gives pupils control over how to approach a given problem and obliges them to attempt to identify the significance of their findings before the teacher offers an explanation. HMI's surveys of teaching in primary schools (HMI, 1978) and in secondary schools (HMI, 1979) both noted a more widespread use of expository teaching than discovery learning.

Teachers spend a large proportion of their time teaching the class as a whole, ie the teacher exposition is directed at the whole class, and interaction with individual pupils is based on teacher selection of pupils as representative of the class response to questions (Good and Brophy,

1980; Rutter *et al*, 1979). Such whole class teaching clearly poses two major tasks for the teacher. First, the exposition must gain and sustain the attention of the pupils. Second, the exposition must be appropriate for all the pupils in the class. These two tasks are not easily met, and represent an important phase in the development of a teacher's competence. Gaining and sustaining attention depends on a mixture of clasroom management skills (eg use of eye contact) as well as the content of the exposition itself (eg clarity). Keeping the exposition appropriate for the whole class depends on the teacher's ability to fully take account of the pupils' previous level of knowledge and understanding and the level of cognitive demands the exposition is making upon them. Obviously, all classes will contain a range of pupil interests, abilities and motivation, and in general the exposition tends to be pitched so that the least able or least receptive pupil can be carried along with the rest. However, where the range of differences amongst the pupils is particularly large, a teacher may decide that some pupils may well be left behind in the early part of an exposition, but that subsequent elaboration and questioning, or indeed individual help once the academic tasks have been set, will deal with this problem. Two dangers arise when such whole class exposition has not been fully successful. First, the teacher may need to give a large number of pupils individual help (indeed some pupils may come to be inattentive during the exposition because they know they can rely on subsequent individual attention); second, some pupils will either disguise or simply not realise their misunderstanding and will approach the academic tasks set using faulty techniques or simple memorisation of the essential elements necessary for task success.

Recent research on the quality of teacher exposition has indicated that an overwhelming proportion of teacher exposition comprises simple information and data giving, with a contrastingly small proportion offering a consideration of concepts, reasons, explanations and generalisations. This imbalance is also reflected in the types of questions teachers ask and the types of academic work teachers set, and appears to be the case in both primary schools (Bennett *et al*, 1984; HMI, 1978) and secondary schools (HMI, 1979; Kerry, 1984):

> A typical task was a request from the teacher for the class to write a story, usually accompanied by exhortations on neatness and appropriate grammar. Here the demand was for the practice of well-understood routines and rarely did such tasks impart or demand the acquisition of new knowledge. This staple diet of little new knowledge and large amounts of practice was rarely varied to include tasks which required either the discovery or construction of new or different ways of perceiving problems, or the application of existing knowledge and skills to new contexts. (Bennett *et al*, 1984, p. 213)

There were many examples of lengthy monologues without pause for questions, often accompanied by dutiful note-making by pupils; competent though they were, those teachers who gave them might not realise that there would be several other such monologues for pupils to listen to in any one day. Pupils who spend so much of their time listening may need more opportunities than they are given to confirm their understanding and relate it to other experience. (HMI, 1979, p. 95)

Fortunately, in the 1980s we are witnessing a move away from such expository teaching towards much greater use of questions, explanations and academic tasks which foster a greater quality of mental activity HMI, 1985a). Following detailed research on teachers' verbal interactions with pupils in the 1960s and 70s (eg Eggleston *et al*, 1976), aspects of effective explaining and effective questioning have received much recent attention (eg Wragg, 1984).

With regard to effective explaining, it is interesting to note that a teacher's ability to explain things clearly is widely perceived to be one of the most important teaching skills (Kyriacou, 1986a; Wragg and Wood, 1984a). Brown and Armstrong (1984) distinguished between three main types of explanations:

1 *The interpretive* which clarifies, exemplifies or interprets the meaning of terms (what is . . .?).
2 *The descriptive* which describes a process or structure (how is . . .? How does . . .?).
3 *The 'reason giving'* which offers reasons or causes (why is . . .?).

The essential elements of the teacher's ability to explain 'what, how or why?' to pupils involve taking account of the pupils' current knowledge and understanding, clarifying the nature of the problem of knowledge or understanding in hand and the nature of the type of explanation appropriate, and using a combination of explanation, questioning, example giving, and a learning activity to facilitate the knowledge and understanding required. In much teaching the difference between informing, describing and explaining is not clear. This is because some explanations are fairly low level; for example, when a pupil asks a teacher to explain how to use semi-colons, a simple statement of a rule together with some examples may be sufficient. Other explanations, however, concern the elaboration of meaning which may be quite sophisticated; for example, when a pupil asks a teacher to explain why water freezes at the surface of a pond first, the teacher needs to relate the explanation to the pupil's current understanding of the properties and processes involved in this phenomenon.

Brown and Armstrong have noted much diversity in how teachers offer explanations. Of particular interest is the current trend in a number of subjects, such as science and history, to encourage pupils to explore their own thinking when seeking an answer; this is often linked to the notion of how evidence might be interpreted. Such a trend is desirable both because it links the explanation generated explicitly to the pupil's understanding, and because it fosters the pupil's ability to communicate ideas clearly.

3 Using questions and discussion to facilitate and explore pupil learning

During a professional career, the number of questions asked by a teacher runs into tens of thousands. Indeed, there can be no other profession where one asks so many questions that one already knows the answer to. In recent years a great deal of attention and emphasis has been given to effective use of questions as a key teaching skill (Brown and Edmondson 1984; Kerry, 1982; Perrott, 1982). What makes questioning such a useful but complex skill is that it can be used in a number of different ways, ranging from a simple and quick check that a particular pupil has been paying attention, to an integral part of developing a dialogue and genuine discussion with pupils about the topic in hand.

With regard to the types of questions teachers use, one first needs to consider the type of thinking that the question is designed to promote, for example in terms of Bloom's categories of cognitive processes: knowledge, comprehension, application, analysis, synthesis and evaluation (Bloom *et al*, 1956). One important distinction in categorising question types is between those which merely require recall and reporting of facts or information (lower order questions) and those which require some manipulation of information – reasoning about, evaluating or applying it (higher order questions). Whereas lower order questions tend to have answers that are clearly right or wrong, higher order questions tend to be judged in terms of general qualities related to the thinking involved.

A second and related distinction is that between 'closed' questions which only have one right answer and 'open' questions where a number of correct answers are possible. Studies of teachers' use of questions indicates a much greater use of lower order and closed questions rather than higher order and open questions (eg Hargreaves, 1984; Kerry, 1982). In view of the widespread advocacy of the latter as having greater effects on pupil learning, this difference may seem to be a cause for concern (McNamara, 1981). However, a teacher's use of questions to promote thinking amongst pupils is inter-related with its use for other purposes, particularly of a social and managerial nature. Brown and Edmondson (1984), for example, have noted the following reasons given by teachers for asking questions (in order of popularity):

- encouraging thought, understanding of ideas, phenomena, procedures and values;
- checking understanding, knowledge and skills;
- gaining attention to task, to enable teacher to move towards teaching points, as a 'warm up' activity for pupils;

- review, revision, recall, reinforcement of recently learnt point, reminder of earlier procedures;
- management, settling down, to stop calling out by pupils, to direct attention to teacher or text, to warn of precautions;
- specifically to teach whole class through pupil answers;
- to give everyone a chance to answer;
- to prompt bright pupils to encourage others;
- to draw in shyer pupils;
- to probe children's knowledge after critical answers, re-direct questions to pupil who asked or to other pupils;
- to allow expressions of feelings, views and empathy.

In looking at the skills underlying effective questioning, four key aspects stand out: quality, targeting, interacting, and feedback. The *quality* of the question itself, in terms of clarity and appropriateness for meeting its intended function, is clearly of importance. In part this depends on the teacher's ability to take account of the pupil's perspective when asking the question. The *targeting* of questions refers to the way in which teachers select pupils to answer. Of major importance here is the need to distribute questions to as many pupils as possible, and certainly not to focus on volunteers. At the same time, targeting also involves matching the question to the target pupil.

Interacting refers to the techniques used by teachers to deliver questions and to respond to pupils. They involve making use of eye contact, the manner and tone of voice used, the use of pauses to give pupils thinking time, the use of prompting to help pupils in difficulties, and using follow up questions or points to enable and encourage pupils to elaborate or improve the quality of their initial answer. Teachers' use of questions often involves stringing together several questions to develop a particular theme or explore the issue in hand. This technique of sequencing can be a very effective form of dialogue, particularly when the teacher is sensitive to and takes account of pupils' responses. The greatest danger in sequencing is that of sticking too rigidly to a pre-planned sequence, so that pupils' responses become no more than objects against which the dialogue rebounds (a particular pitfall if only volunteers are utilised or ambiguous answers are accepted). One suspect technique occasionally employed by teachers is that of sentence completion: where questions take the form of points in the teacher's exposition at which pupils are asked to insert what might be in the teacher's mind (this may be ambiguous or to some extent arbitrary which is extremely frustrating for learners). At the other extreme, where sequencing sets up a genuine dialogue and exchange of ideas, the educational benefits are clear.

The role of *feedback* concerns the effects on pupils of the teacher's use of questions. Answering questions is often a high risk and emotionally charged activity, in part because it is usually public and in part because it usually involves explicit teacher judgement. The teacher's use of questions can thus have a profound influence on the whole tone of a lesson and on the rapport which develops between the teacher and pupils. In order to protect a pupil's self-esteem and develop pupil self-confidence the teacher needs to ensure that questioning takes place in an encouraging and supportive atmosphere. In particular, this requires praise and encouragement to develop pupils' answers and to convey the message that all attempts to answer will be respected and valued; a teacher should certainly avoid scorning an answer or allowing other pupils to do so. Pupils are very sensitive and alert to such aspects of interaction in forming their views of the teacher's expectations of their efforts; teachers need to be aware of the many unintended consequences which may follow from their use of questions. For example, if a teacher frequently corrects the language used by pupils in answering, these pupils may feel reluctant to contribute answers because of their perception that 'correct language' is as important to the teacher as the meaning of what is said (Barnes *et al*, 1969; Hull, 1985).

Effective questioning overlaps with the use of discussion to explore the topic in hand. Both the National Primary Survey report (HMI, 1978) and the National Secondary Survey report (HMI, 1979) pointed to the need for teachers to make greater use of genuine discussion to explore and develop pupil learning. Two main skills are involved here. First, the ability to get as many pupils as possible to make a contribution. In the case of discussion this means that the teacher can afford to be more uncritical and less censoring of pupils' contributions (compared with the dialogue approach to questioning). Second, the teacher needs to probe and encourage pupils to develop their contribution. Such teacher-directed, discussion-based interaction most often occurs when teachers are exploring general aspects or perspectives of a topic (such as the advantages and disadvantages of 'family life', in a social studies lesson) which are later to be shaped and refined in terms of identifying key issues or attributes. In such cases, the teacher is often leading with hints or suggestions as to the range of contributions being sought. Full and genuine discussion will take place when pupils are given more control over the course of the contributions and indeed when pupils begin to comment on each other's contributions. The teacher's skill in relaxing control over the direction of contributions, while at the same time retaining appropriate control over the nature and procedure of the discussion, is important here. The increasing emphasis now placed on developing pupils' communication skills suggests that in future years such discussion will become an increasingly common occurrence in almost all subject areas both in primary and secondary schools (HMI, 1985a).

Before leaving teacher exposition, a special note is required in relation to the teaching of a foreign language. The traditional approach to foreign language teaching, with its emphasis on grammar and translation, is not very different in many respects from the teaching of other subjects. However, more recently there has been an increasing emphasis on oral interactions in the foreign language and attempts to immerse pupils in the language experience. This approach to foreign language teaching stresses the need for pupils to use the foreign language in response to academic tasks as the means of developing competence skills. These developments, although certainly not the norm, do require some special attention (Dulay *et al*, 1982; McDonough, 1981; Partington, 1981). In this more recent approach to foreign language teaching, the role of teacher exposition and the use of questions basically takes on the form of coaching, with a mixture of practice and extending skills in response to language demands. Given the potentially high risk aspect of oral work of this nature for pupils, the importance of a supportive and encouraging classroom atmosphere cannot be overstated. The use of language games and role playing has been very useful in fostering such an atmosphere.

Academic work

Academic work refers to the academic tasks, activities and experiences used by teachers, usually in conjunction with teacher exposition. In essence this is based on pupils learning by doing, and the learning derives from the thinking involved in undertaking the academic work. Of particular interest here are the findings of a number of studies which have focused on the way in which pupils approach academic work (eg Bennett *et al*, 1984; Doyle, 1983). Such studies have indicated that the type of thinking used by pupils to meet the academic demands set, and the strategies they employ, may often be very different from that intended by teachers. Research has pointed to the ways in which pupils are continually attempting to make sense of what is required of them by the teacher: 'what do I have to do and how do I do it?'. From the pupils' perspective, attention is primarily focused on how to perform successfully (or at least give the teacher that impression) and not on thinking and learning in a genuine intellectual sense. Doyle (1983) notes that this seems to be particularly well documented in primary school teaching with respect to the occurrence of 'buggy algorithms' (solution strategies which are systematic but wrong) in mathematics and reading. When pupils give incorrect answers it is important that teachers explore the method the pupils used to obtain their answer, rather than merely repeating the correct method. In addition, if a teacher wishes to foster understanding rather than performance competence this must be reflected in the nature of the academic demands made; for example being able to add fractions competently will not of itself foster an understanding of fractions. Pupils gear their learning towards the type of assessment they expect the teacher will be employing. This, in part, explains why pupils may be reluctant to pay attention to learning which will not be tested.

There is a large variety of academic work teachers can set. In looking at the range of such tasks, two important aspects seem to be central to the pupils' perception of their appeal. First, the degree of teacher control and direction over the nature of the task. This aspect is often characterised as the difference between 'direct instruction' and 'indirect instruction'. In direct instruction, the activities and tasks are highly structured and organised by the teacher and usually involve written work which enables the pupils to acquire, demonstrate and practise the knowledge, skills and understanding covered during an initial phase of teacher exposition. A common example of direct instruction would be in mathematics teaching, where an exercise consisted of examples of a type of question explained at the start of the lesson. In contrast, indirect instruction involves tasks where pupils are given a significant degree of initiative and responsibility in deciding how the tasks are organised and undertaken and in deciding on the nature of the learning which takes place. An example of indirect instruction would be in the teaching of a foreign language, where pupils are asked to form groups of four and then script a short sequence of interaction (eg arriving at a hotel and booking a room) which the pupils choose, and are then asked to perform in front of the class.

The second important aspect of a task's appeal concerns the degree of risk and cost involved for the pupil engaging in the task. This aspect relates to pupils' perception of how likely it is that they will succeed at the task in hand (which relates to its intellectual difficulty), the nature of the work itself (eg copying out), the nature of the mental effort involved (eg memorising, applying rules, applying understanding), and its apparent value in terms of interest and relevance.

It is important to note that pupils differ markedly in the extent to which certain characteristics of the task set by teachers increase or decrease its appeal. In addition, it appears to be important that teachers employ both direct and indirect instruction, and both high and low risk/ cost tasks, in order to foster a broad range of educational outcomes; the skill involved in doing this lies in matching the best combination of characteristics to the particular context and desired outcomes (Doyle, 1983; Good and Brophy, 1980).

There are five main categories of academic work employed by teachers to complement teacher exposition. These will now be considered in turn:

1   structured reading and writing tasks
2   investigational work
3   individualised programmes of work
4   small group work
5   experiential learning

1 Structured reading and writing tasks

Structured reading and writing tasks refer to those activities where what is read and written is tightly prescribed and directed by the teacher. Such a task often takes the form of an elaboration or consolidation of what has been presented during teacher exposition. The most classic example of such tasks is the use of exercises or lists of questions in a textbook where the pupils' ability to answer correctly is derived from the preceding teacher exposition or material presented in the textbook itself. Other examples of such structured tasks are copying a map out of a book, copying notes out (from dictation, from a book or off the blackboard), or simply being asked to read some text. The essential feature of such structured tasks is that they are passive, in the sense that they provide the pupil with little initiative or control over the work. This is not to decry their importance, particularly in enabling pupils to practise and apply a whole variety of skills. However it has been noted with some concern that structured tasks appear to occupy perhaps too great a proportion of the academic work undertaken by pupils. This point has recently been made with particular reference to primary education (Bennett *et al,* 1984) and to the teaching of mathematics (Cockcroft Report, 1982). Where such tasks are less structured and offer more initiative, they begin to take the form of genuine investigational work, which will be considered in the next section.

The HMI surveys of primary and secondary education (HMI, 1978, 1979) provide a good insight into the use of structured tasks. In the latter survey, HMI made the following important observation:

> Over nearly 400 schools the lasting impression was of a general uniformity of demand. There were considerable differences of format and custom among subjects as there always have been. But the pattern most frequently found could be described as essentially one of 'notes' and 'essays', interspersed with the practice of answering examination questions alongside the drills of exercises and tests. This pattern did not make it easy for pupils to feel that their individual reactions were valued, or that their variations of information or opinion were welcome. Their files at times demonstrated the successful imprinting of a standard language, arising from teacher or textbook. (HMI, 1979, p. 83)

In recent years teachers have become increasingly aware of the hidden messages communicated to pupils by the teaching practices and demands they make, and many have attempted to take greater account of how pupils actually experience schooling. This shift in the consciousness of teachers over such issues is in part a reflection of the large number of changes currently taking place in schools, such as the introduction of life and social skills courses (Hopson and Scally, 1981) and the *Technical and Vocational Education Initiative* (MSC, 1983), which has created a climate of debate about the purposes of schooling and the types of teaching practices and demands which best foster educational objectives.

Even in the last few years there has been a perceptible shift away from the use of structured reading and writing tasks towards other types of academic work, a shift advocated in recent DES and HMI documents (DES, 1985a; HMI, 1985a). Along with such changes a number of significant developments have meant that structured reading and writing tasks have been set with different aims in mind. In the context of learning to read, for example, two notable developments have occurred. First is the use of paired reading schemes, which involve pupils being asked to read books at home in the presence of a parent. Such reading schemes appear to have marked benefits for pupils, in part because of the help parents give through prompting, and in part through the message communicated to pupils that their parents value the activity (Topping and Wolfendale, 1986). The second is the greater use of diagnostic assessment tasks in order to facilitate and extend the development of reading skills (Fyfe and Mitchell, 1985).

In the context of structured reading and writing tasks, specific mention needs to be made of the use of tests. Regular tests and examinations act as a stimulus both for teaching and for learning. In addition, they serve to provide both teacher and pupils with feedback concerning the quality of learning which has taken place and the general standard of attainment that has been achieved. Tests and examinations can, however, have a corrupting influence on education, particularly where both teacher and pupils gear teaching and learning towards success in tests and examinations. Indeed, many teachers and educationists have noted that the importance placed on test and examination results as the prime index of educational success is the single most influential barrier against the development by teachers of many desirable forms of educational experiences (Hargreaves, 1982). Furthermore, the fact that some pupils must inevitably do less well in their test and examination results than others, communicates to many pupils an unequivocal message of failure. One of the greatest challenges facing effective teaching is to devise methods of monitoring progress and attainment which do not alienate those pupils who do relatively less well. One interesting development in this respect is the use of objective criteria of performance whereby pupils progress through various levels of attainment. Such criteria take the form of knowledge or skills required for a given level of competence to be displayed. Attainment tests thereby emphasise what pupils can do and succeed at by setting an appropriate level to be aimed at for each pupil; success is dependent on achieving the set criteria, and is not explicitly measured by performance relative to other pupils. Examples of this approach are the use of graded tests in the teaching of modern languages (Buckby *et al*, 1981) and the development of GCSE (discussed in chapter 9).

2 Investigational work

Investigational work refers to those activities where pupils are given a degree of initiative, autonomy and responsibility towards planning and conducting their own learning in order to investigate some topic or task set by the teacher. The essential ingredient of genuine investigational work is that it involves a degree of problem solving and/or discovery which is in part or totally independent of teacher support. Its prime value lies in the qualities and skills it fosters in pupils, although in addition it has been widely advocated as an effective way of promoting deeper understanding. One of the shifts that has characterised the development of educational aims in schools over the years has been the greater emphasis now placed on pupils developing investigational skills rather than simply acquiring knowledge. Two notable examples are the teaching of history and of science in both primary and secondary schools, where investigational activities have become increasingly prominent. The DES (1985a) has stated in a discussion of science in primary education:

> What should primary science include? In the view of the Secretaries of State, pupils need to grow accustomed from an early age to the scientific processes of observing, measuring, describing, investigating, predicting, experimenting and explaining. Appropriate work can and should begin in infant classes. Pupils should also use their science in technological activities which pose realistic problems to be solved and involve designing and making. Science and technology in the primary school should form, and be experienced as, a continuum. (pp. 8–9)

Advocates of the use of discovery learning and problem solving (eg Heywood, 1982) have emphasised the importance of teachers clearly formulating the problem which is to be undertaken, explicitly fostering the types of information gathering skills which are required, and systematically debriefing pupils on the learning which should have occurred. The ability of pupils to undertake investigational work has to be cultivated carefully, otherwise such activities may result in little learning actually occurring. Indeed, one of Doyle's (1983) observations is that pupils are adroit in presenting teachers with the product they require in ways which circumvent the processes teachers assume have taken place.

An important aspect of investigational work is that of developing the pupil's ability to go beyond the information collected by identifying some rule or principle or by offering some interpretation or explanation. Some problems may appear to involve investigational work but in fact merely foster simple information gathering. For example, asking pupils to give three reasons why the Romans invaded Britain after reading a page of a textbook which lists three reasons is not investigational work, although it is an early precursor of such work. Now, asking pupils to analyse some information about both Britain and Rome at the time from which to identify possible reasons for the invasion would involve a genuine investigation based on analysis and interpretation.

Investigational work does not only foster intrinsic motivation but also those qualities and skills which pupils need to be able to apply to meet many demands in adult life. Attempts to facilitate such transfer of skills from school to the real world have involved the use of practical problem solving tasks. For example, Foxman *et al* (1984) have described types of practical problems that have been used by the APU to assess pupils' problem solving skills. One such problem involved pupils being asked to plan a class trip, using maps, train timetables and a budget, including the selection and organisation of activities and meals.

Another benefit claimed for the use of investigational work is that it fosters creative thinking. One of the key skills of effective teaching in this context is indeed to encourage pupils to explore their own ideas. Quite naturally, teachers often have in mind the type of responses and comments they are seeking from pupils. Unfortunately, this can sometimes foster an atmosphere where pupils are encouraged to guess what the teacher has in mind (often assisted by the teacher through clues and prompts). It takes a fair degree of skill by the teacher to enable pupils to retain the intellectual initiative and to encourage genuine exploration of their own thought. Furthermore, the high degree of risk for pupils in offering comments or ideas which are publically judged to be incorrect makes it imperative for the teacher to be very supportive of all pupil efforts, particularly as the giving of such efforts is exactly what investigational work is attempting to foster.

A particularly interesting development in a number of schools is the use of resource centres to support investigational work. Such centres have tended to develop from their original function as school libraries to include a whole range of materials and equipment (tapes, slides, photographs, objects . . .). These resources are then linked to particular pieces of investigational work which a pupil or group of pupils can undertake. The work will specify the type of information that needs to be gathered or the problem to be addressed, along with the sources and activities housed in the resources centre which need to be consulted. Such centres have been developed widely in both primary and secondary schools, and appear to be very successful.

3 Individualised programmes of work

Individualised programmes of work refer to a substantial piece or course of academic work extending over a number of hours or days, which the pupil is able to undertake on an individual basis. The two major facets of such an individualised programme of work are that it enables the pupil to work at his/her own pace and at his/her own level. Given the importance of matching pace and level to the pupil in maximising the quality of the pupil's learning experience, such programmes of work have been widely advocated and employed.

Three main types of individualised programmes are commonly used in schools: project work, computer-assisted learning programmes, and work cards. Waterhouse (1983) has made two important observations about such programmes. The main danger facing effective teaching, he argues, is that the teacher spends too much time dealing with a range of trivial resource and organisational matters, rather than actually teaching; over-reliance on the content of the materials used for the development of pupil understanding can lead to problems. Indeed, the main rationale for such schemes is not that they replace the teacher, but rather that the teacher is given more time to teach on a one-to-one basis. Waterhouse's second point is that it is commonly asumed that the most crucial task for teachers is indeed to help pupils when they get into difficulties. In fact, the major task is to properly brief pupils before they begin about what they are expected to do and achieve as a result of the activities.

Project work has been widely used in schools as a means of developing independent study skills, and is increasingly being incorporated into national examination assessments at the age of 16. Project work is a very important motivator (particularly of intrinsic motivation) through the degree of choice and control it offers to pupils in undertaking the work. It also enables pupils to apply a number of the skills they have developed. In secondary schools, the use of project work in history (Shemilt, 1980) and geography (Beaumont and Williams, 1983) has received particular attention. In primary schools it normally takes the form of topic work where a particular theme or topic (eg water) is used as a common link between various subject areas and activities (eg creative writing, history, biology). This form of activity is used extensively and imaginatively at primary level (Gunning *et al,* 1981).

Perhaps the single most significant development in recent years regarding individualised learning has been the growth of schemes based on computer-assisted learning (Hartley, 1985; Wellington, 1985). The advent of the micro-computer, coupled with the commercial development of educational packages ('software') for schools has led to a number of exciting initiatives. The simplest type of development has been the production of programmed learning texts. These commonly consist of a number of questions together with multiple choice answers; depending on the choice of answer the text then moves on to further information (if the answer was correct) or a repeat or further elaboration of previous information with a repeat of the same question (if the question was answered incorrectly).

Since the 1950s programmed learning texts have been advocated as an effective teaching aid (Stones, 1979). Their use has been limited because they were time-consuming and expensive to produce, and quite demanding to work with for long periods. However, micro-computers have enabled such texts to be displayed on a screen in a more animated and exciting form. For some reason, the use of a micro-computer seems to appeal to almost all pupils. A more sophisticated type of development has been the use of computer programs to display the results of answers to different questions. So, for example, what would happen to a population of mice with a given gene pool for pigment can be displayed for any particular set of conditions specified by the user (such models have now been produced in many subject areas; one obvious example being economic forecasting). Particularly exciting developments have occurred in the use of programs to develop conceptual understanding. A very good example is a package entitled *Making Numbers Make Sense* (Bailey and Lienard, 1984), aimed at primary school children. One program uses an array of objects on the screen to develop number estimation of an array; another program uses a golfer putting to develop number estimation of length; another program uses a submarine firing at a tanker to develop number estimation of angles. The programs in the package all use a game format to develop real conceptual understanding of the size of a number across various areas of application (array, length, angle, etc).

The biggest brake on the development of computer assisted learning, particularly in primary schools, is the need for in-service training and support for teachers. Other problems, such as the unreliability of some equipment, the time involved in setting up equipment, and the lack of time available to monitor and modify programs, will all be increasingly overcome as the technological and information services available to teachers gradually improve.

The use of work cards as a basis for individualised programmes of work has also become widespread in recent years. The most common form such schemes take is a specified series of tasks and activities which together make up a course of academic work. The course may be a published one used in a number of schools, or one devised by a teacher. The tasks and activities are usually printed on cards, but may be printed on paper or contained in a folder. The tasks and activities may direct pupils to textbooks, worksheets or explanatory texts and accompanying exercises. For some courses, the cards must be followed in a set order, for others, the pupil may be allowed to select the order. The most crucial aspect in using work card schemes is the need to have a good record of progress maintained for each pupil. While some degree of pupil self-assessment and record-keeping is often involved, teacher assessments are essential if a whole range of qualities (spelling, handwriting, presentation, explanation) are to be monitored. There are many examples of such schemes; a number of particularly interesting developments along these lines have taken place regarding the teaching of mathematics (Watson, 1976). Both Bennett *et al* (1984) and Waterhouse (1983) have noted the potential danger of time being wasted in waiting for teacher help, marking and direction. Attention to organisation which minimises such problems is thus very important. Indeed, there is little doubt that supervising pupils who will be working on different topics and presenting a whole range of demands (from needing intellectual help to requesting materials) requires sound planning and organisational skills as well as a fair degree of mental energy.

4   Small group work

One particularly healthy development in schools has been the greater use of small group work. Small group work refers to academic tasks and activities undertaken by a group of pupils, which involves some degree of discussion, reflection and collaboration. The optimum size for small group work for most types of tasks is probably about five (Waterhouse, 1983) although small group work can be undertaken by groups as small as two. Advocates of the value of small group work (eg Barnes and Todd, 1977; Whitaker, 1984) have stressed the importance of the skills developed by the processes involved in small group work (eg social and communication skills) as being educationally as important as – if not more important than – the intellectual quality of the work produced (ie the aims may often be process rather than product oriented in emphasis). Indeed, the importance of collaboration involved in such work has received particular attention, under the term of 'collaborative learning' (eg Salmon and Claire, 1984).

Whitaker (1984) has listed the value of such work:

1   It creates a climate in which pupils can work with a sense of security and self-confidence.
2   It facilitates the growth of understanding by offering the optimum opportunity for pupils to talk reflectively with each other.
3   It promotes a spirit of cooperation and mutual respect.

Studies of group work (eg Kerry and Sands, 1984) have indicated that it is more successful where the teacher shows skill in handling and understanding groups, gives a positive lead before the group work begins, and follows up the group work by pooling the discussion and giving feedback on the work produced. Good and Brophy (1980) have also emphasised the importance of the follow up if the value of such work is not to be undermined by it being regarded merely as a time filler. Many might regard science practicals as a common example of small group work (usually involving two or three pupils working together). However, the vast majority of science practical work involves pupils carefully following instructions and directions given by the teacher; it thus offers little room for discussion and collaboration other than the cooperation required for the conduct of the practical. In fact, small group work occurs most often in English, history and social studies, in the secondary school, and in topic work and collaboration on projects in the primary school. The greater use of small group work in science and mathematics will depend on these subject teachers recognising the value of the skills being fostered as an important part of their own subject area and not regarding them as the more proper concern of others.

There are two main types of small group work: where the pupils are given a specific task to achieve (eg 'Prepare a leaflet about the working conditions a sailor could expect to find on the seventeenth century ship from the materials given'); and where the pupils are asked to explore an issue through discussion (eg whether fox hunting should be banned). In addition, a number of other activities are used to a lesser extent. These range from activities based on pairs of pupils interacting (a common feature of foreign language teaching) to 'buzz sessions' (where pupils are asked to list as a group as many ideas, features or whatever connected with some problem).

The use of group work in the primary school has, however, been the subject of some controversy, in part because it has been discussed in the context of the debate over 'formal' versus 'informal' teaching styles and 'traditional' versus 'open' education. Group work has been seen as part of more progressive teaching which may be adopted at the expense of maintaining academic standards (Bennett, 1976; Cohen and Manion, 1981). Some of this debate has confused the term 'group work', used here in its educational sense as collaboration between pupils, with its use as a type of classroom organisation to denote pupils sitting in small groups around a table rather than at individual desks or in rows (Bennett *et al,* 1984). While many pupils do not possess the skills or maturity to produce a high quality of work within the context of small group activities, it must be stressed that part of the educational benefit derived from small group work is the fostering of such skills and the development of such maturity. One of the most common, and to my mind flawed, reasons given for not using certain teaching methods or activities, is that the pupils lack the appropriate skills. This has been argued in relation to using discussion and investigational work in particular, on the basis that when such an approach was tried the quality of work produced or the activities undertaken seemed rather poor. It must be remembered, however, that developing such skills takes practice and confidence; a substantial period of teacher support and guidance is necessary before pupils can show just what they are capable of.

A particularly interesting development in schools has been the use of peer group tutoring, which involves one pupil helping or teaching another on a one-to-one basis (Allen, 1976; Morgan and Foot, 1985). The most common application of peer group tutoring has involved older pupils helping young pupils, for example in learning to read or in arithmetical computations. Interestingly, the older pupils themselves often benefit from the exercise for having to teach leads them to improve their own competence (Goodlad, 1979). This form of tutoring has been widely used to help less able older pupils as well as younger tutees. At the same time, peer group tutoring has also been successfully applied using older pupils to help remedial younger pupils (Wheldall and Mettem, 1985). Earlier in this chapter, mention was made of paired reading programmes which involve pupils reading to their parents at home. Studies of such programmes indicate that it is often an older brother or sister, rather than a parent, who acts as tutor – particularly among ethnic minority communities – which is in fact a form of peer group tutoring. For some reason the use of more able pupils helping less able pupils within the same class appears to have been less successful than the use of older pupils, in part perhaps because a classmate as tutor may serve to highlight one's sense of failure and relatively lower status.

5 Experiential learning

It is important to note that there are two common usages of the term 'experiential learning'. The first denotes the process of coming to understand and make sense of oneself and one's own experiences, particularly aspects of oneself or experiences one has sought to suppress (Claxton, 1985). In education this definition is applied to the need to develop 'the whole person' and is an aspect of the humanistic psychology which essentially sees the teacher's role as involving a degree of emotional help and support in fostering such learning (Rogers, 1983). The second use of the term 'experiential learning' refers to the use of activities such as role-playing, or direct experiences such as spending some time working at a local firm, which are employed by teachers to enable pupils to better understand and appreciate, both intellectually and emotionally, an issue being explored. These two meanings are sometimes linked (eg Whitaker, 1984), but it is the second use of this term that will be considered here.

Experiential learning, as defined above, involves providing pupils with an experience which will totally and powerfully immerse them in 'experiencing' the issue which is being explored, and will as a result influence both their cognitive understanding and also their affective appreciation (involving their feelings, values and attitudes).

The most common examples of experiential learning are role-play (utilising drama, simulation activities and games); watching plays performed in the school by professional acting groups; viewing professionally made videos which focus on a particular person's perspective; and direct experiences (based on tasks or visits). Examples of the use of role-play include acting out life on an eighteenth century ship crossing the Atlantic, or acting out an industrial dispute at a factory with pupils allocated various roles such as managers, shop stewards and workers.

Plays and videos can provide particularly powerful experiences, for example, exploring prejudice or war through the experience and perspective of victims. Direct experiences can utilise visits in various ways; for example pupils can discover much more about the nature of working on a production line in a factory from a visit to one than is possible by more 'indirect' means. An interesting opportunity for a visit which also includes role-play is offered in some historic houses where pupils take on roles (including period dress) in the household at an appropriate historical period. Direct experiences can also utilise a whole variety of tasks in the authentic situation (work experience in a local firm) or in some contrived way (such as being asked to wear a purple arm-band for three days in school, without divulging the reason to anyone, in order to parallel aspects of racial discrimination).

Many areas of the school curriculum now make use of experiential learning, although the most extensive use and development seems to be in the area of social studies and social education. Two particularly fascinating examples have been an exploration of the world of work through industrial simulation and games (Holmes, 1984) and an experiment establishing small businesses in a school, which were developed and run by a group of pupils (Moore and Crisp, 1984).

Where the use of experiential learning has been employed in social studies and social education as a means of fostering personal development in the sense of coming to understand oneself and one's experience, its links with the first usage of 'experiential learning' outlined above become apparent.

As with group work, careful planning, briefing and de-briefing by the teacher is of fundamental importance for the success of experiential learning. In addition, this approach calls for a very different form of teacher–pupil relationship and classroom climate than that which commonly pertains during expository teaching, as discussed earlier in this chapter. In experiential learning the role of the teacher is to set up a learning experience which encourages the pupils to reflect upon their own feelings, ideas and values; the climate of the classroom during de-briefing work needs to be supportive and enabling rather than intellectually prescriptive.

In thinking about experiential learning it is interesting to note that the pupil's whole experience of schooling is in itself an example of experiential learning. After all, the myriad of experiences that the pupil has throughout the school years shapes that pupil's feelings, ideas, values and attitudes about him- or herself as a learner, and to some extent about him- or herself as a person. If one thinks of schooling in terms of experiential learning, one can focus upon a number of experiences schooling typically offers to pupils. First, as a result of the comparative nature of much of the assessment that is made, the majority of pupils are not deemed to be academically successful. Second, academic knowledge and understanding is held to be of fundamental importance and value. Third, that the role of the teacher is one of authority in imparting and directing the accumulation of such knowledge and understanding. Fourth, that the role of the pupil is to accept and accumulate such knowledge and understanding in an essentially passive and biddable manner.

It is interesting to contrast these four aspects of schooling with the characteristics of experiential learning put forward by its exponents. It is perhaps not surprising that both teachers and pupils often find experiential learning uncomfortable at first. Teachers tend to feel drawn to impose a degree of exposition and interpretation; pupils often approach such sessions with caution and may feel unsure what is expected of them. As with group work, both teachers and pupils need to develop the skills to make such learning successful; they should not be disheartened or put off by early experiences with such forms of teaching. Indeed, it is worth noting that schooling involves experiential learning for teachers themselves about their capabilities, their strengths and weaknesses. Like pupils, teachers also prefer the safe ground of tried and tested learning situations. Perhaps one of the major challenges facing schools is to develop an experience of schooling for pupils which adopts two implicit assumptions of experiential learning: that each pupil will benefit from the experience, and that all pupils will be held in equal value and esteem.

Conclusions

In this chapter the diversity of the learning tasks, activities and experiences which a teacher can set up to facilitate learning have been considered. While a number of distinct categories have been used to make this diversity clear, in practice effective teaching involves a complex combination of such tasks, activities and experiences. Effective teaching involves a number of skills concerned with the planning and organisation of such tasks and their presentation, and with matching the tasks as appropriate to the educational outcomes the teacher wishes to foster. Much discussion of effective teaching has relied heavily on an image of teaching which is traditional both in terms of the teaching style it implies (expository teaching) and in the educational outcomes it focuses upon (performance on attainment tests). If there is one thing that has characterised schools in recent years, it is the greater diversity of teaching activities which are adopted, ranging from computer assisted learning to role play. Our thinking about effective teaching needs to keep pace with such changes in the character and nature of learning.

5 Taking account of pupil differences

There are a large number of differences between pupils and between groups of pupils which may influence teaching and learning. Many of these are capable of sustaining books in their own right, and indeed some have. This chapter, however, will focus on the six major pupil differences which warrant particular attention: ability, motivation, social class, gender, race and special educational needs.

Taking account of pupil differences is a key factor in thinking about effective teaching. It enables the teacher to be more sensitive to the context of the educational experience to be set up and the issues involved in ensuring that this educational experience will facilitate the desired learning by a particular pupil or group of pupils. Essentially, the same message occurs from each pupil difference considered: that teachers need to carefully monitor the match between teaching and the pupil or pupils being taught. The skills involved in getting this match right, and the implications for the teaching methods and processes adopted, will almost always benefit *all* pupils, not just the specific individual or group being considered. For example, in considering how best to sustain the interest of gifted children, it becomes evident that the strategies and considerations involved are relevant to sustaining the interest of all children. Each of the six major pupil differences that will be considered in this chapter in effect thus serves to raise a number of agenda items about teaching and learning which carry with them similar implications, although the details of the prescriptions that emerge may be different. This similarity of implications is perhaps not surprising, given that the categories of pupil differences commonly identified as important are not mutually exclusive. Indeed, such categories overlap to a considerable extent, as for example in the case of 'ability' and 'social class' which will be discussed later. In looking at pupil differences, the central message invariably says something about *all* pupils and about *each* pupil. This point needs to be borne in mind throughout the chapter.

Ability

The 1944 Education Act states as a legal requirement that all children receive an education related to their 'age, ability and aptitude'. While the need to take account of age is currently reflected in the widespread grouping of pupils into single year-span classes (although not exclusively so), ability and aptitude are currently the subject of diverse provision. Ability is closely linked to the notion of 'intelligence', which refers to a child's ability to learn and to meet cognitive and intellectual demands through the application of current knowledge, understanding and intellectual skills. Indeed, the notion of intelligence arose from research findings which indicated that children appeared to differ in performance in a consistent way across a wide variety of cognitive and intellectual tasks; this indicated the existence of some 'general ability' which contributed to relative success in each such task. Aptitude refers to particular talents, such as mathematical, musical or in foreign languages.

Two important points need to be made concerning this view of general ability (or intelligence). First, it is clear that at any given moment a pupil's general ability is in part a reflection of previous learning experiences. Second, a pupil's level of educational attainment is not simply a function of general ability but is influenced by a number of other considerations, such as the pupil's motivation and aspirations; parental encouragement and help; and the nature of the content and processes involved in the school curriculum, such as relevance, interest and familiarity. Thus, distinguishing between 'less able' pupils and 'low attainers' is important in its implications for effective teaching; after all, low attainers may well include some able pupils.

In recent years there has been much discussion concerning the teaching of 'very able' and 'gifted' children (eg Povey, 1980; Wallace, 1983). The major concern in this respect is that such pupils are not sufficiently stretched by the teaching they would normally experience in schools, and that this may well result in gross underachievement. Given that gifted children may well be able to make a very significant contribution to society in their future working careers (particularly in science and technology), additional support for the education of such children can be justified not only in terms of the pupils' needs, but also in terms of the possible future benefit to society as a whole.

However, providing additional provision for gifted children is no easy matter. One problem lies in the implicit élitism involved and the feeling that extra resources may be directed at pupils who are quite capable of doing well from the education system anyway. Another problem is the difficulty involved in identifying such children. For many years the label 'gifted' has been restricted, by some, to those with very high IQ test scores (the cut-off point differs from author to author, but the top ½ to 2 per cent of the age population is fairly common). Recently, however, there has been a tendency to focus on the needs of 'very able' pupils; sometimes this term has been used synonymously with giftedness, but more properly it denotes a broader range of IQ test scores, covering the top 5 or 10 per cent. At the same time there has been much concern about the use of IQ scores as a rigid method of identifying gifted pupils, and other authors have advocated focusing on the quality and style of work produced by a pupil, which can take account of motivational factors and more specific aptitudes (eg Denton and Postlethwaite, 1985). However, those gifted pupils who attempt to mask their ability (for example, so as not to appear to be too different from their peers) may be overlooked whichever approach to identification is used.

Three main types of additional provision are available for gifted pupils. The first involves acceleration through existing provision, such as when a pupil is promoted to a class of older pupils. The second involves specialist provision for groups of gifted pupils, such as specialist schools for particular talents (such provision in this country is largely restricted to music) or specialist centres where gifted pupils can meet perhaps once a week to engage in advanced work of various types. A number of specialist centres of this sort have been organised by voluntary associations of parents. The third type of provision involves school-based enrichment materials and activities, normally used by the class teacher.

At present, in the vast majority of schools no additional provision is being specifically directed at gifted pupils. Teachers have been given neither additional time nor additional resources to gear specific provision to this select group. With a few notable exceptions, LEA policy has been to give gifted pupils low priority. The most central need of gifted pupils is to be stretched; this does not mean to work faster or to do more of the same, but rather to engage in a higher quality and more stimulating course of work. Fortunately, a more general awareness of the need to stretch *all* pupils has led to changes in teaching methods and activities, such as a more widespread use of topic work, project work and individualised learning programmes, which may well benefit very able and gifted pupils by allowing them more control over their own learning.

At the other end of the range of ability and attainment are pupils variously described as 'the less able', 'low attainers', 'slow learners', 'backward' and 'remedial'. Unfortunately the meaning of these terms has not been consistently employed. Following the 1981 Education Act (see p. 97, we now speak of children in the ordinary school as having *mild learning difficulties* if their attainment falls well below the average expected of their age. Some children come into this category largely as a result of low general ability. Others are seen to do so because of environmental, motivational, emotional, behavioural or health problems. The current expectation is for pupils with mild learning difficulties to remain with their normal classroom teacher, in 'mainstream' teaching. Their educational needs may be met by their normal classroom teacher alone; with support from colleagues; or through a period of withdrawal for remedial attention.

Pupils with a very low general ability, whose educational needs an ordinary school is unable to meet in the normal way, may be described as having *moderate learning difficulties* and may, if assessed as appropriate, attend a special school. These pupils were formerly described as educationally subnormal – ESN. Pupils with *severe learning difficulties* linked to very low general ability include those whose needs can best be met, in the most serious cases, by residential (rather than day attendance) special schools or hospitals (for an overview see Galloway (1985); see also the section later in this chapter on special educational needs).

The picture is complicated by the fact that many pupils with a very low general ability (say with an IQ test score of less than 80) remain in ordinary schools, while some pupils with a higher general ability may attend a special school. Indeed, a further term frequently employed is that of children with a *specific learning difficulty,* which refers to apparently normal pupils who have a marked difficulty in one area of basic educational progress, such as in reading, writing, spelling, or number work (Tansley and Panckhurst, 1981). Such children may be found in both ordinary and special schools. Overall, the relationship between pupils' general ability, learning difficulties, and attendance at an ordinary or special school, is not a simple one.

Much has been written about teaching children with learning difficulties in the ordinary school (eg Gulliford, 1985). Perhaps the most sensitive problem concerning such pupils is that they have often experienced failure in the school. Hence they may well have built up an emotional resistance regarding future effort to succeed, largely because it exposes them to further risk of painful failure. In such cases, remedial teaching can often involve counselling, and activities based on building up the pupil's academic self-confidence and self-esteem. A particularly interesting development in schools is the use of a centre to provide additional teaching both for pupils needing remedial attention and also for pupils undertaking individualised programmes of work in the normal way. This dual purpose, in catering for the whole ability range whilst concentrating on the remedial aspect, to some extent reduces the overt labelling that occurs in many schools if a centre is only used by pupils requiring remedial attention. It is important for the classroom teacher to be sensitive to pupils' learning difficulties which may arise from an inadequate base of understanding and competence (either linguistic or mathematical) and thus require remedial attention. This is no easy task, since many pupils are quite adept in masking the real nature of their difficulties, particularly in indicating that a problem lies in motivation rather than in their level of understanding.

The fact that the teaching of very able and less able pupils has received particular attention in writings on teaching methods does not, of course, mean that teaching average ability pupils is in any sense less of a problem. Clearly, because a majority of pupils are of average ability, the classroom tasks and activities, together with resources and materials, tend to be more specifically geared to them. In practice, however, the problem of meeting the needs of the very able, average and less able pupils faces not only the school as a whole but also the individual class teacher, since even in classes composed of pupils selected as being of relatively similar ability there exists a marked range of ability.

In thinking about effective teaching across the ability range, a teacher needs to take account of the fact that some types of teaching activities may be more successful for some ability groups and for particular desired outcomes than others. For example, in relation to success in 'O' level Physics, Chapman (1979) noted that use of dictated notes contributed to success amongst the weaker pupils but time on private study contributed to success among the more able pupils, even though the range of ability involved was quite narrow – as all the pupils were 'O' level Physics candidates.

Given the range of individual differences which may influence the effectiveness of teaching (Riding, 1983), maintaining an ideal match for each pupil is difficult. However, some general considerations do apply. Overall, probably the most important is to assess the size of step in understanding that pupils of different abilities can benefit from. There is a real danger, here, of viewing relatively less able pupils as simply needing more practice in, and consolidation of, lower level work. In fact, such pupils need to be excited, challenged and stimulated by their learning just as much as their more able peers, particularly if intellectual skills rather than content are to receive emphasis.

One final aspect of individual differences related to ability which requires attention is the use of mixed ability teaching. This refers to classes which are composed of pupils drawn from the whole ability range of the school. Although many arguments have been put forward to justify mixed ability teaching, perhaps the most central one is that it avoids the labelling and depressed expectations of less able pupils which occurs when they are grouped together by setting or streaming into a class. In the discussion surrounding mixed ability teaching (eg Cohen and Manion, 1981; Davies and Evans, 1984), it has been noted that this trend was strongly associated with a move towards using a variety of teaching strategies and activities and towards an emphasis on broader social and academic development. Where such developments have been sufficiently resourced and the teachers involved committed to the schemes, much success has been achieved. However, in a number of schools, such schemes have been undermined by an emphasis on too narrow a view of educational attainment, an inability to broaden teaching activities sufficiently, or an inability to sustain the degree of effort such teaching and organisation demands. Currently a large number of schools use mixed ability groups as class units, although in the secondary school this is often restricted to the younger year groups and may exclude subject areas where it is argued that an overtly hierarchical and cumulative nature of progress would cause difficulties (eg mathematics and modern languages).

Motivation

Motivation towards learning is undoubtedly one of the key aspects of pupil learning, and it is also a source of particularly important differences between pupils. Yet, whereas differences in ability between pupils are almost taken for granted, differences in motivation are subject to extensive debate and discussion. In my own research on stress among teachers, for example, 'pupils' poor attitudes towards work' and 'poorly motivated pupils' were rated by teachers as major sources of stress (Kyriacou and Sutcliffe, 1978a). The notion that the vast majority of pupils 'could do better' is so commonly used it has the status of a cliché.

Differences between pupils in their academic motivation are a reflection of a number of influences, ranging from experiences in their upbringing to their responses in school to previous success and failure at academic tasks and activities. The role of the home and parental encouragement is widely acknowledged, and received particular prominence in the Plowden Report (1967) on primary schools. More recent studies of the relationship between home and school (Craft *et al,* 1980; Newson and Newson, 1977) have highlighted that such pupil motivation is fostered through developing a child's self-confidence concerning his or her own ability, by direct help from parents with school related tasks (eg reading, project work), by pressure exerted concerning the importance of school attainment, and, particularly importantly, by the experience in the pre-school years of school learning type activities in the home. Such characteristics vary in extent from home to home, but appear to be more prevalent in middle-class homes than in working-class homes (the influence of social class is explored in the next section). Such differences between pupils in self-confidence and perseverance, and in their attitudes regarding the importance of school attainment, can underlie the relative success of some pupils in contrast to the relative failure of others; for a vast number of pupils in the latter category, a vicious circle of poor motivation and relative failure has resulted in gross underachievement in school.

Another aspect of the influence of the home stems from the tendency for pupils to identify with and take on the aspirations of their parents. To the extent that becoming like their parents (or living up to their parents' aspirations) in lifestyle and occupation may require educational success, such pupils may be prepared to tolerate school and school learning to a remarkable extent. This is most noticeable in the learning strategies pupils are prepared to adopt to be successful. Countless pupils have used rote learning to memorise information or techniques, without understanding what the learning addresses. This strategy of reproducing what a teacher appears to require without any underlying understanding is often used by highly motivated pupils. In contrast, poorly motivated pupils often complain that they do not understand or see the importance and relevance of the learning; this, in effect, is a more intellectually honest response than rote learning.

Teachers' concern about poor motivation in pupils, however, is not just restricted to a small, relatively low attaining group of pupils within the school. Rather, it is a concern about the vast majority of pupils. Teachers themselves are aware that the compliance towards learning of many pupils (across the whole range of ability) lacks that quality of intellectual involvement and excitement about academic work which is the hallmark of the highest quality of educational progress. Teachers often contrast the attitude of most pupils with the enthusiasm that adult learners bring to a subject during evening classes. For teachers, improving pupil motivation reflects a concern to develop and foster a more positive and enthusiastic approach to their studies, involving a degree of autonomy, independence and self-generated activity; the problem does not only relate to pupils alienated from school work altogether.

Increasing pupils' motivation depends on giving pupils more control over their learning, fostering greater self-confidence, and increasing the perceived relevance and interest of the academic work undertaken. It is quite crucial, however, that the teacher is skilled in identifying the source of a particular pupil's low motivation. Underlying a pupil's low motivation may be a lack of understanding; poor self-confidence; reluctance to apply the required mental effort; or fear of failure. In giving remedial attention to a pupil's lack of progress, the teacher needs to diagnose the problem accurately. This requires an element of individual attention, which most teachers give in conjunction with whole class teaching.

A particularly important influence on pupils' motivation appears to be the teacher's expectations, as noted in chapter 3. The interplay between pupils' and teachers' expectations of each other and its relationship to the nature and level of motivation pupils display towards learning is a complex one. Teachers clearly need to have expectations, since such expectations are crucial to their ability to match the learning experience to pupils. What is problematic is that such expectations inevitably reflect pupils' previous attainment rather than reflecting what they are capable of producing if fully motivated. This problem is central to HMI's frequent reference to low expectations by some teachers (HMI, 1984). At its worst, the interplay of expectations can create a vicious circle of declining motivation, as was graphically described in Hargreaves' (1967) seminal study of the attitudes of some lower stream boys in a secondary modern school:

> The allocation and attitudes of teachers increase this divergence between upper and lower streams. Whilst the fact that lower stream pupils are not entered for external examinations must inevitably lead to a reduction in motivation to achieve, the tendency to assign teachers with poorer qualifications and weaker discipline to these forms reduces even further the

pressure exerted on such boys towards academic goals. Once teachers remove the incentive of examinations from these pupils, provide greater opportunities for indiscipline, and begin to expect little from them, it is hardly surprising that they become progressively retarded and alienated from the school's values. (p. 169)

However, teachers' expectations need to be more than just encouraging; they must also be educationally sound. For a teacher to indicate that a pupil is well capable of memorising the technique for solving quadratic equations in mathematics and to encourage that pupil to do so, may not be sufficient if the pupil is neither convinced of the relevance of doing this work nor prepared to accept the lack of understanding such learning may involve. What does seem to be of great importance, is that the teacher's actions and expectations convey that the academic work is interesting, worthwhile and of value, and that the progress of each pupil really does matter.

Pupils differ not only in their overall level of academic motivation, but also in the underlying make up of that motivation. In particular, pupils differ in the extent to which they are intrinsically and extrinsically motivated. Whilst all pupils will respond to some extent to intrinsic motives (eg making the learning interesting and eliciting curiosity) and to extrinsic motives (eg merit awards for good work and pride from parents), some pupils appear to be more responsive to some aspects of the learning experience than to others. Indeed, some forms of motivation, such as an extreme authoritarian coercion towards academic effort, may elicit higher attainment for some pupils but may produce lower attainment among others (particularly if high levels of anxiety are aroused). This interaction between teaching style and pupils' personality characteristics was noted in Bennett's (1976) study of teaching styles in primary schools.

A number of authors have explored the relationship between pupils' personality and their educational attainment (Gammage, 1982; Riding, 1983). The most frequently explored overview of pupils' personality has focused on the dimension of introversion–extraversion (inward looking and reserved versus outgoing and sociable). In addition, a number of studies have focused on more specific aspects of personality, such as 'locus of control' (a generalised belief that things in life are to some extent within one's own control rather than outside it). Although many of these studies have indicated that personality characteristics may be associated with educational attainment, such findings have varied somewhat depending on the age of the pupils and the type of learning being explored. These findings have typically been interlinked with a number of other factors (eg teachers' perceptions of personality types) and thus make it difficult to identify any clear and consistent implications for effective teaching. More helpful to thinking about effective teaching has been the exploration of how pupils react to their academic success and failure, in particular the extent to which they consistently attribute success or failure to their ability, luck, effort, aspects of the task, or some other factors (Rogers, 1982). A major task for effective teaching involves influencing pupils' perceptions in an educationally more desirable and beneficial way, as was indicated in the earlier discussion of teachers' expectations.

Social class

The relationship between social class and educational attainment has been the subject of much discussion and research. The term 'social class' has not been used in a single and consistent way (Shaw, 1981), but it is generally taken to include two main elements. First, the relative power, wealth and status that derive from one's occupation; second, the set of cultural values, attitudes, and aspirations that typify the different occupational groups. The main distinction made is between 'middle class' and 'working class', but different authors have placed differing emphasis on how individuals are assigned to these two categories. The most widespread categorisation is based on the Registrar General's classification of occupations into six social classes, also termed 'socio-economic status' (SES):

1 *Professional occupations*: eg doctors, lawyers
2 *Intermediate occupations*: eg sales managers, schoolteachers
3 *Skilled occupations*
    (N) Non-manual: eg clerical workers, shop assistants
    (M) Manual: eg railway guards, bricklayers
4 *Semi-skilled occupations*: eg bus conductors, barmen
5 *Unskilled occupations*: eg office cleaners, road sweepers

Groups 1, 2 and 3(N) are categorised as 'middle class', and the others as 'working class'. Pupils with middle-class parents achieve higher educational attainment markedly more often than their working class counterparts. A number of influences have been analysed in accounting for this (Gammage, 1982; Shaw, 1981). First, middle-class homes are more likely to provide the child rearing experiences which foster greater intellectual development, motivation towards success in school, and greater academic self-confidence. Second, middle-class parents provide a stronger identification model which requires and expects higher educational attainment if pupils are to enjoy the same lifestyle as their parents or relatives, which shapes their aspirations towards gaining middle class occupations. Third, working-class homes are more likely to contain the extremes of poverty, overcrowded and poor housing, and the associated social tension and distress, which may undermine a child's capacity to deal positively with the demands of schooling. Fourth, the middle-class home is more likely than the working class to provide a cultural milieu of experiences, interests, tone and use of language, and assumptions about worthwhile activities that is in tune with the cultural milieu of schools. Thus to some extent, working-class pupils are more likely to experience a type of culture shock on entering school, particularly as they are also less likely to have attended pre-school playgroups or nursery classes.

It is extremely important to bear in mind, however, that 'pro-schooling' characteristics may be present or absent in both middle-class and working-class homes. Indeed, working-class homes display the whole range of such characteristics: parental encouragement, high aspirations, high income and good housing, and a cultural milieu similar to the school. In addition, in working-class homes where all these are absent, many pupils are still educationally successful. Nevertheless, it remains the case that the social class of pupils' parents is a strong predictor of their educational attainment, ranging from learning to read in the early years of schooling to 'O' level and 'A' level success in the later years, and beyond, including university entrance (Davie, 1979; Mortimore and Blackstone, 1982).

It is clear that a number of factors influence educational attainment, including ability and motivation. To the extent that differences in social class are bound up with differences in the ability and motivation of pupils then it is not social class *per se* which influences attainment, but rather the underlying psychological experiences associated with middle- and working-class homes respectively. A crucial question is thus whether the notion of social class draws attention to the way social class may influence educational attainment over and above its influence through general aspects of ability and motivation.

There appear to be two main ways such an additional influence may operate. The first is the school's response to pupils from working-class homes. Indeed, many authors have criticised much of the research on social class and educational attainment for focusing overmuch on the home rather than the school in seeking to explain the association, and have highlighted a number of aspects concerning schools and schooling which may also contribute. In looking at the school's response, particular attention has been paid to the greater degree of culture shock for working class pupils which stems from the way teachers use language in the classroom and the type and content of the curriculum experience and activities they employ, which are based on shared assumptions about common interests and lifestyles. Teachers need to be sensitive to the way in which they and pupils use language in the classroom and the way in which they focus on particular types of interests and activities within the curriculum. This is not to say that teachers should use the working-class vernacular, but rather that they should avoid discouraging pupils' contributions to lessons by unnecessarily correcting language use. Nor is it implied that working-class pupils should be given specialised activities based on working-class areas of interest; this would create a danger of educational apartheid. Rather all pupils, both working- and middle-class, should undertake activities based on a broad range of cultural and community-based interests, so that the overtly middle-class bias is reduced. Indeed, this is the point which lies at the heart of Bernstein's (1970) widely quoted statement:

> If the culture of the teacher is to become part of the consciousness of the child, then the culture of the child must first be in the consciousness of the teacher. This may mean that the teacher must be able to understand the child's dialect, rather than deliberately attempting to change it. Many of the contexts of our schools are unwittingly drawn from aspects of the symbolic world of the middle class and so when the child steps into school he is stepping into a symbolic system which does not provide for him a linkage with his life outside. (p. 120)

The second main way in which social class may have an additional distinctive influence on educational attainment is through the influence of class consciousness. This refers to the extent to which working-class and middle-class families adopt a general view of the world (a set of general attitudes, expectations, values and ways of behaving) which derives from their type of occupation and associated status and method of working. In general, this view is reflected in the middle-class emphasis on the virtue of individual enterprise and personal advancement, in contrast to the working-class emphasis on a collectivist outlook (Roberts, 1980). Until recent years, this meant a much better match between the middle-class emphasis and the nature of schooling. In this respect, the trend towards greater use of group work and cooperative activities in schools should benefit working-class pupils (as long as the activities and social skills required do not undermine this). In many respects Hargreaves' (1982) advocacy of changes in the school curriculum towards community based studies and cooperative styles of working addresses the problem of the lower educational attainment of working-class pupils. This was impressively developed as a theme in the two recent reports commissioned by the ILEA on improving the educational achievement of primary and secondary school pupils in ILEA schools (Thomas Report, 1985, and Hargreaves Report, 1984, respectively).

Two important caveats need to be borne in mind, however, concerning the notion of social class. First, that each class in practice covers a great diversity of experiences. Second, that social changes in life styles and occupations over the years have influenced the nature of class consciousness and identification. Having said this, the extent to which social class still operates as an area of pupil differences with an impact on pupils' educational attainment is surprising. Part of this continuing influence would appear to derive from the strong tendency for middle-class and working-class families, and in particular pupils, to associate primarily with others from their own class, and thus reinforce and consolidate their class associated values and attitudes.

In the context of discussion about social class, the term 'educational disadvantage' has been widely used to refer to pupils whose opportunity for educational attainment has been markedly constrained by either 'social disadvantage' (eg poor housing, poverty) or 'cultural disadvantage' (eg impoverished mother–child interactions, absence of cultural experiences in the home) or any other set of factors (eg poorly-resourced local school). While some writers have discussed the aspects of disadvantage stemming from being working class, the term has more usually been applied to a smaller group of pupils, normally within the working class, who experience the extremes of such disadvantage or deprivation, typically accounting for about 5 per cent of the pupil population (Chazan and Williams, 1978; Davie, 1979; Mortimore and Blackstone, 1982). Such pupils are much more likely than their peers to be identified as having learning difficulties stemming from both low ability and emotional or behavioural problems.

A number of 'compensatory education' programmes have been launched to meet the needs of educationally disadvantaged pupils (Demaine, 1980; Nisbet and Watt, 1984), initially stimulated by the establishment of *Educational Priority Areas* recommended by the Plowden Report (1967). Two main problems have handicapped the success of such programmes. First, the whole nature of what compensatory education meant was unclear and controversial. Was it to address all working-class pupils or merely the extremely disadvantaged minority? Was it correct to refer to aspects of working-class culture, and in particular their use of language, as deprived or impoverished, or is this simply a reflection of a bias towards middle-class norms? Second, educational provision would appear to have little impact on the effects of gross deprivation. A successful intervention programme needs to deal with the underlying deprivation, which involves both the family's social interaction and their material circumstances. Despite some lavish intervention programmes in the United States during the 1970s, stemming from 'Head Start', once the period of support finishes, the educational gains made typically regress back towards the norm for the deprived group.

Before leaving the discussion of social class, particular attention needs to be given to the use of language by middle-class and working-class pupils. A very influential theory has been developed by Bernstein (1971). In an early exposition of his theory, he argued that a distinction could be made between two kinds of language used by speakers: 'elaborated code' and 'restricted code'. The former is characterised by a richer use of language to make the meaning of what is said explicit to the listener; the latter is characterised by a grammatically more simple utterance, shorter in length, and depending on shared understanding. An example would be 'Would you like a cup of tea?' versus 'How about one?'. Bernstein argued that middle-class pupils were able to use both codes while working-class pupils were limited to using the restricted code. He further argued that as a result working-class pupils were severely disadvantaged in their intellectual growth, and were less able to meet the demands of schools. This crude version of the theory is extremely dubious, and is no longer subscribed to by Bernstein; however, it did influence much of the discussion about compensatory education, and to a large extent entered the educational folklore about working-class pupils.

More recently, however, Bernstein has developed a more sophisticated notion of these codes, closely related to child rearing practices and socialisation patterns. He now argues that middle-class homes foster a use of language which emphasises a more generalised and explicit use of speech, and it is this which may advantage middle-class pupils in schools. At this stage in our understanding, however, it would appear that the impact of social class related speech patterns (be it dialect or grammatical qualities) as an explanation of lower educational attainment may be based on the teacher expectations such characteristics elicit about the pupils' ability and motivation, and to some extent the pupils' feelings that the way teachers use language in the school is somewhat alien. The notion that use of non-standard English limits educability *per se* now appears to be very suspect (Stubbs, 1983). This broader view of the role of language used in the classroom, and its differential impact on working-class and middle-class pupils, will be developed in chapter 7.

Gender

In recent years, the word 'gender' has been widely used in place of 'sex' in discussing the educational attainment of male and female pupils. This trend is a reflection of the fact that sex is based on biological differences, thus in discussing sex differences in education there is an implicit hint that these are in part a reflection of underlying biological differences. In contrast, gender refers to the ways in which boys and girls in our society typically see themselves and are seen by others; in discussing the role of gender in education, therefore, attention is drawn to the influence of such perceptions on educational attainment. Clearly, sex and gender overlap, and the choice of term made by a particular author to some extent indicates where the author wishes to place emphasis in the exploration of educational differences between male and female pupils.

The complex inter-relationship between pupils' biological makeup and development on the one hand and their perceptions, attitudes and values concerning their sex (ie gender) on the other hand, makes the examination of their individual and distinctive influence on educational attainment difficult to conduct (Archer and Lloyd, 1982). For example, the onset of puberty for female pupils during early adolescence seems to be coupled with a heightened awareness of themselves as 'female' and an increasing concern with their own sex-role and sex-appropriate behaviour. While some aspects of differences between male and female pupils in education may have a biological basis, the vast literature in this area now seems to indicate that the main differences reported during the school years (ranging from learning to read in the early years to the choice of option subjects taken and levels of subject attainment achieved in the later years) appear to result from pupils' sex-linked attitudes, values and aspirations, their child-rearing experiences and socialisation, and the response of the school to gender (Davies, 1984; Whyld, 1983). Indeed, even such developments in infancy as the use of language or spatial ability (the former favouring girls and the latter boys) may be markedly influenced by the type and degree of mother–child interaction and play rather than sex differences in biological development *per se*.

The challenge for effective teaching is to try to ensure that both male and female pupils are able to receive a broad-based education, with opportunities to follow up specific interests and activities, without their progress and choice being unjustifiably constrained by gender. Recent studies have highlighted the ways in which pupils' and the school's response to gender can contribute to these constraints, particularly by fostering the perception that attainment in some subjects is more appropriate to boys or to girls. Such influences include:

- whether the subject is usually taught by a male or female teacher;
- whether the subject is related to sex-stereotyped career aspirations;
- whether the sexes differ in their perceptions of the subject's interest and their general ability in the subject;
- whether the activities and materials used in the subject display sex-bias, making it more appealing or more related to the experience of boys or girls;
- whether the pupils' and teacher's behaviour in the classroom reinforces sex-stereotyped perceptions;
- whether school documentation or organisation relating to the curriculum includes in-built assumptions about sex-stereotyped behaviour.

The recent GIST project (*Girls into Science and Technology*) aimed to explore the reasons for girls' underachievement in physical science and technical crafts, and to introduce an intervention programme in eight co-educational comprehensive schools to mitigate this (Whyte, 1986). The GIST project reported findings in line with the influences listed above; for example, in physics, third year boys typically dominated the teacher's time and use of equipment, taunted girls who made mistakes, perceived their ability to be much higher than girls', and saw physics as useful for their careers and chose it for that reason more than did girls. The intervention programme used workshops with the teachers to heighten their awareness of the problems; visits by women scientists and crafts-people; and modifications to curriculum materials, content, aspects of classroom interaction and activities, to improve girls' perceptions and attitudes. Discussions were also held with parents and pupils concerning option choices. The findings of the study indicated that the project had influenced pupils' attitudes and aspects of school practices, although the impact on subject choices was less marked.

Anti-sexist initiatives in schools, however, can often themselves involve sexist assumptions. For example, the belief that girls are more interested in people than things has been used as a basis for advocating that the science curriculum be broadened to consider the social implications of science, and thereby make science more appealing to girls:

> 'Subjects' like physics are supposed to be neutral or 'pure'. But the teaching of scientific principles without any parallel discussion of how this knowledge might be applied (the bomb, space programmes) is an incredibly partial and short-sighted stance. Girls' reluctance to do science is inextricably linked to the way 'science' is (abstractly) presented in school: I will make this inevitable plea for my own sex and claim that women, for whatever reasons, *do* show more concern about social issues, do have a greater sense of social responsibility. (Davies, 1984, p. 63)

Despite the complexities involved in developing policies and practices in schools which will offer a more genuine equal opportunity for both sexes to enjoy a broad education, this development has received particular attention and advocacy in a number of recent DES and HMI publications (eg DES, 1985a; HMI, 1985a). Although factors outside schools have a powerful impact on sex-stereotyping that occurs within schools, there is still much that teachers can do to mitigate such influences. Already a number of developments, such as compulsory home economics and woodwork for both sexes, are commonplace. In particular, there has been a conscious effort by teachers to ensure that a more equal distribution of participation in lesson activities (including dialogue with the teacher) takes place. This is, in fact, no easy matter; the tendency for boys to receive more attention arises in part because this is used as a method of sustaining their interest and thereby pre-empting any likelihood of misbehaviour occurring when such interest wanes. A particularly interesting and related development is the exploratory use, in some co-educational schools, of single-sex science lessons. This is a reflection of the finding in some studies that the up-take of physical science in single-sex girls' schools appears to be greater than for girls in co-educational schools (although the slightly greater average ability of the intake of girls in single sex schools may contribute to this). After years of advocating the social benefits which accrue to co-educational schools compared with single sex schools, some authors have now had to re-assess the relative costs and gains (Deem, 1984).

Race

As with the consideration of social class and gender, the concern with race stems from the apparent lower average educational attainment of particular ethnic minority groups. To some extent the greater under-achievement among pupils from some ethnic minority families can be attributed to the effects of poorer housing, relatively lower income and different cultural values, attitudes regarding the role of schooling, use of language, and patterns of family life; all this parallels the earlier discussion of educational disadvantage and the working class. But the readily identifiable nature of coloured ethnic minorities appears to have added to the problem. Successive immigrants to Britain in this century have often faced initial problems in achieving parity of educational attainment with the indigenous community. By and large this has not been a continuing problem for those pupils born in Britain, be they Jews, Italians or Cypriots. More recently, however, it has become apparent that black West Indian pupils born in Britain, in particular, have not attained the expected level of attainment. A number of reasons for this have been postulated. The most significant factor would appear to stem from a mixture of racial prejudice and West Indian cultural values which has meant that black West Indian families have not become more prevalent in middle-class occupations – and thus this group's spectrum of social class composition has not increased. In this respect, the under-achievement of black West Indian pupils is very much a reflection of their tendency to remain in relatively low income occupations or unemploy-ment and in poorer housing, together with the associated social tensions and pressures of such circumstances. In contrast, pupils from Asian families have achieved levels of educational attainment close to that of the indigenous community (with some exceptions such as the Bangladeshi community). It is no coincidence to note that Asian families have been able to establish themselves in a range of middle-class occupations (ranging from shopkeepers to doctors), and that their children share this range of educational and career aspirations. If black West Indian families continue to remain proportionately more economically and socially disadvantaged than other ethnic minority groups and the indigenous community, this will be a major barrier against their achieving edu-cational parity.

The Swann Report (1985) provides an excellent overview of the issues and problems concerning the education of ethnic minorities. In addition, it stressed the importance of taking a wide view of these issues and problems by considering the role of education for all pupils within a multi-racial society.

In considering the role of racism in schools, the report distinguished between direct racism, which refers to prejudiced attitudes concerning ethnic minority groups (both hostile or well-intentioned) and indirect or institutionalised racism, which was outlined thus:

> We see institutionalised racism as describing the way in which a range of long established systems, practices and procedures, both within education and the wider society, which were originally conceived and devised to meet the needs and aspirations of a relative homogeneous society, can now be seen not only to fail to take account of the multi-racial nature of Britain today but may also ignore or even actively work against the interests of ethnic minority communities. (p. 28)

These two forms of racism are seen to relate to underachievement in that they may contribute to a vicious circle of teacher and pupil perception about the educational performance of particular ethnic minority groups. At the same time, such racism in the school is unlikely to be a major influence on attainment in comparison to its operation outside school and in particular its influence on the quality of life as discussed earlier. This is not, of course, to imply that racism in schools is of minor importance, and a number of schools and LEAs have specifically addressed such problems.

The school's proper response to the twin concerns of meeting the demands of ethnic minority pupils and preparing all pupils for a multi-racial society is the subject of much discussion (Jeffcoate, 1984; Willey, 1984). Two main themes have been developed. The first is 'multicultural education' which is based on teaching and learning about the different ethnic cultures. Advocates of this approach argue that it fosters a better understanding and respect for the different ethnic minority cultures and thereby undermines prejudice, and also boosts the self-respect of ethnic minority pupils by showing that their culture is deemed of value to the school community. The second main theme is 'anti-racist education' which is concerned specifically with addressing questions of race and prejudice as they operate in our society, with a view to undermining prejudice among pupils. Anti-racist education has utilised a range of teaching activities to do this, such as group work based on cooperation between pupils of different ethnic origins, role play and simulations. Clearly, these two themes overlap in many respects. They both place emphasis on fostering a critical and sensitive appreciation of the different ethnic minority cultures which make up our society, and developing a pluralist and non-prejudiced perspective. To do this successfully, however, requires the whole school to consider and deal with both direct and institutionalised racism within the school. This involves establishing a non-racist bias in the curriculum and dealing with racist attitudes and behaviour such as racist graffiti and harassment. It is important to note, however, that this whole area is emotionally charged, and can involve intense clashes of value judgements among and between teachers and pupils, both inside and outside the classroom. In addition, certain

developments may also invite criticism from parents. The developm
school policy regarding race needs to be carefully thought out
implemented with sensitivity.

As well as developments concerned with racist attitudes and behav
a number of initiatives have been primarily concerned with helping
ethnic minority pupils to achieve higher levels of educational attainment.
In doing this, particular attention has been paid to the role of language.
For many such pupils, the acquisition of communicative competence in
standard English is crucial for educational success. Ethnic minority
pupils include those who speak no English at all and whose mother
tongue may be based on a non-western alphabet script, and those who
speak fluent English but with a strong accent or dialect. The main
implication of this for effective teaching is the importance of teachers
being aware of the degree of pupils' linguistic competence in monitoring
their progress across the curriculum. In particular, pupils' lack of
confidence about their own linguistic skills may result in their appearing
more inarticulate or reticent than their underlying understanding should
allow in their contributions to lessons – for example, if asked to develop
their ideas verbally in front of peers. (A similar phenomenon commonly
occurs in modern language oral work.)

In effect, the main question a teacher or school should be asking about
their current practice is in what ways their practice has changed in order
to take account of accommodating the multi-racial nature of Britain. It is
still all too common to find schools (including those with or without
ethnic minority pupils), whose curriculum activities appear to be no
different than they would be had the debate concerning the need to
prepare *all* pupils for a multi-racial society never taken place at all.

One final point concerning teaching in a multi-racial school involves
the way in which race is an important construct for ethnic minority
pupils in perceiving their educational experiences. Such pupils may
interpret the reasons for their own educational progress and relationships
with teachers as largely influenced by their race. Many pupils share the
racist assumptions and expectations of others, including to some extent
those about their own ethnic minority; and will readily attribute such
perceptions to others, including their teachers. Such tendencies reflect
complex underlying psychological processes concerning developing self-
respect, and developing feelings of group solidarity (influenced by
whether the group one identifies with is the indigenous community or
one's own ethnic minority). These tendencies can create acute and
painful tensions, and can only be understood by taking careful account of
each pupil's particular circumstances. In the light of the Swann Report,
and an increasing awareness of race as a social and educational issue, it is
likely that schools will need to pay more attention to developments
aimed at meeting the implications of the multi-racial composition of our
society.

Special educational needs

Until 1983, special educational provision primarily referred to the education of pupils in special schools or in special classes and units attached to ordinary schools, or, in the most severe cases, in residential homes and hospitals. The education of these pupils was catered for in a context separate from that of pupils in ordinary schools. These pupils were categorised as having handicaps (mental, emotional, social and/or physical) which resulted in ordinary schools not being able to adequately meet their educational needs. Ten such categories of handicap were recognised: blind, partially sighted, deaf, partially hearing, educationally subnormal, epileptic, maladjusted, physically handicapped, speech defect. and delicate. Approximately 2 per cent of the school population received such special and segregated provision.

In 1978 the Warnock Report introduced a broad notion of 'special educational need'. The report recommended the abolition of these ten statutory categories of handicap and their replacement by a system of identifying pupils' special educational needs which focused on the pupils' actual *educational needs*. In addition, the report advocated that this system should not only apply to those pupils whose needs were typically being met by special and segregated provision ('the 2 per cent') but also to a much larger proportion of pupils whose learning difficulties (in the short or long term) would benefit from special provision in the ordinary school. The report estimated that about one in six children at any time. and up to one in five children at some time during their school career, will require some form of special educational provision as advocated:

> Our conclusion that up to one child in five is likely to need special educational provision in the course of his school career does not mean that up to one in five is likely to be handicapped in the traditional sense of the term. The majority will be unlikely to have such long-term disability or disorder. Their learning problems, which may last for varying periods of time, will stem from a variety of causes. But, unless suitable help is forthcoming, their problems will be reinforced by prolonged experience of failure. We refer to the group of children – up to one in five – who are likely to require some form of special educational provision at some time during their school career as 'children with special educational needs'. (p. 41)

The report placed emphasis on the child having a 'learning difficulty' as the essential criterion for identifying the child's special educational needs; such learning difficulty might be described as 'mild', 'moderate' or 'severe'. The term 'children with learning difficulties' was seen to include both those previously described as educationally subnormal and those who received remedial support. In very broad terms, the report saw special educational need as likely to take the form of the need for one or more of the following:

- the provision of special means of access to the curriculum through special equipment, facilities or resources, modification of the physical environment or specialist teaching techniques;
- the provision of a special or modified curriculum;
- particular attention to the social structure and emotional climate in which education takes place.

While the report advocated that children's special educational needs should be met by the ordinary school wherever possible, it envisaged that special schools (and other segregated special provision) would still be required for three groups of pupils:

1   Children with severe or complex physical, sensory or intellectual disabilities.
2   Children with severe emotional or behavioural disorders.
3   Children with less severe disabilities who do not perform well in an ordinary school.

The recommendations of the Warnock Report were embodied in the 1981 Education Act, which took effect in 1983. The Act defined the key terms involved thus:

- A child has 'special educational needs' if he has a learning difficulty which calls for special educational provision to be made.
- A child has a 'learning difficulty' if *a* he has a significantly greater difficulty in learning than the majority of children his age; or *b* he has a disability which either prevents or hinders him from making use of educational facilities of a kind generally provided in schools for children of his age.
- 'Special educational provision' means educational provision which is additional to, or otherwise different from, the educational provision made generally for children of his age.

The Act included pre-school age children for such provision, and also added an interesting caveat of relevance to the discussion earlier in this chapter of race; this was that a child is not to be taken as having a learning difficulty solely because the language (or form of the language) in which he is, or will be, taught is different from that spoken in his home.

The wide-ranging nature of the current developments concerning special educational needs is the subject of much discussion (eg Galloway, 1985; Lindsay, 1983). It is particularly interesting to note the major influence which thinking about children with special educational needs has on thinking about the educational needs of *all* pupils in the school, as has been similarly observed throughout this chapter in relation to the other pupil differences considered.

With regard to effective teaching, these current developments require teachers in ordinary schools to undertake two important tasks; first, to identify children with special educational needs, and second, to arrange for those needs to be met. Both these tasks highlight the needs of teachers for in-service courses and support services if the procedures and practices developed in schools are to be effective.

In identifying children with special educational needs, four main procedures operate:

1   LEA-based screening programmes
2   school-devised screening programmes
3   classroom teachers' concerns
4   parents' concerns.

Screening programmes are prevalent in the primary school years and typically include a reading test and other measures of checking educational progress. Often such testing is used in conjunction with a broad system of record keeping and as an aid to curriculum development. Such screening programmes, however, differ markedly from school to school. The classroom teacher has a very real responsibility to be alert to the problems which may underlie pupils having difficulties in learning. Parents' concerns may also be a starting point for considering a pupil's needs in detail, and current developments have stressed the importance of involving parents at an early stage in any consideration of pupils' special educational needs. In addition, many pupils starting primary school at age 5 or transferring to a new school will already have had special educational needs identified, and it is vital to ensure that the new school is made fully aware of these immediately.

Once concern has been expressed about a pupil, an 'informal' assessment is carried out to gather a wide range of information about the pupil: the exact nature of the concern, the pupil's progress and type of learning difficulty, the pupil's general circumstances, and any medical problems if appropriate. Wherever possible, parents should be involved at this stage. On the basis of this assessment, the school will make a decision about the nature of the provision it can make from its own resources to meet the pupil's special educational needs. The school may decide to involve other professionals to assist in decision-making, and to utilise the resources and support generally available to schools in the locality to meet pupils special educational needs. Most LEAs have now set up active support services to assist schools in this way.

If the school feels it is unable to meet the pupil's special educational needs using the resources and support generally available, it will then institute a formal assessment to be undertaken by a multi-professional team. On the basis of this assessment, the LEA will determine what 'additional' special educational provision is required. This formal assessment must involve parents. Indeed, under the 1981 Education Act parents have the right to demand such an assessment, to see the reports making up the assessment, and to appeal against the judgements being made. The assessment will result in a 'statement' being made by the LEA of the special educational needs of the pupil and the special educational provision to be made to meet those needs. Only after such a formal assessment and the making of this 'statement' can the LEA decide to provide segregated special provision (eg placement in a special school). However, the LEA is required to attempt to meet the pupil's special educational needs in the ordinary school context wherever possible.

The Warnock Report envisaged four main types of special educational provision located in the ordinary school:

1 Full-time education in an ordinary class with any necessary help and support.
2 Education in an ordinary class with periods of withdrawal to a special class or unit or other supporting base.
3 Education in a special class or unit with periods of attendance at an ordinary class and full involvement in the general community life and extra-curricular activities of the ordinary school.
4 Full-time education in a special class or unit with social contact with the main school.

Given the range of types of learning difficulties pupils may have and of types of provision which may usefully be made, the task of identifying and matching a pupil's special educational needs with the provision to be made is no mean one. Such matching will also inevitably be affected by the views and wishes of parents, and by the school's perceptions of what provision may feasibly be offered. In addition, in many cases it is extremely difficult to decide exactly what is the special nature of a pupil's educational needs. Poor reading attainment in the primary school, for example, may involve one or more of a mixture of underlying causes: mental, emotional, social or physical in nature. An identification of educational need and provision requires a sound diagnosis of the learning difficulty. In reaching a diagnosis reference may be made to underlying causes which are themselves the subject of much controversy. Two such causes have received particular attention. The first is 'dyslexia', which, it is argued, is a constitutional brain dysfunction that impairs reading development specifically while not affecting general intelligence. It is true that there are many apparently able pupils whose progress in reading is poor, but evidence of a constitutionally-based syndrome of dyslexia is the subject of much debate. The second such cause is 'emotional and behavioural disorder' (formerly 'maladjustment') characterised by disturbing behaviour, either emotional and/or anti-social, that impairs educational progress. Such pupils are seen to require special educational provision to effect their personal, social and educational adjustment.

At one level a teacher may feel that special educational provision primarily concerns remedial attention to help pupils improve their reading competence. Schools using screening tests on a regular basis may well see such provision in this way, and may set up a remedial centre to give specialised support. At another level, however, the teacher needs to be aware of and sensitive to the possibility that poor reading progress is not simply a matter of poor educational progress, needing educational remediation *per se,* but may be a result of other factors such as dyslexia or emotional and behavioural problems. What is important to note is that the pupil's response and the school's response to poor reading attainment could well influence the nature of the diagnosis, and that the processes and considerations involved in making such a diagnosis are often very problematic.

In most ordinary schools the main difference of opinion over meeting children's special educational needs in a remedial context has been between those who advocate setting up a withdrawal scheme of some sort within the school where pupils receive such special provision, and those who argue that remedial or special needs support staff should be used as a resource to work alongside teachers in the normal classroom, providing remedial materials and also helping individual pupils. A large school is likely to have one or two such teachers available, while a small school is likely to utilise peripatetic teachers employed by an LEA to support such work in a number of schools. A very interesting development along these lines is the use by some schools of parents and other volunteers to increase the amount of one-to-one teaching a pupil may receive, although such developments need to be implemented by schools with great care to ensure such teaching is of the appropriate quality and approach.

Conclusions

In this chapter a number of important differences between pupils have been explored: ability, motivation, social class, gender, race and special educational needs. This theme of pupil differences highlights some very important concerns and observations. First, the importance of knowing the pupil as an individual with his or her own particular educational history and perspective towards schools, teaching and learning. Second, that there are certain groupings of pupils (of which the six most important were explored in this chapter) which serve to highlight a number of major issues concerning teaching and learning that bear upon the question of why certain pupils appear to be more successful than others in terms of educational attainment. Third, that the highlighting of these major issues raises fundamental questions about the nature of education in schools, such that in attempting to meet the needs of *some* pupils more effectively, one is forced to consider changes in curriculum content and activities and in aspects of pupil–teacher interaction which are relevant to meeting the educational needs of *all* pupils more effectively.

6 Key classroom teaching qualities and tasks

At this point it is worth reminding ourselves of the theme which has been developed so far. It has been argued that in thinking about effective teaching, it is important to take account of the *context* of the lesson (eg the subject matter, the age and ability range of the pupils, and the school ethos) and the desired educational *outcomes* the teacher wishes to foster (eg increased interest in the subject matter, and development of some particular intellectual skill). What may constitute effective teaching in one context and with one set of desired outcomes in mind may not be as effective in a different context and with a different set of desired outcomes in mind.

The earlier chapters of this book paid attention to how pupils learn, the ways in which pupils learn, and the types of pupil differences which have a major bearing on the effectiveness of teaching and learning. I argued that pupil learning required the pupil to be *attentive* to the learning experience, and *receptive* (ie the pupil must be motivated and have a willingness to learn and respond to the experience). In addition, the learning experience must be *appropriate* for the desired learning to take place. In thinking about the qualities and tasks of effective teaching, the question is one of how to effectively marshal aspects of one's teaching and set up a learning experience such that it:

- elicits and sustains pupils' attention;
- elicits and sustains pupils' motivation;
- fosters the type of learning desired.

In looking at effective teaching a useful distinction can be drawn between the general *qualities* of effective teaching and the component *tasks* involved. The qualities focus on broad aspects of teaching which appear to be important in determining its effectiveness, such as good rapport with pupils or pitching the work at the appropriate level of difficulty. The tasks refer to the activities and practices involved in teaching, such as planning a lesson or assessing pupils' progress. Clearly, qualities and tasks are closely inter-related; however, discussion of the former tends to be in answer to a question such as 'what qualities would you expect to find in an effective lesson?' whereas consideration of the latter tends to be in answer to a question such as 'what tasks are involved in teaching?'. In effect, the search for qualities is explicitly judgemental in character and may cut across a number of different tasks involved in teaching. The first part of this chapter will explore the key qualities involved in effective classroom teaching; the second part will explore the key tasks involved.

Key classroom teaching qualities

Over the last two decades many studies have sought to identify those characteristics of teaching which contribute to effectiveness (see chapter 2). At one extreme are those studies which attempt to itemise in detail the numerous attributes which may characterise a lesson, and then to explore the extent to which each of these attributes is associated with some measure of effectiveness (the criteria used may range from teachers' perceptions of their importance, to performance on a standardised test of educational attainment). A recent study of my own, for example, explored the perceptions of a sample of 142 heads of departments in comprehensive schools regarding the extent to which they associated each of 38 teacher characteristics with the likelihood of pupils' success at 'O' level (Kyriacou, 1982). In this study, which sought to compare heads of departments in four teaching areas: biology, English, geography, and mathematics, the ten characteristics which overall were reported as having the strongest association with 'O' level success were (in order of strength):

1 Explains points clearly and at pupils' level
2 Conveys an enthusiasm for the subject to pupils
3 Has a genuine interest in the subject
4 Pays attention to revision and examination technique
5 Tries to make lessons interesting wherever possible
6 Conveys high expectations for work pupils produce
7 Teaches for understanding rather than reproduction of learned material
8 Is confident and at ease when teaching
9 Stimulates pupils to think for themselves
10 Is constructive and helpful in criticism of pupils

Such studies give a fascinating insight into teachers' perceptions; whilst there is some degree of consensus across some studies, it is also interesting to note the extent to which teachers disagree. This disagreement is evident not only between teachers of different subject areas but also between teachers of the same subject. In addition, their perceptions are also different when alternative criteria of effectiveness are considered.

A major problem with approaches that attempt to itemise the characteristics of effective teaching, is that they tend to produce fairly long checklists of these characteristics. Thus there is a danger of losing sight of the holistic quality of teaching. We should not forget that 'the whole is more than the sum of its parts'. In making judgements about teaching, we react to the sense of the whole lesson as a single unit. While this unit can then be usefully broken down into a number of key teaching qualities, once such a list of qualities becomes too lengthy, the interplay between the qualities is lost; yet it is that interplay which, in many respects, is the most important aspect of the analysis of teaching.

A number of very useful attempts to identify such key teaching qualities have been reported, most often in the context of teacher education programmes – either as part of initial training courses or aimed at in-service professional development. In the United States, for example, the *Stanford Teacher Competence Appraisal Guide* (a copy of which may be found in Stones and Morris, 1972) lists a total of 17 qualities, grouped together under five headings: 'aims', 'planning', 'performance', 'evaluation' and 'community and professional'. Each of these qualities is then rated by an observer of a lesson on a seven-point rating scale, labelled from 'weak' to 'truly exceptional'. The six qualities grouped together under the heading of 'performance', for example, are:

- *beginning the lesson*: pupils come quickly to attention; they direct themselves to the tasks to be accomplished.
- *clarity of presentation*: the content of the lesson is presented so that it is understandable to the pupils; different points of view and specific illustrations are used when appropriate.
- *pacing of the lesson*: the movement from one part of the lesson to the next is governed by the pupils' achievement; the teacher 'stays with the class' and adjusts the tempo accordingly.
- *pupil participation and attention*: the class is attentive; when appropriate the pupils actively participate in the lesson.
- *ending the lesson*: the lesson is ended when the pupils have achieved the aims of instruction; there is a deliberate attempt to tie together the planned and chance events of the lesson and relate them to the immediate and long-range aims of instruction.
- *teacher–pupil rapport*: the personal relationships between pupils and the teacher are harmonious.

The development of similar schedules in Britain using this approach has also been reported (eg Norris, 1975; Povey, 1975).

In the 1970s the research community also began to adopt this approach in their exploration of effective teaching. In large measure this move within the research community received its major impetus from the work of Kounin (1970). Kounin's seminal study attempted to identify the effective techniques used by teachers in dealing with pupil misbehaviour by contrasting the videotaped classroom behaviour of teachers known to be successful with that of teachers who had continuing discipline problems. Surprisingly, the two groups differed little in how they dealt with actual misbehaviour. Rather, what seemed to differentiate the two groups was that the successful teachers were much more effective in their teaching (in terms of instructional management and keeping pupils actively engaged in the lesson), thereby minimising the time in which pupils were bored or restless. The qualities identified by Kounin included:

- *withitness*: the teacher communicating to pupils through actual behaviour that he knows what the pupils are doing (has 'eyes in the back of his head').
- *overlapping*: being able to deal with two matters at the same time, particularly that of dealing with a pupil's misbehaviour while other pupils remain task engaged with the teacher.
- *smoothness*: maintaining the flow of academic activities – avoiding 'jerkiness', such as sudden interjection while pupils are busy, or leaving an activity too early and then returning to it later, rather suddenly.
- *momentum*: maintaining an appropriate rate of flow – not staying on a point (either academic or concerning misbehaviour) too long, or breaking down an activity into parts that could be better performed as a single unit (avoiding 'slowdowns').

While any set of key classroom teaching qualities identified by an author cannot be regarded as being an unequivocal analysis of effective teaching, such sets do provide a very useful list of agenda items which serve to focus on the way in which different aspects of classroom teaching combine to convey these qualities. There are three components to the analysis involved. The first component consists of all the *tasks* involved in teaching (eg classroom organisation, planning a lesson, dealing with misbehaviour). The way in which these tasks are carried out involves the application of teaching *skills* (eg vigilance, giving clear instructions); these teaching skills constitute the second component of the analysis. How these skills are applied to the tasks results in the particular *qualities* the teaching displays. The discussion here of the search for key classroom teaching qualities and their relationship to tasks and skills serves as an elaboration of the first part of the model presented in Figure 2 (p. 26) dealing with a pedagogical (craft of teaching) level of analysis.

This approach has recently been adopted by HMI (1982) in their study of probationary teachers, in which each of 294 probationers were observed teaching two lessons: 186 lessons in the primary sector and 402 lessons in the secondary sector. Each lesson was then rated by the observing Inspector on a five-point scale for each of 24 attributes. These 24 attributes were grouped together in terms of five qualities. Each attribute was described in terms of two extreme statements, scored 1 and 5 respectively; a score of 2, 3 or 4 denoted an assessment within the range of these two extreme statements. The five qualities with their constituent statements scoring 1 were as follows:

Quality of teacher–pupil relationships and class management
- teacher has good relations with the pupils
- teacher manages the class well

Quality of planning and preparation of work
- the aims and objectives of the lesson were appropriate
- lesson had been well planned
- lesson appeared to draw appropriately on previous work
- teacher had made a good choice of books/materials/equipment
- pupils' work thoroughly and constructively marked
- the aims and objectives of the lesson were achieved

Quality of teaching process and match of work to pupils
- teacher adopted appropriate teaching style
- teacher had a mastery of the subject
- pupils were given appropriate opportunities to organise their own work
- the needs of the more able within the group were catered for
- the needs of average ability pupils within the group were catered for
- the needs of the less able pupils within the group were catered for
- pupils' capabilities were suitably stretched
- pupils' interest maintained throughout period of observation
- pupils appeared to enjoy the lesson/activity

Quality of language used in the classroom
- many useful dialogues between teacher and pupils
- pupils encouraged to express their own thoughts and ideas
- pupils' language suitably extended
- teacher's use of language was always appropriate to the occasion

Quality of questioning techniques
- teacher varied questioning techniques appropriately
- teacher's questioning well distributed among pupils
- teacher made good use of pupils' responses

As noted earlier, the search for such key qualities of classroom teaching appears to have its greatest value in providing a framework of agenda items which can be used to discuss the interplay between such qualities and the underlying interplay of classroom teaching tasks and skills. The HMI's study exemplifies this strength in a most informative way. In looking at the five qualities and the 24 statements listed, many of the central issues concerning effective teaching are evident, particularly the HMI's emphasis on the importance of matching work to pupils and on the use of language (and questioning) in the classroom.

The HMI assessment identified two attributes in primary schools and five attributes in secondary schools which received ratings of 4 or 5 (the undesirable extreme) for more than 35 per cent of the lessons observed.

In the primary schools surveyed the following statements were most frequently given a rating of 4 or 5:
- pupils' work over-directed (42 per cent)
- pupils' capabilities not extended at all (36 per cent)

In the secondary school the statements were:
- pupils' language not extended (47 per cent)
- questioning techniques narrow in range (44 per cent)
- pupils' work over-directed (39 per cent)
- the needs of the less able within the group ignored (39 per cent)
- self-expression not encouraged (37 per cent).

The HMI report elaborates in a very informative way their view of effective teaching in terms of the five qualities considered. For example, in their discussion of the quality of language used in the classroom, they comment thus:

> Where dialogue and discussion are a common feature of lessons, pupils are more likely to express their own thoughts and ideas and to engage in the sort of talk which allows them to make new ideas of their own, which leads them to understand a process, or which gives them practice in forming and testing an hypothesis. Examples of exploratory uses of language were to be found at every stage from the infant class onwards. An example comes from a secondary fourth-year English lesson to low-ability pupils. The teacher told the class briefly about an imaginary unidentified accident victim. She brought in a few 'possessions' and then encouraged the class to speculate about what kind of person the victim was and how the police had set about identifying her. The talk which ensued allowed pupils to develop hypotheses and test them against each other. (p. 17)

In looking at the five qualities and their constituent attributes, it is clear from the HMI's discussion how these qualities and attributes interact and influence each other. For example, good questioning techniques contribute both to sound classroom management and the development of good teacher–pupil rapport, as is illustrated by the following comment:

> Where questioning was well distributed, there was often a careful balance between questions addressed to the whole class and those addressed to named individuals. Teachers were observant and did not allow silent or timid pupils to remain uninvolved for the whole lesson, but questioned them directly, drawing them out, if necessary, with encouragement. They did not content themselves with calling on only those pupils who were ready to answer, but made a point of involving every pupil during the lesson. In such classes it was useful to find that an atmosphere had been created in which pupils' contributions were valued by the teacher and by the rest of the class. (p. 18)

In summarising their findings, HMI identified the following characteristics as being associated with good practice: pupils' participation, interest and involvement; good organisation with a balance and variety

of activities and efficient use of materials and equipment; good relationships – often characterised by a shared sense of purpose and mutual
respect; productive and lively discussion – usually associated with
appropriately varied questioning techniques; good planning and preparation and a choice of content appropriate to the ages and abilities of
the pupils. In discussing the characteristics associated with lessons of low
quality, HMI noted that in nearly all the least successful lessons, teachers
were working under external constraints which exacerbated serious
weaknesses of teaching technique or failure to form satisfactory relationships with pupils. The four main external constraints which had this
effect were the difficulty of the class, the limited expectations of the
school, the non-availability of teaching materials, and the absence of
guidelines covering the work.

HMI's view of the qualities of effective teaching has also been
elaborated in their recent report on the qualities of 'good teachers' based
on their inspection of schools (HMI, 1985b; see also McNamara, 1986).
Here the HMI state their view thus:

> Good teachers need a variety of approaches and patterns of working, and
> the flexibility to call on several different strategies within the space of one
> lesson. Sound planning and skilful management are needed to blend class,
> group and individual work, to provide a wide range of learning activities,
> to observe, to solve problems, to offer explanations and to apply skills and
> ideas. Pupils of any age need a satisfying balance between oral, practical
> and written tasks providing scope for extended discussion as well as for
> sustained writing of many different kinds. (p. 4)

The growing emphasis on pupils engaging in a variety of learning
activities, exerting greater initiative over the course of their work and
greater control over the development of their understanding, most
characterises the HMI's advocacy of how the quality of teaching should
improve.

An exploratory study

Any attempt to break down the holistic quality of teaching into a number
of key qualities of effective teaching presents a major challenge for those
involved in teacher education to 'lay their cards on the table' and make
explicit their own view of such qualities. This challenge led me to
formulate my own set of qualities, drawing from the wide-ranging
research on effective teaching that has been reported. My initial 'melting
pot' of attributes included the whole variety of specific teacher behaviours
at one extreme (frequently maintains eye-contact with pupils, follows up
pupils' ideas, etc) to general qualities at the other extreme (withitness,
enthusiasm, warmth, etc). It became clear that any attempt to define an
unequivocal set of qualities which would describe effective teaching was

doomed to failure; there are a number of different ways in which teachers may be effective, and these different ways appear to rely on different characteristics. However, what did seem to be justifiable was an attempt to formulate a set of qualities which have been widely identified in writings and studies on effective teaching. Such a set of qualities could then be used as a basis for exploring the extent to which lessons given by different teachers might be usefully described and discussed in terms of variations in – and from – these qualities. If the set of qualities proved useful in this way, it could then be further explored in terms of its relationship to effectiveness. If it failed to describe differences between lessons, that in itself might be important for our thinking about effective teaching. I felt that the most useful approach in developing such a set of key classroom teaching qualities, would be to outline each quality in terms of teacher and pupil behaviour and lesson characteristics, which would typify the two extremes of a dimension of appraisal based on that quality. Following a development study based on classroom observation and discussion with teachers, a set of eight such qualities was identified. The corresponding dimensions and the descriptions are shown in Figure 4: the *Teaching Assessment Rating Scales*.

The basic theme of each of these dimensions was as follows:

1 Preparedness
The notion of preparedness was intended to be seen from the viewpoint of the pupils in the class in terms of the appearance that the lesson gave of being well-organised, having a coherent structure, and creating the impression of purposefulness from the teacher. Attached to this notion was also the idea that the unexpected could be catered for in the lesson without disrupting its structure or intent.

2 Pace and flow
This dimension dealt with two complementary notions. Pace concerned the idea of keeping up the rate of events within the lesson so that all pupils are kept involved and attentive; the idea of flow was seen to have more to do with maintaining the lesson as a single unity. The key concept here is Kounin's notion of overlapping: the teacher being able to deal with more than one thing at a time so that the thread of the lesson was not lost while an individual pupil's problem concerning work or discipline was dealt with.

3 Transitions
Transitions focuses on two key elements in the lesson. First, the establishment of attention at the start and maintaining attention when moving between activities. Second, the teacher's sensitivity in deciding when to move from one activity to the next.

4 Cognitive matching

This dimension contains three key elements: whether the lesson is suited to pupils' abilities and interests, whether the work is challenging and instructive, and whether individual differences between pupils are accommodated.

5 Clarity

The notion of clarity refers to the extent to which the teacher's instructions and explanations are clear and are pitched at the appropriate level for pupil comprehension.

6 Business-like

This dimension is concerned with the manner in which the lesson is conducted. It focuses on matters of authority, reaction to misbehaviour, and teacher expectations which together create an impression that the teacher is in control. This impression is conveyed by a tone of confidence and firmness regarding teaching and control, together with positive expectations regarding the quality of work and behaviour occurring in the lesson.

7 Withitness

This notion, developed by Kounin, deals with the teacher's monitoring of the lesson so that he or she is alert to and can pre-empt pupil misbehaviour, or take swift action when it does occur. Such monitoring includes taking note of inattention by pupils and an inability to do the work set.

8 Encouragingness

This dimension explicitly examines the nature of teacher–pupil inter-action in terms of the extent to which the teacher uses a mixture of praise, instructive criticism, enthusiasm and good humour to develop a positive and encouraging tone in the lesson which will foster and support pupils' self-confidence and self-esteem.

While these eight qualities overlap in some respects, they appear to represent the main key classroom teaching qualities which warrant particular attention in the consideration of effective teaching. In an ESRC-funded study, 40 lessons (each given by a different teacher) were observed in two secondary schools, and the observer rated each lesson in each of these eight dimensions on a rating scale of 1 to 5, where 1 denoted the righthand (less desirable) description and 5 denoted the lefthand (more desirable) description (see Figure 4). The findings of the study, reported by Kyriacou and McKelvey (1985a, b) indicated, sur-prisingly, that for all but one dimension over half of the 40 lessons

Figure 4   The Teaching Assessment Rating Scales

1 Preparedness

Well-organised and prepared both for teaching during the lesson and for setting work; lesson well structured; teacher knows where s/he is going and how to get there.

vs Teacher not sure how s/he wants lesson to start or develop; frequently not sure what s/he wants to do next; materials required not to hand; some problems caused by lack of foresight.

2 Pace and flow

Keeps up an appropriate pace for maintaining interest and attention; lesson flows smoothly; able to attend to more than one thing at a time and thereby does not break flow of lesson in order to give individual help or discipline individuals.

vs Dwells on minor points; talks longer than necessary for children's understanding of points and tasks; holds up lesson whilst disciplining, or whilst dealing with minor matters (eg getting a pupil a pencil); distracted by questions or actions of individuals; lesson progresses slowly and is disjointed.

3 Transitions

Able to quickly establish attention at the start of a lesson and re-establish it when required such as at transitions between activities; lesson begins smoothly and moves smoothly between activities; teacher is sensitive to how lesson is progressing in deciding when to initiate transitions.

vs Beginning of lesson and transitions are jerky, long and awkward; unable to establish and maintain attention when required; jerkiness caused by having to repeat instructions or by referring back to previously omitted points or instructions; new instructions are disruptive because they contradict earlier ones or because they are not relevant or appropriate for the whole class.

4 Cognitive matching

Lesson is well suited to pupils' ability and interests; teacher is able to accommodate individual differences by varying the difficulty and pace through individual attention where appropriate; work is challenging as well as instructive.

vs Lesson is boring and ill-suited to pupils' ability and interests; no attempt is made to meet the requirements of individuals.

5 Clarity

Teacher's instructions and explanations (both verbal and written) are clear and at pupils' level.

vs Teacher's instructions and explanations are vague, ambiguous, or take no account of pupils' level of comprehension.

6 Business-like

Lesson is essentially conducted in a business-like manner; authority is firm; reacts calmly when dealing with misbehaviour; teacher exudes confidence and positive expectations for quality of work and behaviour.

vs Lesson conducted hesitantly; authority is uncertain, and reactions are over-emotional; teacher lacks confidence and conveys expectation of underachievement and misbehaviour.

7 Withitness

Teacher is aware of and continually monitors what is going on in all parts of the classroom; frequently maintains eye contact with pupils, and scans whole class; pre-empts misbehaviour or acts with speed when it appears.

vs Gets wrapped-up in what s/he is doing and is unaware of parts of the classroom; is slow to recognise and react to misbehaviour, and when s/he does so fails to identify the culprits correctly.

8 Encouragingness

Interaction with pupils is essentially encouraging and positive, such as to build up pupils' self-confidence and self-esteem; uses plenty of praise and instructive criticism (explaining where pupil went wrong or how he could do better rather than criticising pupil himself); teacher conveys enthusiasm and some good humour.

vs Interaction with pupils is hostile and deprecating; teacher frequently uses personal criticisms; remains aloof; teaches with little enthusiasm and shows no sense of humour.

---

observed received a rating of 5, the exact numbers (out of 40) being:

preparedness	31
pace and flow	24
transitions	24
cognitive matching	24
clarity	33
business-like	26
withitness	22
encouragingness	14

The fact that only 14 of the 40 lessons received a rating of 5 on encouragingness reflected some teachers' tone being somewhat tired or bored, and instances of teachers using sarcasm or being deprecating in their interaction with pupils.

Four of the 40 lessons rated all 5s. These were all characterised by a coherence of presentation; a pace that seemed to suit the pupils' needs and maintain their interest; an ability to deal with matters of discipline without interrupting the lesson (although it is also noteworthy that very little misbehaviour was evident); ease in moving between activities without spending time repeating explanations or controlling the class and in a way that seemed appropriate to what the class appeared to do next; a general awareness of what was going on in the class at all times so that the teacher was able to ensure that pupils were engaged with the lesson as much as possible; and a positive and enthusiastic relationship with pupils. Nevertheless, there were also notable differences between these four lessons: one lesson was very formal and highly structured, requiring a great deal of individual seatwork from pupils and little discussion; in contrast, in another lesson the teacher either read or talked to pupils or they talked among themselves as part of the lesson plan, then reported back to the teacher. Although these two lessons received identical ratings, they had very different atmospheres.

Of the 40 lessons, a further 14 received a profile of ratings which contained only 5s and 4s. This bias in the lessons observed towards ratings of 5s and 4s (the desirable descriptions) was no doubt in part a reflection of the fact that the 40 teachers observed were all experienced teachers, and all had agreed to allow the researcher to observe a lesson (some teachers who were approached did not agree to take part in the study). In this respect, the descriptions used for the eight qualities did not sufficiently discriminate between such lessons.

Using such rating scales in the context of initial training courses has been very useful indeed. It raises an agenda of qualities against which student teachers can discuss and compare their views about effective teaching and their assessment and evaluation of videotaped lessons.

The views of student teachers, together with the lack of discrimination between the lessons of experienced teachers, in many instances, seem to point to three important observations concerning the search for the key qualities of classroom teaching. These apply not only to the qualities discussed here, but to all such sets, including those used by the HMI and in the *Stanford Teacher Competence Appraisal Guide,* already discussed. The first observation is that such ratings fail to do justice to the intellectual quality of the lesson (how the content and learning activities are marshalled to set up the educational experience appropriate to achieving the teacher's intended outcomes). In part, this requires one to consider the development of the lesson as a whole unit, which is why some of the lesson descriptions produced in the study were so interesting, as indeed were the HMI's lesson vignettes.

The second observation is that such ratings also fail to do justice to the nature of the rapport between teacher and pupils, and to measure how such rapport is developed over the course of the lesson. Such rapport extends beyond its purely affective tone to include the hidden curriculum, in terms of the types of activities used; the 'language climate' of the classroom and the messages that are thereby conveyed to pupils about their role and the teacher's view of pupil learning. In addition, the rapport between teacher and pupils often changes many times during a lesson as the teacher puts on 'different hats': encouraging, reprimanding, explaining and counselling, among others.

The third observation concerns the importance of teachers being able to see the progress of a lesson from the pupils' perspective, and make the appropriate decisions and modifications to the lesson while it is happening. This quality of social sensitivity is an important contributory factor to all eight of the qualities considered in the study.

Together these three observations have a common thread: that the dynamic nature of a lesson (in terms of how the scenario unfolds and is inter-related) is fundamental to the consideration of how judgements about qualities are made.

What can now be concluded about the search for the key classroom teaching qualities? First, that the set of qualities discussed here, as is the case with a number of other such sets, provides a very valuable set of agenda items for discussion and reflection. In part, it is *how* one discusses these qualities that is of importance. Whether one uses the qualities adopted here or another set such as HMI's, it is likely that the same underlying points about teaching and learning will need to be considered. In effect, valuable as such a set is, it is really only a heuristic device that enables one to probe the nature of effective teaching.

Second, while such sets are valuable in highlighting the shortcomings of less successful lessons, they appear to be of much less use in discriminating between the more than adequately effective lessons given most of the time in schools and those lessons which are particularly effective and more exceptional in quality. The latter owe something to the notion of 'master classes' in that they go beyond 'what you do' to 'the way that you do it'. Such exceptional lessons seem to involve a variety of additional factors: exceptional teaching skills, charisma, first class commitment and preparation, and an ability to tailor a learning experience perfectly to the needs of pupils. At such an extreme of qualities, one begins to deal with case studies of unique teachers and teaching, rather than a consideration of general qualities.

Key classroom teaching tasks

The key tasks involved in classroom teaching can usefully be grouped under three main headings: 'planning', 'presentation and monitoring', and 'reflection and evaluation'. These three groupings form a continuous cycle underlying the teacher's decision-making. *Planning* involves the teacher's decisions about the aims of a lesson, its context, and the learning activities which will effectively achieve its aims. *Presentation and monitoring* involve decisions the teacher makes about the progress of a lesson while it is taking place. *Reflection and evaluation* involve decisions made after a lesson has finished, which feed into future planning activities. These three main groupings of key classroom teaching tasks are reflected in many of the discussions of effective teaching in terms of practical craft knowledge (eg Calderhead, 1984; Heywood, 1982; Marland, 1975; Perrott, 1982; Waterhouse, 1983), and will be considered here in some detail.

Planning

Good planning is a crucial aspect of effective teaching. Many experienced teachers have a store of wisdom concerning the ingredients of a successful lesson, which enables them to spend much less time in planning than is the case for most younger teachers. However, all teachers need to have clear ideas about the lesson they wish to set up and have carried out the necessary preparation if it is to be successful.

Three main elements are involved in planning a lesson. First is the need to consider the general aims and specific educational outcomes the lesson is intended to achieve. The second element, taking account of the context (eg the type of pupils, the school's resources) and desired outcomes, is to consider what will be the most effective learning environment, activities, and sequencing of these? Third is the need to monitor and evaluate pupils' educational progress, so that the teacher can assess whether the lesson has been successful. Planning is essential for the success of all lessons; but it is particularly crucial in taking account of important differences between pupils, such as learning difficulties indicative of special educational needs, and in the use of teaching and learning activities designed to combat any problems which may be linked to ability (both high and low), motivation, social class, gender and race. The main questions involved in planning are detailed in Table 2.

Table 2 Planning a lesson

1   What level and range of ability is there in the class?
     What level and type of motivation can I expect?
     What is the composition of the class in terms of ethnic minority pupils, social class and sex?
     Do any of the pupils have special educational needs?
     What do the pupils already know and feel about the subject/topic?
     How have the pupils behaved in previous lessons?

2   What do I want the pupils to learn in this lesson:
     • cognitively (eg knowledge, understanding, intellectual skills)?
     • affectively (eg interest, attitudes, self-confidence)?
     How does this relate to their present knowledge, feelings and needs?
     How does this relate to the course as a whole (both past and future)?

3   What constraints need to be accommodated:
     • time available for lesson, preparation time available?

- number of pupils in class, layout of classroom?
- teacher's knowledge and skills?
- acceptability of lesson to significant others (colleagues, parents)?

4   Are there any other considerations of note:
- has this lesson been successful with a similar class?
- what time of day, week, term, etc is it?

5   What teaching method (type of learning tasks, activities and experience) will best foster the cognitive and affective outcomes desired, given the context and the constraints which need to be accommodated (as outlined above):
- discovery methods, exposition plus practice, individualised learning, work sheets, small group work?

6   Having chosen a particular method and general academic topic for the lesson, what sequencing of the tasks/activities/experience, level of difficulty and structuring of the topic, and pace of lesson will be best for the lesson to be successful in terms of maintaining the pupils' attention, interest, understanding and motivation, and achieving the desired cognitive and affective outcomes?

7   What level of pupil performance will be expected, and how will the degree of success of the learning taking place be determined (eg questioning of pupils, written work, follow up tests)?

8   What preparation is necessary before the lesson:
- are there sufficient textbooks available, is the equipment in working order, which questions and/or exercises will be set and what are the answers to these?

9   What teacher behaviour is required during the lesson to ensure its success:
- quality, style and tone of presentation and monitoring?
- use of questions, reinforcement and feedback?
- monitoring of general progress and the management of discipline?
- adjustment to the lesson (eg pace, content) as appropriate?
- helping individual pupils?

10   How will the lesson be perceived and experienced by the pupils:
- of interest/relevance/importance/difficulty?
- their comprehension of instructions and task requirements?

11   What problems might arise?

The most important aspect of planning is to ensure that the learning experience fulfils the three psychological conditions necessary for pupil learning to occur:
- *attentiveness*: the learning experience must elicit and sustain pupils' attention
- *receptiveness*: the learning experience must elicit and sustain pupils' motivation and mental effort
- *appropriateness*: the learning experience must be appropriate for the educational outcomes desired.

Consideration of these three psychological conditions must underpin all discussion of how the key classroom teaching tasks are to be met if effective teaching is to take place.

Considering the general aims and specific educational outcomes the lesson is intended to achieve involves a complex web of concerns: short-term and long-term outcomes; cognitive and affective outcomes; and the fact that different outcomes may be directed at particular pupils within the class. The most important question for the teacher to ask is 'what should pupils have learnt from the lesson?' whether it be in terms of knowledge, understanding, skills or attitudes. Interestingly, Calderhead (1984) has observed that such an approach, although widely advocated, rarely matches established practice:

> Research on teachers' planning suggests that teachers engage in a process that contrasts sharply with the prescribed rational planning model. Whereas the prescribed model starts with a statement of aims and objectives, followed by a reasoning of the content and organisation to be adopted and how the pupils' performance is to be evaluated to assess whether the objectives have been achieved, teachers' plans reflect little concern either with objectives or with evaluations. In reality, the process of planning seems to be more appropriately conceptualised as a problem-solving process. Teachers, faced with a variety of factors such as pupils with certain knowledge, abilities and interests, the availability of particular textbooks and materials, the syllabus, the timetable, the expectations of headteachers and others, and their own knowledge of previous teaching encounters, *have to solve the problem of how to structure the time and experiences of pupils in the classroom*. Teachers, it seems, adopt a much more pragmatic approach than that prescribed for curriculum design. Rather than start with a conception of what is to be achieved and deduce which classroom activities would therefore be ideal, teachers start with a conception of their working context and from that decide what is possible. (p. 74)

The import of Calderhead's observation is that the teacher's planning takes place against a background of concerns and constraints which influence the selection of the learning activities more than the rational model suggests. These range from resources available to problems of discipline.

In considering the selection of learning activities, a useful distinction can be made between content and lesson organisation. With regard to content, the most important consideration is to take account of what pupils already know: the lesson must start 'where the pupils are'. This means not only ascertaining their present knowledge, understanding and skills connected with the topic in hand, but also building upon any related or relevant knowledge and interests. Of particular importance is the need to check rather than presuppose the existence of knowledge, understanding and skills which are necessary if a lesson designed to achieve certain educational outcomes is to be successful. If a lesson builds upon work covered in a previous lesson given some time ago, some revision may be necessary, along with an explanation of how the work in hand will relate to the previous work. Indeed, Bruner (1960) has argued for a system of content selection whereby each topic is gradually developed and extended by being met periodically within a course. Such a procedure of periodic development linked by revision, he argues, would be particularly effective in allowing the structure of the knowledge to be consolidated in the pupil's memory. Bruner calls this arrangement 'the spiral curriculum', and it is a common feature of many subject textbooks.

With regard to lesson organisation, a host of concerns are involved during planning. Of prime importance is the need to ensure that the type of activity to be used is right for the type of learning which is desired. For example, if the teacher wishes to extend pupils' use of language, then pupils must be given opportunity to talk; if the teacher wishes to foster pupils' ability to frame scientific hypotheses, they should be asked to do so. The single biggest danger facing teachers is to slip into an informing mode of teaching when such a mode is not the most effective for the intended objectives of the lesson. Indeed, the fact that pupils learn more effectively by doing rather than by listening indicates that a greater emphasis should be given to pupil involvement and activity across the curriculum than is typical at present.

The planning of a lesson is also an important opportunity to think carefully about the way in which the educational objectives to be achieved may need to be broken down into conceptually appropriate steps, each of which may require practice and consolidation. In terms of the sequencing of activities within a lesson, the most basic sequence for a lesson is one which has a beginning (in which the topic is introduced), a middle (comprising the main learning activities) and an end (which may review the learning which should have occurred). The possible variations of this basic sequence are numerous; what is important is that the rationale underlying the sequencing and activities adopted take account of attentiveness, receptiveness and appropriateness.

Another key point about the planning of lesson organisation is that the outline of a lesson must always be flexible. The ability to extend parts of a lesson further than originally intended, or even to omit certain elements and tasks when appropriate, is essential. Teachers always need to be ready to modify their plans in the light of how the lesson progresses, and to have additional tasks at hand if the work planned is completed by some or all of the pupils before the end of the lesson.

Finally, in planning lesson organisation one needs to take account of the learning environment in terms of the tone or atmosphere created. Above all it needs to be borne in mind that learning, with its risk of failure, is an emotionally charged and high risk process, which needs to be carefully nurtured and supported. Some activities are more high risk than others, and the teacher needs to be alert to this. The learning environment generated in a lesson is in part a reflection of the style of relationship which develops between teacher and pupils in terms of both the learning activities and the disciplinary strategies used. These will be considered in later chapters. What is important to note here, is that the tone of the learning environment may have a marked influence on the effectiveness of achieving certain educational outcomes.

With regard to planning how the success of a lesson is to be evaluated, a teacher needs to build in strategies that will enable him or her to monitor the progress of learning during the lesson and to assess such learning after the lesson. Given the importance of quick corrective feedback to facilitating pupil learning and to ensure that the progress of the lesson maintains its effectiveness, the teacher needs to be continually assessing pupils' learning by checking their work, asking questions and responding to difficulties. More formalised assessment made on the basis of tests and, to some extent, marking homework provide both the teacher and pupils with feedback about progress. A careful match of learning experiences with such assessment is important in the cause of fairness to the pupil and in order to achieve a valid measure of progress.

At this point some attention must be given to the role of lesson notes. Compiling an outline of a lesson in terms of notes about the aims of the lesson, the sequence, timing and type of learning activities to be used, and details of the learning materials (including textbooks, worksheets, and equipment) serves a number of extremely important functions. Firstly, it forces the teacher to consider the logistics of successfully implementing the plan of a lesson. For example, it becomes immediately apparent whether too much or too little time is available for the intended learning activities. Second, such outlines provide a script to which the teacher can refer during the lesson to check on what should come next. Third, they can alert the teacher to activities and aspects of the lesson which will require preparation in advance; for example, the need to ensure that equipment and resources are available: is there an adequate number of log books available for distribution? Is the apparatus for the demonstration already set up? Is the equipment in working order? Fourth, lesson notes can usefully include the questions which the teacher intends to ask, the answers to be expected, and the correct answers and results for work set, all of which will enable marking and feedback to progress smoothly. Fifth, they provide the teacher with a record of the lesson which can be referred to and modified for future use. Making lesson notes is so useful as a part of planning effectively, that it is an essential activity for student teachers. Among experienced teachers, however, the use of lesson notes varies extensively, in part because such formalised planning is time-consuming and in part because experienced teachers have largely developed the ability to speedily envisage a script for a lesson, and to teach as though all was well planned and prepared.

Finally, in planning lessons, one has to make sure that the demands placed on oneself as teacher and on the pupils are sensible and realistic. It may seem odd to state that a staple diet of apparently excellent, exciting lessons would not be desirable. Both teachers and pupils need to have a curriculum which gives opportunity for low-key demands, during which they can take a mental breather, as well as periods when the demands on the teacher and pupils are very high. Such considerations apply not only to the whole school week, but also to individual lessons; lessons more than 40 minutes in length will certainly benefit from containing a mixture of learning activities and demands, in terms of the mental health of pupils as well as of the teacher.

Presentation and monitoring

The two key tasks involved in the activity of classroom teaching are presentation and monitoring. Presentation refers to all the aspects of lesson organisation and its implementation; monitoring refers to the ways in which the teacher needs to assess the progress of a lesson to ensure its success. In practice, presentation and monitoring are closely interlinked; many of the tasks and activities carried out by the teacher during a lesson (eg questioning pupils' understanding) are part of both presentation and monitoring. These areas also overlap within the field of classroom management which in its broadest sense refers to the general management and organisation of pupil learning and discipline. The main characteristics underpinning the task of effective presentation and monitoring are shown in Table 3.

In essence, the effectiveness of presentation and monitoring rests on establishing the three psychological conditions necessary for pupil learning: attentiveness, receptiveness and appropriateness. The teacher's classroom teaching *skills,* involved in carrying out the *tasks* of teaching, will determine the extent to which these three conditions are effectively realised.

A key factor in presentation is the effective use of time. Pupils should arrive promptly for lessons and lessons should end on time. The speed with which the lesson can commence is helped by establishing well-used procedures so that the pupils are familiar with the routines and conventions linked to one's teaching; this should cover entry to the classroom and the way pupils settle into the rhythm of the lesson presentation. The amount of time wasted at the start of a lesson – by having to settle latecomers, deal with pupils without pencils or pens, and wait for all pupils to pay attention – can be minimised by having established clear demands and expectations regarding these problems (eg spare pens will be dealt with at the appropriate time by the teacher and should not

---

Table 3 Presenting and monitoring a lesson

In considering those characteristics of presenting and monitoring a lesson which will contribute to its success, one needs to bear in mind that these may well vary depending on the context (eg topic, type of pupils); on the particular type of outcomes the teacher wishes to emphasise most (eg developing an interest in the topic, ensuring recall of certain facts); and on the type of learning experience or teaching method adopted (eg group work, discovery learning).

Nevertheless, a number of characteristics of effective presentation and monitoring apply across a range of lesson types.

1 The teacher appears to be self-confident, is normally patient and good humoured, displays a genuine interest in the topic, and appears to be genuinely concerned with each pupil's progress.

2 The teacher's explanations and instructions are clear, and pitched at the right level for pupil comprehension.

3 The teacher's voice and actions facilitate pupils maintaining attention and interest.

4 The teacher makes good and varied use of questioning to monitor pupils' understanding and to raise the level of pupils' thinking.

5 The teacher monitors the progress of the lesson and pupils' behaviour, and makes any adjustments necessary to ensure the lesson flows well and that pupils are engaged appropriately.

6 The teacher encourages pupils' efforts.

7 Pupil misbehaviour is minimised by keeping their attention maintained on the lesson, and by use of eye-contact, movement and questions to curtail any misbehaviour which is developing.

8 Potential interruptions to the lesson caused by organisational problems (eg a pupil who has not got a pen) or pupil misbehaviour are dealt with in such a way that the interruptions are minimised or prevented.

9 Criticism by the teacher of a pupil is given privately, and in a way likely to encourage and foster progress.

10 Pupil misbehaviour, when it does occur, is dealt with in a relaxed, self-assured and firm manner.

---

interrupt the start of a lesson). Time is also saved if there is a clear routine regarding distribution of materials, including books, equipment or other resources (eg worksheets and apparatus).

Once the lesson is underway, time can be saved (or wasted) in a number of ways. Primarily, the teacher needs to organise and present the learning experience in a way that elicits and maintains pupils' attention and engagement. Attention will easily be lost if the work is too difficult, is boring or appears to lack interest, importance or relevance. In addition, attention will easily be lost if the presentation is poor, for example if the teacher's tone of voice is monotonous; if the pace of presentation is too fast or too slow to follow adequately; if the blackboard work or materials are unclear; if the task is passive and overlong (particularly with respect to teacher exposition) and if the classroom is uncomfortable (too hot, too cold, poor seating arrangements etc). Attention will be most easily maintained by a lively, interesting presentation linked to a variety of activities which enable pupils to be active for some or most of the time, and where the sequencing and content of the learning activities is intellectually and pedagogically sound (ie it makes intellectual sense from the point of view of the pupils and their perception of the nature of the learning which is taking place).

Lest the impression be given here that saving time is the be-all and end-all of effective presentation, it is important to note that many lessons, particularly those involving apparatus or group work, may be costly in apparent non-learning time, where in fact the processes involved in preparing for the activity and in engaging in it (eg waiting for the results in an experiment or long pauses during discussions) may not only be a worthwhile sacrifice of time, but in fact be of educational value in their own right, in terms of developing a range of important learning skills. Excessive time consciousness by a teacher is a danger if it promotes over-controlled and essentially passive pupil learning experiences.

Another major task involved in presentation is to ensure that the learning experience offered is intellectually and pedagogically sound, not only in eliciting and maintaining attention (as already noted) but also in fostering the desired educational outcomes. This involves a careful consideration of the steps that the pupils' learning will need to follow in terms of the learning processes which need to be utilised (eg rote learning, meaningful learning, practice and consolidation, see also chapter 2) and the type of activities which best engage these learning processes (eg teacher exposition, writing tasks, small group work, experiential learning . . . as outlined in chapter 3).

HMI (1985a) have identified four main elements of learning: knowledge, concepts, skills and attitudes. Promoting each of these involves using an appropriate type and range of classroom activities. The teaching of skills is a particularly interesting area. The essence of a skill is that it relates to the ability to perform a task; the emphasis is on doing rather than knowing or understanding *per se*. Thus the teaching of a skill must involve giving the pupil the opportunity to practise and display that skill. Teaching which is mainly expository, where the skill is tested in terms of knowledge and understanding of what it is and how it should be applied, may well not effectively develop that skill. HMI state the position thus:

> The successful development of oral skills, for example, requires opportunities for pupils to put questions and pursue points with the teacher; to give

thoughtful, extended answers; to discuss and explore ideas among them-selves in pairs or in groups both with and without the intervention of the teacher and, on occasions, to talk at some length on particular topics. In developing problem solving skills, teachers have the important task of helping pupils to tackle problems analytically and to adopt logical procedures in solving them. At the same time pupils must be allowed to make mistakes and to follow false scents in what is essentially an exploratory process; and the teacher has to resist the temptation to give the 'right' answer, or to over-direct the pupil, otherwise the skill is not developed or practised. (pp. 40–41)

Recently, a large increase in the number of courses in the area of life and social skills has had a major impact on the development of both diverse teaching and learning activities and of new forms of assessment to ensure that it is really the skills which are developed and assessed (eg Hopson and Scally, 1981; Law, 1984). At the same time, there are numerous such courses where the teaching and assessment has emphasized knowledge despite an explicit reference to the development of skills in the stated aims of the course.

The notion that presentation should be intellectually and pedagogically sound requires that the teacher sees the learning experience from the pupils' perspective. This includes not only attempting to judge how one's own performance, teaching materials, and learning activities might appear from the pupils' perspective, but also an attempt to ensure that the mental activity in which the pupil is engaged is appropriate. Effective presentation may need to give explicit guidance as to the type of mental activity and learning strategy which the pupils are expected to use. Many pupils simply do not know how to go about organising their own learning activity on a mental level (Should they be attempting to memorise instructions? Making notes? Drawing upon previous learning, etc?). Recognition of this has led to the increasingly widespread develop-ment of study skills courses in schools. As was noted earlier, however, too great a degree of spoonfeeding by a teacher may enable a particular lesson to go smoothly, but this may be at the cost of not enabling pupils to develop their own decision-making skills in response to the academic demands made.

Effective presentation goes hand in hand with effective monitoring of the progress of the lesson and of pupils' learning. Indeed, what makes teaching a particularly demanding activity is the need to monitor the whole variety of concerns that need to be taken account of if pupils' attentiveness and receptiveness and the appropriateness of the learning experience are to be maintained. Such concerns include whether the pupils are becoming bored; whether the lesson has been pitched at too difficult a level; whether some or all the pupils are completing the set work faster than expected; whether pupils are encountering problems or making errors; whether the materials and resources needed are to hand;

and whether the organisation of the lesson is leading to problems. In difficult circumstances, the degree of monitoring required – demanding as it does a high level of concentration and complex, simultaneous decision-making – is likely to leave a teacher mentally exhausted. Clearly, sound planning of a lesson pays handsome dividends if it reduces the need for many such concerns to be so vigorously monitored.

For inexperienced teachers the complex nature of such monitoring and decision-making is particularly demanding. However, with time, the teacher becomes more adept at picking up the signals which indicate how the lesson needs to be modified or conducted if attentiveness, receptiveness and appropriateness are to be maintained. Two types of skills, in particular, underpin the teacher's ability to maintain effectiveness in this way.

The first type of skill involves assessing pupils' progress during the lesson: are they paying attention, have they understood the instructions or explanations, are they having difficulties? The main tools teachers use to assess such progress are questions, quick tests, moving around the classroom to check on the work being produced, and reading the facial expressions and general behaviour of pupils.

The second type of skill is the ability to deal with a number of matters and concerns at the same time (in Kounin's terms 'overlapping'). In most classrooms there are times when to ensure that the flow of progress is maintained the teacher needs to deal with a number of different demands, each of which will hold up progress for one or more pupils if not met. For example if, when engaged in teacher exposition, the teacher notices that a pupil is not paying attention, the teacher can continue the exposition while staring at or perhaps moving close to the pupil in question; in this way the pupil's inattention is noticed by the teacher and signalled to the pupil, but the flow of exposition, and hence the attention of others, is not interrupted. In a classroom where pupils may be engaged in different activities or progressing through their work at different speeds, dealing simultaneously with their varied demands is essential. This may mean being able to listen to one pupil reading aloud, whilst checking that another has successfully completed a different task and is ready to move on, and signalling to yet another, seconds later, that some further resources are needed. Over and above all this, the teacher may also be considering whether it is time for pupils to start packing away, whether the noise level is too great, and whether there is a need to circulate around the room to check all is generally well. Problems may occur if the organisation of the lesson and activities leads to too many demands being made on the teacher, which therefore cannot be met. This may result in long queues for help and assessment at the teacher's desk or in pupils being able to get away with very little work without being noticed. Effective teaching requires a lesson organisation which can be adequately monitored.

An important part of monitoring involves giving feedback to pupils concerning their progress. This may be done individually, as when a teacher assesses a pupil's work, or collectively, either by making a statement to the whole class based on the individual assessments and general monitoring, or by getting pupils to mark their own work by giving the correct answers at the end of the activity. The most important aspects of feedback are that it should be quick (particularly if errors are being made or difficulties encountered), constructive, helpful and supportive. Individually-given feedback can be tailored to the pupil's particular needs, but there is a limit to how quickly a teacher can circulate and hence the feedback for some pupils may be slow; collectively-given feedback at least ensures that all pupils can note whether they are progressing correctly, but if they are not, then they need help as quickly as possible. A mixture of both individual and collective assessment and feedback would seem to be the most effective approach, given the constraints on classroom teaching.

In giving feedback, the teacher needs to first establish the root of the pupil's difficulties: initial inattentiveness; not being able to understand the task; a lack of interest in the topic; an application of a faulty learning strategy, or some other factor. Effective feedback needs to diagnose the nature of any problems, and not only give remedial help, but also try to mitigate future difficulties by developing sound study habits and self-confidence regarding learning.

One of the major problems facing effective teaching is how to ensure that those pupils whose progress is less successful than that of their peers do not become discouraged and disheartened. Some forms of learning activity, such as group work, project work, individualised learning, experiential learning, and practical work, can do much to mitigate this effect if emphasis is placed on the process of the activity engaged in and/or on the individual's work in its own right. For a pupil to say 'I'm no good at history (or mathematics, or physical education, or science, or whatever)' is a tragedy. All pupils ought to be able to enjoy and derive pleasure from all areas of the curriculum, for them not to do so because they do less well in their assessed work is unforgivable. This is not to say that pupils should not recognise that others have greater talents in some areas of the curriculum than they do; rather that such a recognition should not undermine their own interest and enjoyment of these areas. The type of feedback and assessment methods used by a teacher is crucial here. To a great extent the examination system places major constraints on teachers' room for manoeuvre. However, in recent years many teachers have attempted to place greater emphasis on the quality of the *processes* which pupils experience during a lesson rather than on the assessment of a final *product*.

One of the problems in planning an objectives-based curriculum using observable and testable performance as the criterion of effectiveness, is hat it tends to squeeze out the development of any educationally desirable behaviour that is manifestly difficult to observe and test; the examination system tends to have a similar effect on classroom teaching. In that respect, it is gratifying to note that new forms of assessment, such as pupil profiling (Law, 1984), are enabling a broader range of pupils' educational development to be monitored. (It should be noted, however, that the implications of this for the recording of progress in a lesson and the type of feedback that now needs to be given are not without problems.) For example, many English teachers have attempted to foster conversation skills amongst pupils, and now some examination boards are including an assessment of conversation skills; it remains to be seen whether this will start to have a major impact on the way such lessons are organised and on the type of monitoring, feedback and assessment methods the teacher will now need to use.

In discussing the major aspects of presentation and monitoring little has been said here regarding the rapport and relationship between teacher and pupils which develops in a lesson and which establishes the tone or climate of the learning environment. In addition, little has been said of the role of teacher authority in establishing discipline and in dealing with misbehaviour. In fact, these questions are so important and fundamental to effective teaching that they will be explored fully in the next two chapters. Suffice to say here that presentation and monitoring are inextricably bound up with these very questions.

Reflection and evaluation

Reflection and evaluation after a lesson are essential if the teacher is to continue to improve the quality of the learning experience offered. Two main tasks are involved. First, to consider whether the lesson has been successful and to act on any implications for future teaching; second, to assess and record the educational progress of the pupils. The key questions underpinning reflection and evaluation are listed in Table 4.

Assessing the success of a lesson involves considering a whole range of concerns. At one level, the teacher needs to consider whether the intended learning outcomes have been effectively achieved. At another level, the teacher also needs to consider a whole host of very practical issues which largely focus on whether the lesson went as planned. It would be naive to believe that teachers' reflection on a lesson is purely a matter of whether intended learning outcomes have been achieved. As was noted in the earlier discussion of planning, teachers are equally concerned, on a day-to-day basis, with whether the organisation of different tasks and activities in a lesson was successfully implemented, in terms of simple logistics. Did the pupils do more or less what I envisaged for the lesson, in the manner I had intended?

In a sense, the question of what learning took place is secondary to the

Table 4   Reflection and evaluation

Reflection and evaluation regarding one's teaching is crucial for the continuing development of teaching skills in general, and for specific knowledge about how a particular lesson could have been improved (with implications for similar lessons). Each teacher has intentions about his or her own teaching; teachers may differ both in terms of the educational outcomes they wish to emphasise and the types of learning experiences they wish to use. In this respect, one teacher may feel a lesson has gone well, whilst an observer may well feel that other educational outcomes or learning experiences could more usefully have been involved. Periodically, teachers need to reflect on the general character of their teaching and relate this to curriculum developments aimed at improving the quality of education.

The following questions form an outline agenda concerning reflection and evaluation. Each can usefully be elaborated in a number of ways.

1   Did this lesson go well?
   - Were the learning activities envisaged successfully implemented?
   - What did the pupils learn in the lesson?
   - How can I be sure such learning occurred?
   - Did the lesson and learning reflect my intended aims?

2   Did any pupil or group of pupils fail to benefit (eg able pupils, average pupils, less able pupils, shy pupils, female pupils, a pupil who missed previous lessons, a disruptive pupil)? If so, could this have been avoided?

3   What changes can I usefully make before giving a similar lesson to another class?

4   What have I learnt about this class, or particular pupils, that might influence future lessons with this class?

5   What have I learnt about this topic or subject matter that might influence future lessons?

6   Are there any immediate actions I should take following this lesson (eg did any pupil appear to indicate some special educational need?)?

7   Am I satisfied with my general planning of this lesson, and its presentation and monitoring? Did the lesson sustain pupils' attention and interest, and did it appear to be intellectually and pedagogically sound?

8   Did any problems occur in the lesson that I should take note of?

9   How can I consolidate the learning which occurred and relate it to future demands and applications?

10 How did this lesson fit in with the teaching in the department and school, and with curriculum developments concerning teaching in this area?

question of whether the lesson organisation was successfully implemented in terms of the envisaged script. However a major danger regarding an emphasis on implementation rather than learning outcomes is that t is all-too-easy to infer that because a lesson has been successfully implemented, effective teaching has taken place. Indeed, some teachers' aims for a lesson may explicitly refer to lesson organisation rather than learning outcomes; for example, the aim of the lesson may be to get pupils to do an experiment, or to make notes on a passage of text, or to discuss the reasons for racial prejudice. Nonetheless, the teacher will usually have in mind, albeit implicitly, some notion of the ways in which successful implementation will foster desirable learning outcomes.

In thinking about the successful implementation of a lesson, the teacher needs to be alert to the strategies and techniques pupils use to give the appearance of attending, understanding and meeting academic task demands, without in fact being engaged in the learning activities in the way assumed and intended by the teacher. Holt's (1969) observations on this aspect of teaching and learning in the classroom had a marked influence on sensitising teachers to such concerns. For example, pupils are adept at not paying attention during teacher exposition until they notice a change in the pitch of a teacher's voice which denotes that someone is about to be asked a question; in answering questions, pupils are also skilful at giving non-committal answers and using prompts from the teacher (including facial expression and tone) to identify the answer required. In a way, both teacher and pupils have a vested interest in the smooth running of a lesson. Thus, if a teacher suspects that a pupil has not been paying attention, it is extremely tempting to ask another pupil to answer the question; if a pupil does little work but keeps a low profile, it is an easy option to ignore the pupil's lack of progress; if a pupil does not appear to understand the work, it is less demanding to encourage the pupil to learn how to produce the right answer or the work required than to help him or her understand the process involved. Throughout teaching and learning, both teacher and pupils are often tempted to take the easy path, and engage in a degree of collusion. It requires great integrity for a teacher not only to resist such temptation when it occurs, but to actively seek, through the teaching activities used, to identify and overcome such classroom processes. In this respect, the teacher's sensitivity in being able to take account of the pupils' perspective of a learning activity is an essential aspect of the effective monitoring of pupils in the classroom, and vital to subsequent reflection and evaluation of the lesson.

Of course the formal assessment of learning, ranging from marking classroom work and homework to use of school-based tests and examinations, also provides the teacher with regular and essential indices of educational progress. Although such assessment will inevitably focus on academic attainment rather than other educational outcomes (eg study skills, moral values), the latter may be to some extent involved in, or inferred from, particular types of assessed pieces of work. In the context of effective teaching, formal assessments serve a number of important functions. They provide both teacher and pupils with feedback concerning the pupils' attainment. They also form a vehicle whereby the teacher can diagnose difficulties and problems which can then be remedied by feedback accompanying the marking, and specifically addressed in future lessons. In addition, formal assessments enable the teacher to maintain a record of the pupils' attainment which can serve as a basis for future planning of courses, for monitoring whether a pupil's progress has declined over a period of time, and for incorporation into reports both purely internal to the school (as used, for example, in discussion of possible special educational needs) and available to those outside the school (such as those made out when a pupil transfers to a new school and sent to parents, employers, and other educational institutions).

In discussing formal assessment, it is important to note the effects on pupils of such assessment. On the one hand, the evaluation of their work and attainment needs to provide pupils with helpful feedback about the standards expected and how the work presented could have been improved. On the other hand, it must also help maintain pupils' motivation and positive attitudes towards learning, rather than discourage and undermine their self-esteem. To achieve both these aims is essential but by no means easy, and is one of the major challenges facing teachers. Moreover, teachers need to provide feedback to pupils which has a balance of both these elements rather than with an undue emphasis on one at the expense of the other.

Recent developments in the assessment of pupils have placed new demands on teachers regarding the evaluation of educational attainment. In particular, pupil profiles (or 'records of achievement') have had a major impact (Law, 1984). The most common application of this development is as a school-leaving report for pupils aged 16. Such a report would typically include four main elements:

1   The expected results of public examinations.
2   Other academic successes and/or an assessment of proficiency in basic subjects.
3   A record of achievement compiled by the pupil (including out-of-school achievements).
4   An assessment of the pupil's personal qualities.

Pupil profiles have highlighted a distinction between two main types of assessment: *summative* and *formative*. Summative assessment focuses on providing a statement of the pupil's level of attainment (either relative to others or in terms of specified objectives which have been met). Formative assessment focuses on giving feedback to pupils during a course rather than at the end and is aimed at promoting self-understanding and motivation. Of particular interest in the development of pupil profiles is the attempt to utilise both summative and formative assessments. Some advocate pupil profiling because it provides potential users (particularly employers) with a more meaningful statement of the pupil's educational progress than do examination results alone; others see the major benefit to lie in the change in learning activities and methods of assessment which has followed. For example, it would be difficult to assess pupils' ability to organise and take responsibility for their own learning if this quality was not explicitly being fostered, monitored and recorded by the teaching and learning activities adopted in the school.

A number of current developments are aimed at improving teachers' ability to critically reflect upon and evaluate their own teaching. Such developments include attempts by LEAs to encourage schools to review their own practices, the move by the DES to introduce teacher appraisal, and attempts to encourage teachers to become 'teacher researchers', actively investigating the effectiveness of their own practices ('teacher action research') (see, for example, DES, 1985c; Nixon, 1981). Within these developments, some interesting attempts have been made to use pupils' observations, comments and perceptions as feedback for the teacher on how a lesson went. In a review of such attempts, McKelvey and Kyriacou (1985) noted that despite evidence that pupils' comments, when solicited in this way, tended to be very helpful and constructive, many teachers are still reluctant to place themselves in a position whereby pupils' judgements (and hence their status) are recognised in this way.

Conclusions

In this chapter, the key teaching qualities and tasks underpinning effective teaching in the classroom have been discussed. The unifying theme has been that effective teaching needs to sustain pupils' attentiveness and receptiveness, and must be appropriate for the educational outcomes desired. The key classroom teaching qualities and tasks outlined here in effect serve as a set of agenda items; using such an agenda, it is possible to identify the major issues and skills involved in effective teaching. Reference to such qualities and tasks thus provides a framework for applying the earlier discussions of chapters 2–5 to the raw stuff of the activity of teaching. However, the discussion does not conclude here, for two aspects of key teaching qualities and tasks are so important that they warrant attention in their own right. These are teacher–pupil rapport and maintaining classroom discipline; they will be dealt with in the following two chapters.

7 Relationships with pupils

The relationship between teachers and pupils is of fundamental importance to effective teaching. It will be argued here that a sound relationship between teacher and pupils needs to be based on two qualities. The first of these is the pupils' acceptance of the *teacher's authority*. The teacher's prime task is to organise and manage pupils' learning. This involves exerting control over both the management of learning activities and the management of pupils' behaviour (including the maintenance of discipline). Unless pupils accept the teacher's authority to organise and manage in this way, effective teaching is likely to be undermined. The second quality that is required for a sound relationship is *mutual respect and rapport* between the teacher and pupils. This refers to the teacher and pupils recognising each other as individuals, holding each other in esteem, and treating each other in a manner consistent with such esteem.

These two qualities are inter-related in a number of ways; behaviour contributing to one will, inevitably, influence the nature of the other. What is important is the need for both to be established in an acceptable form. HMI (1982) stated their view of good teacher–pupils relations thus:

> ... characteristics which were commonly found included: a quiet, calm, relaxed, good-humoured attitude on the part of the teachers, combined with firmness and a sense of purpose; a demonstration of interest in and knowledge of the pupils individually and an appropriate level of expectation of them; and mutual respect, the pupils recognising the personal qualities, knowledge and skills of the teachers and the teachers being sensitive to the needs of the pupils and respecting their contributions whatever their limitations. Where these qualities were shown, pupils were confident enough to play a full part in the lessons, to offer their own ideas and ask questions or seek help when unsure, while the teacher could blend praise and encouragement with an occasional reprimand, the latter without arousing resentment. (p. 7)

The first part of this chapter will focus on the way that the teacher's authority is established and the basis for developing mutual respect and rapport. In the second part, attention will focus on two aspects of effective teaching which encapsulate the qualities underpinning sound teacher–pupil relationships. The first of these is 'classroom climate', which refers to the emotional tone of teacher–pupil relationships in the classroom. Classroom climate is concerned with how the teacher and pupils feel about each other and the learning activities in hand. Of particular interest regarding classroom climate is the subtle way in which, by their behaviour (most notably their use of language), teacher and pupils can communicate a rich collection of messages to each other; this goes well beyond what may appear at face value to have been communicated or even beyond what the communicator directly intended. The second aspect of effective teaching that will be considered is that of 'pastoral care'. In essence, pastoral care is explicitly concerned with the welfare and well-being of the pupil. Although all secondary and many primary schools have a formalised pastoral care system of some sort, the pastoral care role of the classroom teacher forms part of a sound teacher–pupil relationship.

The teacher's authority

An essential task involved in effective teaching is the need for a teacher to establish and maintain authority over the organisation and management of pupils' learning. Such authority can be established and maintained in a number of ways; how this is done will reflect the teacher's personality, character and general approach to teaching on the one hand, and the context (the type of pupils, subject matter, and school ethos . . .) on the other. In establishing and maintaining authority, the teacher needs to create a tone of purposefulness during lessons, as well as sustaining pupils' attention and motivation and ensuring the appropriateness of the learning activities, so that his or her authority is taken for granted by the pupils. Basically, the teacher's authority needs to be based on effective teaching rather than on coercion. This is not to say that disciplinary techniques are not important in establishing authority; rather it is to stress that if the exercise of disciplinary techniques is used to control problems arising from poor teaching, a sorry state of affairs will have been established in the classroom.

There are four main factors involved in establishing and maintaining authority:
1 Status
2 Teaching competence
3 Exercising control over the classroom
4 Exercising control over discipline
Whilst these sources are inter-related in some respects, they each make a separate and identifiable contribution to the teacher's authority.

Status

The teacher derives a certain amount of status from being a teacher, and from the respect that teachers hold in the eyes of society as a whole and in the eyes of parents in particular. Children in infant schools, who come from homes where the child's relationship with parents and other adults has been sound and where a respect for teachers has been fostered, will often hold teachers in esteem and unquestioningly accept their authority. Here, teachers will derive some status simply from being adults. Unfortunately the converse is also true: where pupils' homes have not fostered such respect for teachers and adults, the teacher will derive little such benefit.

Within the context of the school, a teacher's status is linked with his or her position – such as headteacher, or head of department. Status, here, is associated with pupils' perceptions of the teacher's seniority within the school derived from circumstances such as meetings with more senior teachers etc. Also linked with the teacher's position is the exercise of power and control that he or she has recourse to; in dealing with misbehaviour this is usually greater for more senior teachers.

Robertson (1981) has drawn particular attention to the way in which teachers can use behaviour which signifies their status to establish their authority. In effect, it appears that if one behaves like a person who has status, a degree of authority will be assumed. The key examples of how such status is conveyed through behaviour are:

• *by appearing to be relaxed and self-assured*: (as opposed to appearing anxious) one's tone of voice, facial expression, use of gaze, and even posture, all serve to signal one's feelings in this respect.

• *by exercising rights of status*: high status individuals can typically move around freely in the territory of others, and can touch others and others' property. In the classroom this is typified by the teacher moving freely around the room, picking up pupils' exercise books and occasionally touching pupils; at the same time, the teacher needs to deny such rights to pupils except by explicit permission.

• *by communicating an expectation of imposing one's will*: the tone of delivery of instructions and control over who speaks and when, will all strongly imply an expectation that pupils have accepted the teacher's authority; the exercise of one's will is a key element in exercising status, and is exemplified by pupils fitting in with the teacher's intentions rather than *vice versa*. An example is the teacher who will not allow the introduction of a lesson to be sidetracked by pupils requesting pens, or let pupils lead a conversation away from the purpose of the lesson.

If one behaves as though one has authority, it is surprising how far this attitude exerts a momentum of its own, leading pupils to behave accordingly. A need to deal frequently with problems of discipline implicitly indicates lack of authority; effective teachers are adept at pre-empting misbehaviour so that it does not have to be 'dealt with'.

Exercising status is in a sense a game of bluff and couter-bluff; effective teachers are able to take account of subtle signals and cues to know when a clash of wills with a pupil should be engaged in and when averted. The classroom is rich with such signals. For example, if, as the teacher moves around the room, a pupil remains slouched in his or her seat, a signal is being sent about how that pupil feels about the teacher's authority; if the teacher ignores this signal, some degree of authority is lost. Alternatively, a glance at the pupil with a raised eyebrow is likely to be sufficient for the pupil to sit up properly; if this is not sufficient, the teacher may move closer to the pupil, or may quietly ask the pupil if the work required is clear.

There are, however, potential dangers in exercising status, particularly regarding touching pupils and taking pupils' property; again, the need to know one's class is of paramount importance in being able to judge the appropriateness of an interaction, and to avoid unnecessary confrontations.

Teaching competence

There are three main elements involved in teaching competence which contribute to the teacher's authority: subject knowledge, interest in and enthusiasm for the subject, and the ability to set up effective learning experiences. Many pupils will accept the teacher's authority (to manage and organise their learning) in part because they know that the teacher has expertise in the subject being taught. Indeed, it is interesting to note how often pupils will attempt to explore through casual conversation with teachers, details of how they became teachers. Clearly, teachers who have difficulties with the academic tasks demanded by the subject, may well find their authority undermined. In some respects, this may explain why teachers are often anxious about teaching in areas outside their own expertise – as inevitably arises with developments in the curriculum and its content – and when pupils ask difficult questions which require greater subject expertise than the teacher has. There is a danger in being too defensive about subject expertise; pupils should not expect teachers to know everything, indeed it is of educational value for pupils to appreciate that teachers have more to learn too! However, a reasonable degree of expertise is important if subject credibility is to be established.

Interest in and enthusiasm for the subject is a major contributor to establishing authority. Interest and enthusiasm is infectious, and helps to create a climate within the classroom which emphasises the worthwhile-ness of the learning activities. However, it is important to stress that this interest and enthusiasm must be *shared* with pupils, not merely demonstrated in a way that pupils observe but find hard to understand. Learning activities should be presented in a manner which will elicit pupils' interest and enthusiasm. Teachers should not simply hope that their own interest and enthusiasm is sufficient. At the other extreme, a lack of interest and enthusiasm not only acts as a poor model, but is actually expressed through the teacher's tone of voice making it more difficult to pay attention to. Each lesson requires a performance from the teacher which, at its best, will be fresh and authentic for the pupils. When the teacher asks a question, his or her tone of voice will communicate that the teacher is interested in the pupil's reply, and the reply will be listened to and taken account of. When the teacher monitors pupils' progress, his or her delight in good work and helpful concern for those having difficulties will sound genuine.

The ability to set up effective learning experiences is at the core of the teacher's ability to teach. If the teacher's exposition is hard to understand (either because it is spoken inaudibly or because the points are poorly made), if the work set is consistently too easy or too difficult, if the work set does not prepare the pupils properly for the learning they perceive is required, then they are likely to become frustrated and discouraged, and the teacher's authority will be at its most vulnerable. The vast majority of teachers are more than adequately skilful in this respect, but it is important that they keep abreast of the changing demands pupils make on education so that effective teaching can be sustained.

Each generation of pupils grows up in a new context of patterns of interacting with others and in dealing with information; for example, today's pupils will inevitably be influenced by their experiences in watching television and playing with computerised games, and by the style of relationship they have with peers and adults outside the school. Such influences will play a part in shaping their patterns of relating to the world, and these in turn, have implications for teaching and learning in schools. The learning experiences set up by teachers *now* must be tailored to the needs of pupils as they exist *now*; otherwise there is a danger that school will be experienced as an unreal world with out-dated activities. Feedback from pupils, in the form of lack of interest and motivation provides schools with a continuing critique of the quality of the matching between learning experiences and needs. Many current curriculum developments, although advocated on educational grounds, are in a real sense a reaction to the fact that what they replaced simply was not working. The clearest example of this trend is the move away from didactic teaching, where pupils are essentially passive, towards setting up learning experiences where pupils are active and have some control over the course of the learning taking place.

This aspect of teaching competence is thus not something a teacher achieves at one moment in his or her professional development and then maintains in that same form thereafter. Rather, it is an ever-changing requirement based on continuing professional development and critical reflection about one's own teaching.

One final important element in setting up effective learning experiences is the quality of corrective academic feedback pupils receive. Pupils are very sensitive to the speed and care with which teachers monitor and assess their educational progress; written work that is carefully marked and quickly returned is not only effective in increasing pupils' understanding, but also in communicating to pupils the teacher's concern with their work. Similarly, giving helpful and constructive feedback during the lesson to pupils having difficulties and ensuring that those finding the work easy are extended will enhance the pupils' perception of the teacher's competence in teaching.

Exercising control over the classroom

An important aspect of the teacher's authority is his or her control over classroom activities. In order to ensure that such activities do not lead to chaos and conflict, a number of rules and procedures need to be adopted. These are essential if the smooth running of teaching and learning is not to be frequently interrupted. Laslett and Smith (1984) identified the four key rules of classroom management as 'Get them in, get them out, get on with it, and get on with them'!

Undoubtedly, how lessons are commenced and ended has major significance for establishing authority. It is an advantage for the teacher to be present when pupils arrive for a lesson, and to ensure that entry into the classroom is orderly and reasonably quiet. Squabbles over seating are often used as an opportunity to test out the teacher's authority and as such need to be dealt with quickly and firmly. It is also important for lessons to start quickly; pupils should be dealt with effectively if they come late, so that they are not habitually late and teachers should ensure that the start of the lesson is not delayed by matters that could easily be dealt with at some other time. Pupils' remarks at the start of a lesson are important in this respect. While it is part of good rapport between teacher and pupils for some social interchange to take place, the need for the teacher to quickly establish order and to start the lesson must take precedence. Indeed, pupils may often attempt to take the initiative in this respect by some social remark and this may have to be ignored or dealt with quickly by the teacher if control is to be retained. Similarly, it is important for lessons to end on time (neither too early nor too late), and for the pupils' exit from the classroom to be orderly and reasonably quiet; the simplest way to ensure this is by establishing a routine governing how pupils leave the lesson. The final few remarks made by a teacher at the end of a lesson are particularly telling; they should be positive and refer to good work and what was achieved and learnt, rather than being negative and reflecting mutual relief from each other's company!

During the lesson itself, the teacher needs to effectively regulate classroom activities and teacher–pupil interaction, including the circumstances under which pupils can speak and move from their seats. This may sound authoritarian, but it merely reflects the need to have ground rules operating in any social situation where a large number of individuals interact. In classroom observation, Wragg and Wood (1984b) identified

11 classroom rules which were explicitly stated by teachers or could be clearly inferred from their actions; these were (in order of frequency of occurrence):

- no talking when the teacher is talking (public situation)
- no disruptive noises
- rules for entering, leaving, and moving in classrooms
- no interference with the work of others
- work must be completed in a specified way
- pupils must raise hand to answer, not shout out
- pupils must make a positive effort in their work
- pupils must not challenge the authority of the teacher
- respect must be shown for property and equipment
- rules to do with safety
- pupils must ask if they do not understand

Effective teaching is greatly facilitated if clear classroom rules are laid down and enforced, so that pupils act in accordance with them almost as second nature. Establishing such rules clearly and consistently is an essential aspect of the teacher's authority. Pupils are very sensitive to the teacher's ability to establish such rules and will often test out how a teacher will cope with an infringement in order to clarify the rules and how they will be operated.

In fact, almost every classroom activity has the potential for pupils to challenge the teacher's authority and control over their behaviour. Handing in or giving out books, moving furniture about, collecting equipment, closing a window, and even sharpening a pencil, could all be done by pupils in a manner or at a time which tests out the teacher's control. In all such cases, well-established norms and procedures will limit the scope for potential problems occurring. Unpredictable events, such as the appearance of a window cleaner, or a wasp flying about the room, can pose particular problems; often, a touch of humour is useful in such situations.

One major issue related to control concerns the level of classroom noise. The teacher must be able to establish silence before addressing the class, or when pupils are asked to speak; having asked pupils to pay attention, it is important to wait momentarily for quiet before commencing the verbal exchange so that no-one has to speak loudly to be heard over a level of background noise. The level of general noise which occurs while pupils are working is a particularly sensitive issue for most teachers, in part because it may disrupt pupils and teachers in other classrooms and in part because it is often taken to be indicative of a teacher's degree of classroom control or lack of (Denscombe, 1980). This sometimes leads teachers to be somewhat overstrict about noise levels. Some background noise reflecting cooperative talking or group work should not be inhibited by an unnecessary emphasis on low noise levels, but background noise should be kept to a reasonable level if concentration and a climate of purposefulness are to be sustained.

Finally, control over classroom activities requires vigilance. The teacher needs to continually monitor pupils' behaviour, as it is easier to regain control if one acts quickly rather than tackling undesirable behaviour that has been going on for some time. Vigilance is also required to ensure that rules and procedures are effective; for example, if pupils have to put up their hand to gain the teacher's attention, the teacher should be looking around periodically to notice this. Such vigilance is facilitated if the teacher stands centre-stage where the teacher and pupils can clearly see each other; at the same time this helps to establish the teacher's presence.

Exercising control over discipline

Discipline refers to the maintenance of order and control necessary for effective learning. In essence, this involves pupils acting in accordance with the teacher's intentions for their behaviour, be it listening, talking or undertaking the academic work in hand. Unfortunately, most discussion of discipline tends to centre on overtly disruptive pupil behaviour such as noisy non-work-related talking, rowdy behaviour, or insolence. Such discussion tends to imply that exercising control over discipline is solely concerned with how to deal with pupil misbehaviour. In fact, discipline is much more concerned with sound planning, presentation and monitoring of learning experiences, all of which enable the teacher to elicit and sustain the pupils' attention and motivation, thereby minimising the occurrence of misbehaviour. Clearly, however, the teacher does have to adopt a range of techniques for pre-empting and dealing with misbehaviour and these will be outlined in the next chapter.

In terms of the teacher's authority, the central issue of concern here is the contribution that control over discipline makes to such authority. It has been argued thus far that the teacher's authority derives in large measure from status, teaching competence, and his or her ability to exercise control over the classroom. Periodically, however, teachers need to impose their will over pupils in the face of opposition; success in clash of wills is the essence of exercising control over discipline. Such a clash of wills is overt and manifest in the case of disruptive pupil behaviour. However, it may also occur – in some ways more importantly – in the context of the raw stuff of pupils being engaged in the academic work in hand, which involves them paying attention, and applying mental effort and motivation. Indeed, it is interesting to note that in reporting sources of stress, teachers often highlight pupils' poor attitudes towards work as a greater source of stress than overt disruptive behaviour (eg Kyriacou and Sutcliffe, 1978a).

In essence, then, the teacher's prime task is to set up a learning experience, and the question of exercising control over discipline arises whenever the teacher's intentions are being opposed or frustrated by pupils in some way. Examples of such opposition will include what might appear to be quite trivial problems, such as trying to engage the teacher in social conversation when he or she is anxious for the lesson to start; being reluctant to repeat a phrase in a foreign language during oral work; day-dreaming; keeping a low profile; working very slowly; or coming to lessons without a pen. All such examples have a subversive quality about them, in that they are not acts of overt defiance or disruption, but still undermine discipline.

Exercising control over discipline concerns those actions which teachers take to impose their will in such circumstances. Such actions can be categorised into two main groups. The first group consists of actions which the teacher can take during the lesson regarding the learning experience that will re-establish pupils' attention, motivation and ability to meet the academic demands in hand. Such actions might include introducing an interesting anecdote or application of the topic, moving on to a different type of activity such as oral work or a written task, and giving individual help. The second group consists of actions where the teacher exercises power in a dominant manner, such as coercion, threats, intimidation, reprimands and punishments. A firm raised voice, together with an imperative command – 'get on with your work', 'pay attention', 'get back to your seat now' – and an aggressive tone, posture and facial expression are typical of such actions.

It is argued here that the former type of action is more important for effective teaching *per se,* but there are inevitably circumstances where the latter type needs to come into play. What is essential is that the teacher is able to distinguish which type of action is more appropriate for a particular set of circumstances. The major danger is to rely on the latter when problems essentially stem from ineffective teaching. Effective teaching must win the hearts and minds of pupils if the learning experience is to involve intrinsic motivation, curiosity, interest and a proper educational engagement; such a state cannot be achieved if the teacher's authority rests heavily on the exercise of power. Teachers frequently express dissatisfaction with aspects of the school curriculum dominated by examination requirements and with inadequate relevance to pupils' lives, precisely because this often means they have to exercise their power to maintain progress (eg Hargreaves, 1982). In this respect, many of the current curriculum developments in schools, both in terms of content and types of learning activities, are especially welcome. The need to get the curriculum right is explored in chapter 9; it is important to note here that such a need is no academic matter, but strikes at the heart of discipline itself.

The frequency and extent to which the teacher exercises his or her power in a dominant manner is a major issue in a consideration of how best to establish authority in the classroom. If this is excessive, it will almost certainly undermine the mutual respect and rapport necessary for sound teacher–pupil relationships and may contribute to an expectation that pupils must be coerced into working. At the same time, the teacher cannot simply ignore a clash of wills and avoid taking action without undermining discipline. Clearly, a balance of action between these two extremes is required. If overt disruptive behaviour occurs frequently and is widespread in the class, it is clear that the teacher has failed to establish his or her authority. It is much more difficult to re-establish discipline once this has occurred. Effort spent in carefully monitoring and using control in the classroom will pay handsome dividends.

Mutual respect and rapport

The importance of mutual respect and rapport between teacher and pupils cannot be over-estimated. In the discussion of 'good teachers' based on inspections of primary and secondary schools, HMI (1985b) state their view thus:

> It should also be expected of teachers that they are of such a personality and character that they are able to command the respect of their pupils, not only by their knowledge of what they teach and their ability to make it interesting but by the respect which they show for their pupils, their genuine interest and curiosity about what pupils say and think and the quality of their professional concern for individuals. It is only where this two-way passage of liking and respect between good teachers and pupils exists, that the educational development of pupils can genuinely flourish. (p. 3)

In our consideration of the teacher's authority, it was noted that such authority derives from four main sources: status, teaching competence, exercising control over the classroom, and exercising control over discipline. The skill of the teacher in each of these four areas will of itself help earn the pupils' respect – or, if inadequate, contribute to undermining such respect. Pupils generally have a clear idea of the teacher's role and the demands and expectations they have of a teacher who is fulfilling that role. Studies of classroom discipline indicate that much pupil misbehaviour actually stems from a sense that a teacher who is unable to fulfil such demands is felt to be offensive by pupils and thereby provokes them into misbehaviour (see, for example Hargreaves, 1975; Marsh *et al*, 1978). Pupils are typically reported as liking teachers who can keep order (without being too strict); are fair (ie are consistent and have no favourites); can explain clearly and give help; give interesting lessons; and are friendly and patient (Kyriacou, 1986a; McKelvey and Kyriacou, 1985).

Effectively establishing one's authority, therefore, can do much to earn respect from pupils. However, it is essential that the manner in which the teacher attempts to establish such authority does not undermine the development of good rapport. Good rapport between the teacher and pupils refers to their having a harmonious understanding of each other as individuals and is based on mutual respect and esteem. Behaviour by a teacher which indicates that he or she has little respect or esteem for pupils will inevitably undermine the development of good rapport.

The development of good rapport is based on three qualities in the teacher's interaction with pupils: that the teacher shows quite clearly that he or she cares for each pupil's progress; that the teacher has respect for pupils as learners; and that the teacher has respect for pupils as individuals.

Caring for pupils' progress shows itself in a number of ways. First, in a concern to tailor the learning experiences as accurately as possible to meet the pupils' needs and level of understanding. Second, by carefully monitoring pupils' understanding and progress, identifying difficulties, and giving additional help (either individually or to the class as a whole) in a constructive, helpful, supportive and patient manner. Third, by the care and attention given in preparing lessons and in marking work. Fourth, by dealing with lack of progress in a concerned manner which emphasises both a belief in the importance of the pupil doing better, and a belief that the pupil is capable of doing better. Fifth, by giving praise and valuing good work and achievements.

Respect for pupils as learners requires setting up learning experiences where the views and opinions of pupils can be heard, developed and elaborated, and where the pupils are given a large measure of control in shaping and carrying out learning activities. A more active role for pupils not only makes sense in terms of effective learning, but is extremely important in fostering pupils' self-esteem regarding themselves as learners and helping them develop and practise those skills, both practical and intellectual, which are required in exercising control over a learning activity. Of course, this will inevitably result in time apparently being wasted as pupils begin to develop these skills and make mistakes or poor judgements; in addition, less is likely to be covered than would be the case where teacher control over the activity was tight. However, the broad educational benefits of an active learning role for pupils make this well worthwhile. Respect for pupils as learners lies at the heart of the hidden curriculum operating in the classroom. The interaction which takes place between teacher and pupils during a lesson communicates their respective perceptions of each other's role. As well as the overt message of what is said, the way the teacher responds to pupils' answers to questions, whether pupils can initiate questions, and whether the teacher exerts unequivocal control over the learning experiences, all serve to indicate to pupils hidden messages about knowledge (eg all knowledge resides in the teacher *versus* knowledge is gained by exploration of learning activities); about the pupil's role as learner (eg active and enquiring *versus* passive and receptive), and about the status of pupils' knowledge, views and experience (eg pupils have knowledge, views and experience worthy of attention and consideration *versus* such knowledge needs to be tightly constrained, directed, modified and controlled by the teacher before it is of value). Such hidden messages have a fundamental influence on the classroom climate which develops and this will be explored later in this chapter.

Of the three qualities being considered here, respect for pupils as individuals is perhaps the most important contributor to good rapport. Such respect involves an interest in pupils' lives – both within school (outside the subject area of the teacher) and outside school. In effect, the teacher needs to get to know the pupils as individuals. At the outset, this certainly involves learning their names as quickly as possible. Opportunities for social conversation at the beginning or end of lessons, in the corridor, during registration periods, and most important of all through extra-curricular activities, enable the teacher to get to know the pupils in another context. Such remarks as 'anyone go to the match on Saturday?', 'I enjoyed your performance in the school concert', 'Saw you in town last night', are all indicators of good rapport. Such exchanges also need to be a two-way process, with the teacher as an equal, freely mentioning his or her own interests and activities relating to the exchange. Of course, pupils may take advantage of such personal interaction to either ask deliberately embarrassing questions or to adopt a disrespectful attitude towards the exchange. However, if the teacher's authority is well established and secure, such exchanges serve to enhance and develop mutual respect and rapport rather than to undermine such authority.

At this point it is important to acknowledge that friendly relationships between teacher and pupils need to be treated with caution. The development of good rapport needs to be kept separate, to some extent, from the teacher's role in effective teaching. When teaching, the teacher must continue to periodically exert control over classroom activities and discipline in order to maintain an effective learning environment. This inevitably requires the teacher to be able to quickly distance him- or herself when needing to exercise such authority. Certain conventions are employed by some teachers to facilitate such distancing. The most widespread example of such a convention is that teachers must be addressed as 'Sir' or 'Miss' and not by their first names.

In addition, teachers need to be sensitive to the strong affection for them which some pupils may develop. In the primary school years this may involve teachers being regarded as a parent, and pupils may sometimes inadvertently call the teacher 'Mum' or 'Dad'. In the secondary school years, however, a particular problem may arise concerning sexual attraction and fantasies. For this reason, teachers do need to be careful about using ambiguous cues signalling sexual intimacy, particularly touching in an affectionate manner. In general, during the adolescent years, touching is best avoided, despite the fact that some teachers can develop apparently excellent rapport based on a strong 'parental' relationship.

Finally, it is interesting to note that in a study of headteachers' perceptions of teacher competence carried out at ten inner-city comprehensive schools in the ILEA, Grace (1984) reported that the headteachers regarded teachers' rapport with pupils as an extremely important aspect of their general competence. Grace outlined his findings thus:

> In the evaluations of the headteachers, good teachers were not authoritarian martinets or socially distanced pedagogues (since this could provoke discipline problems), nor were they egalitarian participants in dialogue (since this could provoke discipline problems). The good teacher was skilful in developing rapport with potentially difficult and demanding adolescents. Without rapport, which implied a certain giving of consent by the pupils to the business in hand, the institutional life of the school could hardly proceed. The establishment of rapport with pupils was therefore the crucial first step in the pedagogic process, as the headteachers saw it, in the challenging conditions of an inner-city school. It was for these reasons, both institutional and pedagogic, that the teacher's capacity to develop rapport became significant in any assessment and evaluation of teacher competence. (p. 110)

Grace also noted that a high proportion of the outstandingly good teachers were pastoral care teachers or year heads. This link with the pastoral care aspect of teaching illustrates the overlap between effective teaching and the qualities involved in pastoral care activities. Indeed, in Rutter *et al*'s (1979) study of 12 London secondary schools, higher academic attainment occurred in schools where a larger proportion of pupils indicated that they would consult teachers about personal problems. The role of pastoral care will be considered in detail later in this chapter.

Classroom climate

From the discussion so far in this chapter it is clear that teacher–pupil interaction during a lesson involves a very rich flow of information concerning their perceptions, expectations, attitudes and feelings about each other and the learning activities in hand. Indeed, studies focusing on aspects of such perceptions are numerous (Gammage, 1982; Rogers, 1982). The notion of classroom climate draws explicit attention to the emotional tone and atmosphere of the lesson, and is made up of the teacher and pupil perceptions described.

An effective classroom climate is one in which the teacher's authority to organise and manage the learning activities is accepted by the pupils, there is mutual respect and good rapport, and the atmosphere is one of purposefulness and confidence in learning. In discussing classroom climate here, attention will be paid to the ways in which the teacher's behaviour may facilitate or undermine the establishing of an effective classroom climate. A key consideration is the extent to which the teacher is able to foster favourable perceptions towards learning among pupils, most notably by establishing in pupils self-respect and self-esteem regarding themselves as learners (Burns, 1982; Rogers, 1982). The writing of Carl Rogers has been particularly inspirational in demonstrating how effective teaching can facilitate learning (and advocating a pupil-centred perspective in teaching); such teaching, he suggests, should be based on respect for the pupil, and the teacher should have *trust* in pupils as learners. Interestingly, studies of teachers who have adopted such qualities in their teaching indicate that they have positive self-concepts (particularly high self-esteem and self-confidence) and appear to be more effective as teachers in terms of gains in pupils' learning (Burns, 1982; Rogers, 1983).

The classroom climate is influenced even by its physical appearance and layout. The move towards more 'informal' and 'progressive' teaching in primary schools (or 'open education' as it is referred to in the United States) over the last two decades has had a marked impact on the appearance of classrooms (Cohen and Manion, 1981). The increased emphasis in informal teaching on an active pupil role, discovery and exploratory learning and play, group work, and movement between activity areas, shows itself in the arrangement of seats, tables and resource areas. The use of wall displays in the classroom is also important; in the foreign languages classroom, for example, posters can serve to recreate the atmosphere of a different country. A display of pupils' work on the walls also contributes to a positive atmosphere, indicating pride and esteem in the work produced in lessons.

Without doubt the most important aspect of classroom climate is the hidden curriculum: the ways in which the teacher's actions convey information concerning his or her perceptions, expectations, attitudes and feelings about the teacher's role, the pupil's role, and the learning activities in hand. What is particularly interesting about the hidden curriculum is the extent to which much of the information signalled to pupils may be unintended by the teacher, and may indeed serve to undermine the effectiveness of his or her teaching. Particular attention in this respect has been paid to the use of language in the classroom. Who says what, when, and how, lies at the heart of the hidden curriculum.

The importance of language for learning cannot be underestimated. In the wake of the Bullock Report *A Language for Life* (1975) a great deal of attention has been paid to how language is used in the classroom and how schools can adopt the best strategy to foster language development in pupils during the school years (Hull, 1985; Marland, 1977). Indeed, fostering pupils' language skills has been a central feature of a number of HMI writings in recent years (HMI, 1985a, 1985b), as this extract indicates:

> A range of language skills and competences needs to be developed throughout the years of schooling and across all subjects. Pupils should learn to speak with confidence, clarity and fluency, using forms of speech appropriate for a variety of audiences, involving a variety of situations and groupings and for a range of purposes of increasing complexity and demand. As they progress through the early stages of reading they should learn to read fluently, and with understanding, a range of different kinds of material, using methods appropriate to the material and the purposes for which they are reading; to have confidence in their capacities as readers; to enjoy reading for entertainment, for interest and for information; and to appreciate the necessity of reading for learning in most areas of the curriculum and for their personal lives. The pupils should write for a range of purposes; organise the content in ways appropriate to the purposes; use styles of writing appropriate to them and to the intended readership; and use spelling, punctuation and syntax accurately and with confidence. Pupils need to achieve a working knowledge of language so that they have a vocabulary for discussing it and are able to use it with greater awareness and control. That which characterises the achievement of older pupils is not only the accumulation of new knowledge or skills, but an increased ability to use language with sensitivity, sophistication and discrimination and to deal with more demanding forms of spoken and written language used by others. (HMI, 1985a, p. 22)

In terms of classroom climate, the hidden curriculum aspect of 'spoken' classroom language has received the greatest attention. It has been widely observed that the classroom tends to be dominated by teacher talk; when pupils *are* allowed to speak, it tends to be in a context highly constrained by the teacher, such as in answer to closed questions. Comments and observations by pupils tend to be drawn back into the line the teacher has envisaged for the dialogue (Bennett *et al*, 1984; HMI, 1978, 1979). This not only fails to foster pupils' language skills effectively, but also tends to undermine their self-esteem as learners. Barnes' (1969) analysis of the language interaction between teacher and pupils in 12 first-year secondary school lessons illustrates these characteristics most clearly with reference to transcripts of the language interaction. His analysis indicates that teachers' efforts to channel pupils' contributions along pre-determined lines result in certain pupil contributions being rejected as unacceptable or incorrect, not because the contribution did not make sense from the pupils' perspective or was not relevant to the discussion, but primarily because the contribution did not fit closely to the teacher's expectation. From the pupils' perspective, the overriding message was that their contributions needed to match what the teacher wanted. Hence, pupils are led to search for clues to the right answers required, rather than to genuinely enter into intellectual dialogue with the teacher. Barnes also noted that teachers tend to place an undue emphasis on pupils using the correct terminology in their contributions, despite the intellectual quality *per se* of what they are saying. In a later publication (1976) he notes that this 'communication gap' between the teacher and pupils markedly contributes to pupils' failure to learn (see also Hull, 1985).

Effective teaching thus requires that the teacher gives pupils plenty of opportunities to contribute and elaborate their own ideas, and that he or she genuinely listens to what pupils say (or are trying to say) and attempts to consider this from the pupils' perspective. To some extent this means that the teacher needs to accept the value of each pupil's contribution and the relevance of the pupil's experience. Of course, if carried to extremes, such a policy would pose difficulties and would undermine realistic feedback. What is being argued here is the need to maintain a balance between teacher talk and pupil talk which is less markedly weighted in favour of the teacher than is at present the case. Fortunately, the trend in many schools in recent years has been towards this more desirable state of balance.

A particularly difficult issue concerning pupils' language is the teacher's proper response to strong regional and ethnic accents and dialects. On the one hand it is important for all pupils to be accepted as they are, but on the other hand there is also a need for all pupils to be able to communicate acceptably, in standard English. To some extent, the 'more correct' speech of teachers in schools may contribute to some pupils' view of school as an alien environment. There is no easy solution to this problem. However, in some schools attempts have been made, most often as part of English lessons, to look at such differences in speech with a view to recognising these as different rather than intrinsically inferior to standard English. The most important point is that an undue emphasis on correct speech should not be allowed to inhibit and restrict pupils' elaborating their own ideas. Somehow, a balance of concerns needs to be maintained here.

A very important aspect of the classroom climate derives from the choice of words a teacher uses in his or her communication with pupils. Every utterance that a teacher makes during a lesson involves a choice of words; the particular choice made will convey clear messages to pupils – over and above its actual content – concerning the teacher's underlying feelings and expectations. This is particularly evident in how teachers react to pupils' incorrect contributions and how they reprimand mis-behaviour. In both these contexts, it is important that the teacher comments on the contribution or behaviour rather than on the pupil, and thus indicates that it is these rather than the pupil which are at fault. For example, saying 'I might have known you would not have the right answer' or 'you are an insulting little boy' are in effect 'character attacks' which are best avoided. Dealing with the nature of the answer or misbehaviour would be less likely to undermine mutual respect and rapport.

In recent years particular attention has been paid to the way in which the teacher's choice of words may contribute to the effects of 'labelling' pupils: the process by which pupils come to see themselves and act more in accordance with the labels that teachers typically use to describe them (see Bird, 1980; Docking, 1980). As well as overt examples of such labelling, for example when a pupil is described as 'thick' or 'a trouble maker', there are also covert examples, such as when a pupil is never invited to contribute to a discussion or expected to do better. Labelling also arises from organisational characteristics of the school; for example, being in a low set, stream or band appears to foster underachievement through its effect on pupils' attitudes and self-esteem. Overall, it would appear that teacher labelling does have an influence on pupil attainment and behaviour, but it is extremely difficult to separate out the influence of teacher behaviour on pupils and of pupil behaviour on teachers. A number of case-studies of schooling have highlighted just how complex labelling processes are. Ball (1981) in his study of a comprehensive school, noted how the influence of labelling is bound up with other aspects of the teacher's behaviour:

> The band 2 pupils are confronted by teachers who hold very negative perceptions of their intelligence and ability and likely attainment – 'they are not up to much academically'. These perceptions have both attitudinal and practical consequences for the pupils' experiences of learning. That is, lack of enthusiasm for band 2 teaching is transmitted both in the teachers' attitude to the pupils and in their classroom management techniques, their organisation of learning and their mediation of the syllabus. In these ways, the stereotyped notions of band-identity inherent in the teachers' perceptions of the pupils actually contribute to the increasing differences between band 1 and 2 pupils during the first and second years. Several of the teachers certainly attributed the changing attitudes and behaviour of band 2 forms to the pupils' increasing awareness of inferior status. (p. 47)

The crucial question for effective teaching is to what extent a teacher's avoidance of such labelling behaviour in the classroom can mitigate against the gradual erosion of low attaining pupils' attitudes towards themselves as learners. In a school with an ethos of concern for attainment based on comparisons between pupils, the teacher has an uphill struggle. In a school adopting more pupil-centred teaching, emphasising the process of learning rather than merely products, and where attainment is based on individual progress rather than comparisons with age-norms, then the teacher has much more opportunity to mitigate such effects. Whatever the circumstances there is no need to strengthen such an effect by any unnecessary labelling, and character-assassination cannot be justified in any context:

You must therefore firmly resist using words you cannot recant and which leave you in a posture of irrevocable anger and dislike. You can criticize what he has *done* or *said* or *not done* as strongly as you like (although temperateness is advisable), but you must not venture from his crime to himself. You must not criticize *him*. (Marland, 1975, p. 18)

Written comments by teachers are also important in conveying their attitudes and expectations. Here too, a code seems to operate whereby more is signalled by the comments than is apparent at its face value. Marking pupils' work involves more than assessment. It also involves giving pupils feedback about how their work could have been improved. Comments such as 'hopeless' or 'inadequate', are likely only to discourage, whereas positive guidance such as 'this essay would have been better if more material had been covered' or 'always calculate the length of the sides before you attempt to calculate the angles' is more helpful to pupils. An important aspect of classroom climate is the standard of work expected by the teacher. There is, however, a problem if the standard is set so high that most pupils experience prolonged failure (in the form of low marks); on the other hand, too low a standard of expectation may create a false sense of progress, so that the pupil is shocked to find that after years of apparent success, he or she is not to be entered for an 'O' level examination. In this respect, comments made in school reports are of particular interest, both in terms of their ambiguity regarding progress, and of the meaning to be attached to various phrases commonly used, such as 'could do better' (Woods, 1979).

Generally speaking, the most effective classrooms appear to be those in which the atmosphere is task-oriented but where at the same time the social and emotional needs of the pupils are met by establishing mutual respect and good rapport. There is clearly an overlap between the notion of classroom climate and school climate or ethos (see Rutter *et al*, 1979; Strivens, 1985), for each has implications for, and links with, the other. Indeed, Rutter *et al*, in their study of secondary schools, noted that:

> Our observations suggested that it was very much easier to be a good teacher in some schools than it was in others. The overall ethos of the school seemed to provide support and a context which facilitated good teaching. Teaching performance is a function of the school environment as well as of personal qualities. (p. 139)

The final point worth emphasising here is that learning is an emotionally charged and high risk activity for pupils. An effective classroom climate is one that provides continual support and encouragement so that failure, when it does occur, does not undermine pupils' self-esteem regarding their learning.

Pastoral care

Over the last 15 years there has been a massive increase in the attention given to pastoral care in schools (eg Best *et al,* 1980; Lang and Marland, 1985). In essence, pastoral care focuses on a concern for the individual well-being of each pupil. This concern attempts to ensure that each pupil is able to take advantage of what schools have to offer, and involves four main aspects of schooling:

1   Academic progress
2   General behaviour and attitudes
3   Personal and social development
4   Individual needs

In most secondary schools, the pastoral care system has been formalised, in house system or year group system with tutor or form groups, where individual teachers (ranging from the head of house or year to the tutor or form teacher) are given particular pastoral roles and responsibilities. In addition, other members of staff, including the headteacher, deputy heads, and classroom teachers, will also be involved in pastoral responsibilities. Most primary schools utilise non-formalised systems.

Concern with academic progress involves rewarding success, for example through housepoints, as well as exploring the reasons for marked underachievement. In some schools, subject choice and vocational guidance are also included within the responsibility of the pastoral staff. General attitudes and behaviour, particularly misbehaviour in lessons, may be referred to the pastoral staff if guidance and counselling, perhaps involving contact with parents, is felt to be appropriate. Indeed, it is often the tension between a counselling role and the role of disciplinarian that places the greatest strain on pastoral staff.

The concern with personal and social development has led to the development of a pastoral curriculum within schools. This refers to those learning experiences set up within the school which aim to foster personal and social development, often explicitly linked to pastoral care. Such teaching can include almost anything which has a pastoral connection: moral education; religious education; life and social skills teaching; sex education; and study skills. Probably, the most notable development in this approach has been the introduction of 'active tutorial work' (Baldwin and Wells, 1979, 1980, 1981) which involves form tutors utilising extended registration periods to set up a whole range of learning experiences. These often include much use of group work and discussion, and aim to prepare pupils for demands made within the school and beyond.

A concern with individual needs involves a consideration of personal problems threatening the pupil's well-being in some serious way. These may include extremes of poor attainment and disruptive behaviour, as well as other problems, such as juvenile delinquency, truancy, incest, emotional disturbance, and being bullied.

Given the range of concerns involved in pastoral care together with the fact that these are discharged both by teachers designated as pastoral staff and by others discharging a pastoral duty within some other context, an adequate description of the pastoral care system within a particular school will inevitably be fairly complex. Changes currently occurring in schools, ranging from the need to monitor pupils' special educational needs to alternative forms of assessing academic attainment such as pupil profiling, have further served to blur the distinction between pastoral care activities and other aspects of school life.

In the context of effective teaching, it is interesting to note Buckley's (1980) observation that effective teaching is itself the highest form of pastoral care. This reiterates some of the earlier discussion of classroom climate:

> The notion of 'care' for a teacher is the creation of that relationship from which learning may follow. The teacher who 'cares' is the one who teaches effectively. This is the essential 'hidden' curriculum of values and attitudes which must animate any other curriculum if there is to be effective teaching and learning. (p. 183)

Indeed, this theme has been carried further in the argument that much pastoral care work involves containing problems such as disruptive behaviour and truancy, which largely stem from the inadequacy of the teaching processes and curriculum activities offered for many pupils. This aspect of pastoral care, in effect the attempt to 'keep the show on the road' has been termed 'pastoralization': the process by which many pupils, particularly the less able and disadvantaged, are processed to accept a system in which they are destined to be failures (see Williamson, 1980). Most would feel that this is too savage a critique of pastoral care, but it is nevertheless correct in reminding one that all teaching must uphold many aspects of the *status quo* (eg that examination attainment is important, that certain curriculum subjects have greater status; see Turner, 1984), and that effective teaching (and effective pastoral care) must in part foster success within the established framework which operates at the time.

There are many ways in which pastoral care may support effective teaching. The most important of these is in giving pupils a feeling that the school cares about their educational progress and well-being on a one-to-one basis. The pastoral care system adopted in a school should ensure that this message is conveyed to each pupil whenever appropriate. General comments to groups of pupils in, for example, house assemblies or form group meetings, are important, but the message must also be reinforced on an individual basis at moments of crisis and when particular problems arise. In the primary school, the class teacher will almost certainly discharge this pastoral responsibility; in the secondary school, with its typically formalised system of pastoral care, a number of individuals may act in this way.

Indeed, in secondary schools a particularly important function of the pastoral system is that of coordinating information about a pupil that crosses subject boundaries and involves other agencies. This enables the pastoral staff to build up a much fuller picture of each pupil's progress, as well as possible problems, than the individual class teacher can have. This then makes it possible to plan a more effective strategy to meet that pupil's needs.

The crucial features of effective teaching lie in the learning experiences set up by the teacher and the type of learning outcomes desired. In the past, pastoral care was largely distinguished from the explicitly academic and instructional aspects of classroom teaching in normal circumstances. However, in recent years this distinction has become blurred, with pastoral staff playing an active role in offering a critique of how existing classroom practices need to be developed in certain ways in order to combat disaffection amongst many pupils. This healthy dialogue between staff in a school lies at the heart of many important curriculum developments which have attempted to better prepare pupils for learning; it enables staff to utilise content, tasks and activities which enable pupils to be more fully engaged in the learning in hand.

The role of pastoral care in dealing with pupil misbehaviour has been highlighted in a number of recent studies. Galloway *et al* (1982) have been very critical of the way in which the form teacher's pastoral role is often undermined in secondary schools by the fact that discipline problems tend to be referred by subject teachers to the head of department/head of house or year. Galloway *et al* argue that the role of the form teacher is crucial for effective pastoral care if all pupils are to have such care (rather than simply those manifesting particular problems).

Denscombe (1984) has noted that in some comprehensive schools the role of the head of house or year is increasingly becoming one of a discipline specialist or 'trouble shooter', called in to deal with disruptive and emotional behaviour at times of crisis. In order to stem the flow of referrals to them, and in part because classroom teachers' frequent use of referrals may undermine their own authority, most schools will implicitly or explicitly indicate that such referrals should only occur in extreme circumstances. At its worst, this constraint on referrals can lead some teachers to attempt to cope with and contain disruptive behaviour on their own, without support from colleagues. At its best, the classroom teacher is seen as someone who needs support from the pastoral staff (both the head of house and the form teacher) in order to be able to meet effectively the individual needs of any pupils giving cause for concern. Whereas the former involves little or no collaboration with colleagues, the latter requires it. A result of the move towards assessing pupils' special educational needs, has been a much greater degree of collaboration and team work between teachers in schools. This will undoubtedly improve the quality of pastoral care, and – because much disruptive behaviour stems from learning difficulties – it will also support teachers' classroom teaching.

Over the years there has been much discussion of how an anti-school ethos or sub-culture can develop in secondary schools among low attaining pupils. Such pupils may then get caught in a vicious circle where their anti-school views and low attainment progressively reinforce each other:

> The anti-school 'counter-culture' evident in some, but not all, secondary schools may be seen as the pupils' response to a feeling that their achievements are not valued. Feeling that they have little scope for contributing anything useful on the school's terms, they derive a sense of belonging from membership of the counter-culture rather than from membership of the school itself. Failing to win social approval through the curriculum and the school's formal activities they obtain it in other ways. (Galloway, 1985, pp. 104–5)

An important part of pastoral care is to specifically combat the development of such groups of pupils in the school. While many argue that a more relevant curriculum and more effective teaching are the answer, pastoral care requires one to take more pragmatic action. Ball's (1981) case study of a comprehensive school illustrated how the pastoral staff, in co-operation with form tutors, were successful in inhibiting the development of anti-school peer groups by moving key pupils into other forms. Indeed, one of the arguments in favour of mixed-ability groupings rather than streaming, is that it may undermine the development of anti-school peer groups, and there is now some evidence to support this view (Ball, 1981; Galloway, 1985). Success here appears to lie not only in breaking up potential anti-school peer groups but also in the fact that mixed ability groups mean that teachers and pupils are less likely to form stereotyped views about the class and its status than they do in streamed classes.

Finally, attention has also been paid in studies of pastoral care to the worries and anxieties pupils experience at school, ranging from worries about their academic worth and progress, to simply coping with the social demands of school life. Particular attention in this respect has been given to the adjustment problems facing pupils transferring from primary or middle to secondary school. The literature in this area is extensive (eg Brown and Armstrong, 1982; Measor and Woods, 1984), and the issue has also been highlighted by HMI (1985a):

> The secondary school needs to consider how it can make the transition from primary to secondary education as smooth as possible by trying to ensure that children's personal confidence and sense of well-being are

protected, and that their learning continues with the minimum of disruption. On the whole, schools have been more successful at these transfer points in looking after the pastoral welfare of pupils than in achieving curriculum continuity. Yet the two are interdependent and an important aspect of pastoral care lies in promoting success in the main business of the school, which is learning. (pp. 49–50)

The liaison between primary and secondary schools has seen a marked improvement over the last ten years, and the induction programme for first-year pupils in secondary schools now often involves a great deal of preparation. It is now common not only for secondary school teachers to visit pupils in their feeder primary schools, but for the primary school pupils themselves to visit the secondary school during the summer term before transfer. Indeed, in some schemes, pupils are able to experience a few lessons in the secondary school during this summer term, and this appears to have contributed to much more successful transition. Interestingly, similar induction schemes are now becoming more widespread amongst infant and primary schools, involving both visits to the school and experience of school-based activities before the initial entry of pupils at five years of age.

Other pupil worries and anxieties may be the result of reactions to crises at home, such as the death of a parent or marital disharmony, or may be school-based, such as being bullied or having some sort of conflict with the teacher's style of teaching. In most situations, guidance and counselling may be offered by the classroom teacher or pastoral staff. Increasingly, though, in secondary schools with a relatively high proportion of disadvantaged pupils in their intake, use is made of student counsellors, who are able to give extended counselling to pupils with serious or protracted problems (see Fontana, 1981; Saunders, 1979).

Conclusions

In the discussion here of teacher–pupil relationships, it is apparent that such relationships underpin a number of different activities and situations arising in the school. The challenge facing teachers is to establish and sustain the appropriate type of relationship for the particular activity and situation; whether it be the need to exert authority, guiding a pupil with a learning difficulty, or counselling a pupil with a personal problem. The most important quality of such relationships advocated here is that of mutual respect and good rapport. From the discussion of classroom climate and pastoral care it will be evident that sound teacher–pupil relationships lie at the heart of effective teaching.

8 Dealing with pupil misbehaviour

The dominant theme of this book has been the importance of ensuring that the learning experience set up by teachers is effective in terms of maintaining pupils' attentiveness and receptiveness and in terms of being appropriate for the learning outcomes intended. This, along with sound teacher–pupil relationships (as outlined in the previous chapter), can do much to minimise pupil misbehaviour. It cannot be stressed too strongly, that the first concern of a teacher faced with frequent pupil misbehaviour must be to take stock of his or her teaching rather than to seek to establish discipline and control by recourse to the frequent administration of reprimands and punishments.

Of course, all teachers, no matter how effective, will need to deal with pupil misbehaviour from time to time; being able to deal with such misbehaviour is extremely important in complementing their ability to set up and sustain effective learning experiences. If not coupled with effective learning experiences, the techniques and skills involved in dealing with pupil misbehaviour, will at best serve as damage limitation exercises, aimed at establishing some sort of truce between teacher coercion and pupil resistance to the learning activities at hand. At worst, there will be no truce, but a continuing saga of friction, hostility, frustration and mutual resentment.

A great deal has been written about dealing with pupil misbehaviour, ranging from practical advice given by experienced practitioners to sophisticated research studies (see for example, Laslett and Smith, 1984; Lawrence *et al*, 1984). In addition, a number of the teacher unions have produced short guides for student teachers giving advice on discipline and classroom control, and it is interesting to note the points they highlight. In the main, such guides stress the importance of sound preparation and presentation, good teacher–pupil relationships and various teaching skills; interestingly, little is said about how to deal with pupil misbehaviour (as against pre-empting its appearance), except to emphasise that confrontations should be avoided, that punishments must be in line with school policy, and that, generally speaking, extra work and detentions seem to be the most effective types of punishment. Perhaps the single most important piece of advice comes from an (undated) NUT guide: 'try to think out *why* the problem arose in the first place' (p. 7).

The nature and causes of pupil misbehaviour

Pupil misbehaviour refers to any behaviour by a pupil that undermines the teacher's ability to establish and maintain effective learning experiences in the classroom. In a very important sense, pupil misbehaviour lies in the eyes of the beholder, and each teacher will have his or her own idea of what constitutes misbehaviour. While there is a large consensus amongst teachers regarding some forms of misbehaviour (eg refusal to do any work, hitting another pupil), over many circumstances there is a high degree of variation in teachers' judgements (for example, the degree of talking that is allowed). In addition, a particular teacher's judgements may well vary from class to class and from pupil to pupil. Equally, each teacher has his or her own notion of the *ideal* pupil; most usually one who is very attentive, highly motivated and interested in the work at hand, and who is able to remain solely concerned with the learning activities being undertaken (a danger for teachers of such ideal pupils is that they are often reluctant to complain and thus tolerate ineffective teaching). Each teacher must decide, for each individual class and pupil, at what point any deviation from this ideal constitutes misbehaviour. Furthermore the teacher must judge what degree of such misbehaviour can be tolerated (in as much as it will not undermine learning or is unrealistic to attempt to modify) and what degree requires action. There are thus two grey areas: first the point at which misbehaviour is deemed to have occurred, and second the point at which such misbehaviour requires action. Because the notion of misbehaviour inherently involves such ambiguities (see Docking, 1980), an essential feature of effective teaching is that the teacher's expectations and requirements in this area are made explicit and are applied consistently. All pupils wish to know exactly where they stand in relation to a teacher's judgements of misbehaviour; teacher action based on a lack of fair warning and which is inconsistent will invariably cause resentment.

Pupil misbehaviour can range from simple non-compliance (eg not paying attention) to overt disruptive behaviour (eg throwing a missile across the room). Obviously, such overt disruptive behaviour gives teachers the greater immediate cause for concern, but it will be evident from the discussion of effective teaching throughout this book, that the teacher's ability to keep pupils engaged in the learning experiences is of fundamental importance.

Studies of pupil misbehaviour (eg Lawrence *et al*, 1984; Wragg and Dooley, 1984) have shown that the vast bulk of pupil misbehaviour is quite minor in nature. It largely consists of noisy or non-work-related talking, not getting on with the learning activity, and mild misdemeanours and transgressions such as eating, being out of one's seat, and fidgeting. Serious misbehaviour, including direct disobedience, physical aggression or damage, is much less frequent. Most pupil misbehaviour occurs much nearer to the non-compliance end of the continuum than to the disruptive end. Nevertheless, in a number of schools, serious disruptive behaviour occurs sufficiently frequently to be a major source of concern for the school. In recent years the nature of disruptive behaviour in schools and the school's proper response has become a major area of debate. In part, this has resulted from the increasing incidence of disruptive behaviour in schools, particularly those based in inner-city areas with a particularly disadvantaged intake. There have also been organisational developments, such as the establishment of school-based (on-site) and non-school-based (off-site) centres or units for disruptive pupils and truants. Such centres have attempted to offer an alternative to the use of suspension or exclusion as the school's response to serious disruptive behaviour. On-site centres, sometimes referred to as 'sin-bins', were designed primarily to enable persistently disruptive pupils to be withdrawn from the mainstream of the school because teachers could not adequately cope with them there. In recent years, however, attempts have been made to go beyond a simple containment function towards more ambitious programmes of rehabilitation and readjustment.

In a study of suspension and exclusion from Sheffield schools, Galloway *et al* (1982) reported that the most frequent precipitating incidents involved:

- abuse/insolence to teachers (18.0 per cent of cases);
- unspecified bad behaviour (15.8 per cent);
- refusal to accept discipline/disobedience (12.4 per cent);
- bullying/violence to other pupils (10.9 per cent);
- persistent absence (8.7 per cent);
- refusal to accept punishment (7.5 per cent).

The authors noted that although the precipitating incident, if sufficiently serious, might result in suspension or exclusion, more often there was a gradual build-up of problems, which eventually reached a point where the headteacher was no longer prepared to accept a pupil's misbehaviour.

In discussing the nature of pupil misbehaviour it is clear that a wide variety of behaviour is involved, ranging from failure to pay attention to truancy. In addition, a number of related terms are also in use, such as disruptive behaviour, disturbing behaviour, and maladjustment. The Warnock Report recommended that the term maladjustment be retained, as it usefully implies that 'behaviour can sometimes be meaningfully considered only in relation to the circumstances in which it occurs' (p. 44). The 1981 Education Act however makes no mention of this term, while the government white paper, *Better Schools,* states that 'Certain pupils with emotional and behavioural disorders have special needs which fall to be met under the Education Act 1981' (DES, 1985b, p. 57). In general, the term 'maladjustment' has now been replaced by reference to 'emotional and behavioural disorders' or 'disturbed behaviour'.

In practice it has been extremely difficult, if not impossible, to draw clear distinctions between the related terms of disruptive behaviour disturbed behaviour, maladjustment and emotional and behavioura disorders (see Galloway, 1985; Lindsay, 1983; Stott, 1982). In general emotional or behavioural disorder applies when a pupil's behaviour is sc disturbing (either in terms of being detrimental to him- or herself or tc others) that special provision (including possible placement in a specia school) is sought. A distinction may be made between an emotiona disorder and a behavioural disorder underlying a pupil's learning difficulty. The former refers to emotional problems, such as anxieties phobias, depression and extreme withdrawal, which in extreme cases may constitute a psychiatrically-diagnosed neurosis or psychosis. The latter refers to behaviour problems, such as anti-social behaviour truancy, stealing, and violence towards others, which in extreme cases may constitute a psychiatrically-diagnosed conduct disorder. During the primary school years, such disturbing behaviour may well result in a placement in a special school; during the secondary school years. however, difficulty in arranging such a placement due to the limited number of places available may result in large numbers of pupils simply being suspended, excluded or located in centres for disruptive pupils. It thus happens that a large number of pupils avoid being assessed as having an emotional or behavioural disorder. Almost as many pupils are now based in centres for disruptive pupils as are based in special schools because of emotional and behavioural disorders. Galloway (1985) concluded that:

> *all* pupils sent to units for the disruptive could equally well have been
> described as maladjusted if it could have served any useful administrative
> purpose. Their behaviour, according to teachers, is at least as disturbing as
> that of maladjusted pupils. The same applies to their family backgrounds.
> Whether a child is labelled disruptive or maladjusted has nothing to do
> with educational, psychological or medical assessment. It depends solely on
> the type of provision available locally. (pp. 98–9)

Some may feel that this is an extreme view. The term maladjustment tends to refer to pupils whose problems are linked to immature or disturbed personality development. Although some disruptive pupils may be described as maladjusted in these terms, there are others who are quite healthy in this psychological sense, and whose disruptive behaviour can be seen to be primarily a reaction to stress at home (eg family discord), at school (eg frustration stemming from low attainment) or from elsewhere. with which they are unable to cope. Galloway's point is that, in practice. 'maladjusted' disruptive pupils and 'non-maladjusted' disruptive pupils (in the sense described here) may be found both in special schools and in non-special educational provision (such as on-site units for disruptive pupils). The length of time involved in the formal statementing of a pupil's special educational needs (over 12 months is not unusual), which is legally required if that child is to attend a special school, has undoubtedly contributed to this state of affairs. Attempts by LEAs to by-pass statementing for sound educational and administrative reasons have further clouded the distinction between the various labels used in considering behaviour problems.

Given the range of pupil misbehaviour, discussion of its causes could easily form the basis of an entire book. Indeed, each particular form and type of misbehaviour has received its own specialist attention, whether it be vandalism, drug abuse, truancy, or bullying (see Lindsay, 1983). Clearly, many inter-related factors influence the degree and type of misbehaviour that occurs. Even when one focuses on a particular type of misbehaviour, the complexity of this interaction remains. Nevertheless, in trying to understand the causes of pupil misbehaviour, it can be particularly helpful to draw a distinction between those factors outside the clasroom which may predispose or increase the likelihood of mis-behaviour, and those factors operating within the classroom which trigger off the actual misbehaviour (see Docking, 1980; Robertson, 1981).

In looking at the outside factors which contribute to the likelihood of misbehaviour in the classroom, we need to consider the whole range of influences which facilitate or hinder socialisation of the pupil into the ideal pupil role (ie attentive, highly motivated and interested in learning, and able to remain solely concerned with the learning activities at hand). Probably the main influence here is the family and its circumstances; one may contrast those child-rearing practices and family circumstances which contribute to children's intellectual development and self-confidence in themselves as learners with those which undermine such development. There is little doubt that children's experience of schooling in the first few years in the infant school are of crucial importance to their later educational progress, for it is here that children begin to form an image of themselves in the pupil role and lay the foundations for how they will accept and cope with – or react against – the demands that will be made on them.

An important feature of the pupil role is the ability to deal with frustration that occurs over difficulties in meeting the demands that the school makes (both academic and non-academic in nature). The development of impulse control is critically important for the pupil's adjustment to schooling; studies here have indicated that such control is essentially learnt socially and is influenced by child-rearing practices (Maccoby, 1980). A notable aspect of such development is 'delayed gratification', which refers to the ability to behave in a way that will achieve a greater reward in the future rather than a lesser but more immediate reward. In many ways, this is a key feature of being socialised into the pupil role.

Those pupils who see educational attainment as an important requirement for their future (adult) lives are much more likely to strive to meet
the demands of school life (including toleration and acquiescence where
appropriate) than their peers who have not adopted such values or
aspirations. Furthermore, where such motivation does exist, pupils
nevertheless differ in their ability to emotionally sustain delayed gratif-
cation, as is evidenced by those who display a strength of character and
perseverance to sustain school learning in the face of temptation such as
watching television, or adversity such as family discord. It is worth
noting here that such behaviour is influenced by other aspects of the
social-cultural milieu, and also, to some extent, by genetic factors (see
Rutter, 1978).

Whilst such outside factors are clearly important, in recent years
considerable attention has been paid to those aspects of pupils' experience of schooling which increase the likelihood of misbehaviour. Studies
focusing on the pupil's perspective illustrate that what may appear to be
quite senseless misbehaviour by a pupil, may in fact, from the pupil's
perspective, be a meaningful and understandable reaction to his or her
circumstances (eg Marsh *et al,* 1978; Woods, 1980b).

Overall, the most common trigger for pupil misbehaviour seems to be
a threat to that pupil's self-esteem. This often takes the form of being
asked to undertake academic work that he or she finds difficult and is
having little success with. It is not surprising, therefore, that much
misbehaviour is linked with low educational attainment. In such circumstances, the pupil is often caught in a double-bind. By trying to undertake
the work, the pupil risks frustration and further failure; by opting out of
making an effort, the pupil will inevitably become bored, incur teacher
displeasure, and find lessons increasingly hard to bear. Disruptive
behaviour and truancy which result from such a double-bind are, in a
sense, a plea for help.

Second only to learning difficulties as a trigger for misbehaviour is
boredom. There is little doubt that pupils find many lessons boring; this
may be because the content is of little interest, because the learning
activities are too passive, or because the manner of presentation fails to
sustain their attention and interest. Reacting to boredom by misbehaving
is not just restricted to low attaining pupils, but occurs throughout the
ability range. Indeed, for gifted children boredom with lessons may be a
major problem and precipitate disruptive behaviour.

Robertson (1981) has argued that when considering the causes of
misbehaviour it is useful to identify what the motive (or pay-off) for the
pupil might be. He has identified four such common pay-offs: attention
seeking, causing excitement, malicious teasing, and avoiding work. It is
important to recognise that all pupil misbehaviour serves underlying
psychological needs; only by taking account of these needs can the
explanation of such misbehaviour be established. A misdiagnosis may

mean that certain action by a teacher aimed to discourage misbehaviour can be counter-productive; for example, reprimanding a pupil who is attention seeking, or who is trying to establish his or her social standing as a leader within an anti-school sub-group, may actually lead to the misbehaviour occurring again, unless the pupil perceives that the consequences threatened in the reprimand outweigh the pay-offs.

Pre-empting misbehaviour

The adage 'prevention is better than cure' applies with particular force to dealing with misbehaviour. Almost all discussions of misbehaviour make reference to the qualities of effective teaching which sustain pupils' engagement in the learning activities in hand. The skill of pre-empting misbehaviour resides in vigilance and action; the vigilance with which the teacher monitors pupils' behaviour (in terms of attentiveness and receptiveness) and the learning activities (in terms of their appropriateness); the action which a teacher takes to sustain academic engagement in the learning experience whenever it appears to be slipping. Such action may range from changes in presentation (altering the pace of the lesson, moving on to another task, or asking questions) to exerting discipline and control (as was discussed in the previous chapter; examples include moving nearer to a pupil involved in non-task related talking, establishing eye-contact, or a reprimand).

In addition to vigilance and action, a crucial aspect of pre-empting misbehaviour lies in establishing clear rules and expectations regarding classroom behaviour, and this was also considered in the previous chapter. However, of particular interest here is the importance of first impressions created by a teacher with a new class. This has been considered in a number of recent studies. Wragg and Wood (1984b) compared the lessons given by 13 experienced teachers at the start of an academic year with those given by 13 BEd and 15 PGCE student teachers while on teaching practice. In interviews, they noted that experienced teachers were much more clear about which classroom rules were important and how they would ensure compliance. The most commonly-cited rule for both the experienced and student teachers was 'no talking when the teacher is talking', but experienced teachers also made frequent mention of rules governing territory, movement in the classroom, respect for property, the work ethic, and safety. The number of times such rules were explicitly stated, or could be clearly inferred from action taken, was recorded during observations of lessons. Wragg and Wood noted that the types of rules mentioned reflected what had been said in the interviews, but that some student teachers were unsuccessful in making a rule apply. In addition, as was noted in the previous chapter, an important aspect of establishing authority involves the teacher imposing his or her definition of the situation in terms of standards and expectations that are to apply.

Wragg and Wood noted that in September experienced teachers made a clear and concerted effort to establish a working climate for the whole year, based on their authority (see also Ball, 1980; Evertson and Emmer, 1982).

Pre-empting misbehaviour is made much easier if the teacher's authority and expectations can be quickly established and accepted. There is a general consensus that during the first few weeks with a new class, the teacher's behaviour should be firm and serious, in order to establish a climate which is purposeful and task-oriented; thereafter the more human side of teacher–pupil relations needs to develop (see Docking, 1980; Waterhouse, 1983). The advice 'don't smile 'til Christmas' attempts to highlight the importance of the initial relations between teacher and pupil being based on teacher authority rather than friendliness. When the teacher wishes to pre-empt misbehaviour, a quick signal to the pupil that he or she is adopting the initially-established firm and serious role can then be very effective. Attempts to become firm and serious when such authority has not been clearly established during the initial weeks, are not only less effective, but can actually be resented by pupils (Marsh *et al*, 1978). Nevertheless, Wragg and Wood (1984a) warn that if the initial emphasis on authority is too severe and not tempered with humanity, it may be very difficult to establish a positive working relationship later.

Finally, one needs to anticipate problems. This may mean making sure that certain pupils do not sit together or sit at the back of the classroom, that a pupil who has missed previous work is given something to do immediately whilst the rest of the class are introduced to more advanced work, or that clear instructions are given regarding behaviour while disruption is likely (eg allowing only one pupil from each group to collect apparatus).

Reprimands and punishments

Most pupil misbehaviour is either pre-empted or dealt with so quickly (for example, by use of eye contact) that a casual observer might easily fail to notice any such action by the teacher. However, there are many occasions when the teacher is required to take more formal and overt action to deal with misbehaviour, and a number of studies have explored these different strategies. For example, the *Nottingham Class Management Observation Schedule* (see Wragg, 1984) classifies teacher response to 'deviant acts' into three major categories each of which includes a number of sub-categories: *verbal* (which includes order to cease, reprimand, threat of punishment, statement of rule, humour, statements which involve pupil(s) in work, praise or encouragement etc); *non-verbal* (which includes gesture, facial expression, proximity, touch, and dramatic pause); and *punishment* (which includes extra work, moving a pupil, confiscation, detention, physical punishment, ridicule, and involving another teacher). Advice, guidance and research on the relative effectiveness of such actions may be found in a large number of writings (eg Docking, 1980; Lawrence *et al*, 1984; Laslett and Smith, 1984). What must be borne in mind is that when taking action, the teacher needs to take account of its effect on the individual pupil, its effect on the class, its relationship to school policy, and its short-term and long-term consequences. On occasions, these four considerations will each point to a different course of action, and in such cases the teacher is forced to decide on the priorities which apply in that situation.

Some particularly interesting studies have explored pupils' perceptions of different teacher control strategies in terms of their acceptability to pupils and their perceived likely consequences. In a study of 120 comprehensive school pupils in Scotland, O'Hagan and Edmunds (1982) reported that certain control styles appear to be effective in terms of one set of outcomes but ineffective in terms of another. For example, they noted that an 'initiatory hostile teacher aggression' style (typified by a teacher who punishes pupils and seems to like doing so, picking on pupils when no-one was misbehaving) was perceived by the pupils to lead to the least likelihood of misbehaviour in the classroom, but also to the highest likelihood of truancy. Lewis and Lovegrove (1984), in a study conducted in Australia, identified five aspects of secondary school pupils' preferences regarding teachers' classroom control procedures: 'calmness' (teachers remain calm when reprimanding pupils and do not shout, thus minimising embarassment); 'rule clarity and reasonableness' (rules are made clear; reasons for sanctions are stated and based on ensuring that learning is not disrupted); 'appropriate punishment' (avoiding the use of extreme punishments and punishments unrelated to the misbehaviour); 'fairness' (fair warning and correct identification of misbehaving pupil); and 'acceptance of responsibility' (teachers accept responsibility to maintain a sound learning atmosphere). When they compared these with the actual practice of those identified as good teachers by the pupils, they noted that the pupils' preferences appeared to be met in four of these areas, but often not in respect of 'calmness'. Certainly, pupils' preference for teachers whose exercise of control is calm, firm and fair has been widely reported (see for example, Docking, 1980; Wragg and Wood, 1984a).

Before turning our attention to reprimands and punishments, it is worth reiterating the importance of coupling such actions with encouragement and support of desirable behaviour (through praise, merit awards, and the satisfaction of work well done). This is often sufficient on its own to direct pupils' behaviour in the intended direction; certainly an emphasis on reprimands and punishments as the basis for maintaining order and control is likely to undermine the quality of the working relationship between teacher and pupils.

A reprimand refers to a communication by the teacher to a pupil (which can be verbal or non-verbal) indicating disapproval of the pupil's misbehaviour; such action can range from a serious stare to a threat of punishment. Punishment refers to the formal administering of an unpleasant action designed to punish the misbehaviour; such action can range from moving a pupil to a seat at the front of the classroom to suspension from school. The distinction between reprimand and punishment is often very blurred, since some actions, for example a stern talking to at the end of a lesson, appear to be a mixture of both. In essence, however, a reprimand embodies a warning aimed to stop the misbehaviour and prevent its future reoccurrence; a punishment would appear to embody a statement that the misbehaviour is so serious that formal action is required (this definition has been widely discussed, see for example Docking, 1980). Such formal action has one or more of three main aims: *retribution* (justice requires that bad acts are followed by a morally deserved punishment); *deterrence* (the punishment is likely to put off the pupil or other pupils from similar misbehaviour in the future through fear of the consequences) and *rehabilitation* (it is hoped that the punishment will assist the pupil in understanding the moral wrong-doing of the misbehaviour). The role of punishment within the behavioural psychology of classroom management will be dealt with later in the chapter.

A number of qualities have been highlighted which increase the effectiveness of reprimands, and these are described in Table 5. As has been argued earlier, the most effective use of reprimands lies in pre-empting misbehaviour. They form a second line of defence, coming after the use of effective teaching and before the third and final line of defence, punishment. Perhaps the most difficult judgement required of teachers is to know what level and type of reprimands will be most effective for a particular class or pupil. A balance needs to be struck between establishing authority and control to sustain the necessary discipline, and the coercion of reluctant learners. Reprimands are only effective in establishing a sound classroom climate if they are used sparingly to complement effective teaching. Frequent use of verbal reprimands is likely to be regarded by pupils as nagging, this further emphasises the need to employ private and non-verbal reprimands whenever possible.

Many criticisms have been levelled against the use of punishments (eg Fontana, 1985; Laslett and Smith, 1984). These include:

- they form an inappropriate model for human relationships;
- they foster anxiety and resentment;
- they have a short-lived 'initial shock' effect;
- they encourage pupils to develop strategies to avoid getting caught;
- they do not promote good behaviour directly, but simply serve to inhibit or suppress misbehaviour;
- they do not deal with the cause of the misbehaviour;

- they focus attention on the misbehaviour.

Despite such criticisms, punishments are a necessary part of maintaining discipline in schools. It would be nice if schools were so effective in setting up learning experiences which accommodated the needs of pupils that punishments were totally unnecessary. Most teachers will have taught a class for a whole year during which it was not necessary to punish a single pupil. But there *are* occasions when punishment becomes

---

Table 5 Effective reprimands

The following qualities increase the likelihood that a reprimand will be effective in dealing with pupil misbehaviour.

Correct targeting The pupil being reprimanded has been correctly identified as the pupil instigating or engaged in the misbehaviour; a particular danger here is failing to identify the first pupil who engaged in the misbehaviour, or identifying a pupil who simply reacted to another's provocation.

Firmness A verbal reprimand should be clear and firm; its tone and content should not suggest pleading for cooperation or imply damage limitation (eg 'let's get some decent work done for the last ten minutes'); the tone should be authoritative and induce compliance.

Build on rapport and mutual respect The teacher's disapproval should matter to the pupil; hence a statement of disapproval will carry significant weight. On some occasions indicating anger and involving a loud verbal rebuke or a livid expression may be appropriate, but such displays should occur sparingly, and a teacher should not habitually shout at pupils or lose his or her temper.

Emphasise the positive Reprimands should emphasise what pupils *should* be doing rather than complain about what they *are* doing; thus 'pay attention' is better than 'stop looking out of the window'; 'you can talk quietly, but only with your neighbour' is better than 'there is too much noise in here'.

Follow through psychologically When a reprimand is given, it should be accompanied by the appropriate non-verbal cues, such as eye-contact; after the reprimand is given, a momentary prolonging of eye-contact together with a slight pause before continuing the lesson, increases the force of the exchange.

Avoid confrontations Do not force pupils into a situation where an emotional and heated exchange results; where such a situation seems to be likely, postpone the exchange by asking the pupil to stay behind at the end of the lesson, and quickly resume the lesson in order to curtail the exchange.

Criticise the behaviour, not the pupil Criticism of the behaviour and not the pupil allows the pupil to dissociate him- or herself from the act, and emphasises that the teacher disapproves of the misbehaviour and not the pupil.

Use private rather than public reprimands This minimises the tendency for reprimands to disrupt the flow of the lesson and causes less embarrassment to pupils as well as less likelihood of a confrontation. Such private reprimands might include a quiet word, eye-contact, physical proximity, and asking a question in a context where being asked implies a reprimand.

Pre-emptive Reprimands aimed at pre-empting misbehaviour are more effective than those which follow only after repeated or extended misbehaviour.

State rules and rationale A reprimand can usefully consist of a statement of the rule being transgressed, together with an explanation of why the rule is required for the benefit of teaching and learning (eg 'please put up your hand and wait until I ask you to answer so I can give everyone a fair chance to speak and we can hear what is said').

Avoid making hostile remarks Hostile and deprecating remarks should be avoided; once a pupil feels personally disliked, disaffection and alienation may quickly follow. Sarcasm and ridicule are often felt by pupils to be an abuse of authority and can seriously undermine rapport and mutual respect, to the detriment of the classroom climate.

Avoid unfair comparisons Pupils are particularly sensitive to reprimands that involve stereotyping, labelling or comparisons with other pupils (such as high attaining pupils or family members who are or have been pupils), which describe their behaviour as typical or disappointing in terms of the teacher's expectations (eg 'your sister's work was much better than this', 'just because this is set three doesn't mean you don't have to pay attention').

Be consistent Reprimands should be consistently applied to pupils so that they are able to establish what behaviour will be dealt with; pupils resent inconsistency both in terms of whether certain misbehaviour is reprimanded and in terms of the severity of the reprimand.

Avoid idle threats Avoid reprimands which explicitly threaten certain consequences; when it is necessary to make such threats, they should be carried out and, as such, threats which will not be carried out must not be made.

Avoid reprimanding the whole class Having to reprimand the whole class is very serious, and implies that the teacher has been unable to stem the tide of individual acts of misbehaviour; the need for such reprimands may occur from time to time, such as when the noise level has crescendoed whilst the teacher was out of the room, or when a group of pupils collude to subvert the teacher's authority by surreptitiously tapping under desks.

Making an example Occasionally a public reprimand to an individual is necessary; this tends to be when the teacher needs to convey to the whole class with particular force the seriousness of the transgression, or when the teacher feels that his or her authority needs to be displayed publicly, such as when the misbehaviour itself can be seen by pupils to be a public challenge or test of the teacher. Indeed, making an example is commonly used by some teachers during their first few lessons with a new class to establish their authority; making an example of pupils should be done sparingly or it will quickly lose its impact and may also start to undermine teacher–pupil rapport and mutual respect; reprimands are more effective when targetted at individuals rather than at the class or at some imaginary pupil at the teacher's feet or in mid-air; this may mean selecting one particular pupil as an example after fair warning has been given to the whole class.

necessary, when the teacher's use of reprimands has not been sufficient to prevent or curtail certain misbehaviour, and he or she decides that unless punishment is administered the misbehaviour is likely to reoccur and become more widespread, and thus undermining. The vast majority of incidents leading to punishment involve a clash of wills between the teacher and pupil in which the pupil is deemed to have refused to accept the teacher's authority. Typically, in such incidents, the expectations of the teacher were clear but despite this the pupil misbehaved. Indeed, it is persistent misbehaviour, following repeated reprimands, or a direct challenge to the teacher's authority (such as a refusal to undertake the work in hand or verbal abuse), that precipitates punishment. An alternative to punishment in such circumstances is to defer dealing with the matter until the end of the lesson, when an investigative interview, which seeks to explore the reasons for the misbehaviour, can take place (see later in this chapter).

Some teachers occasionally use punishments to emphasise their authority without due warning or use of reprimands. While some incidents (eg fighting between pupils) may be punished immediately, it is wisest and most effective to use punishments very sparingly and only as a last resort.

Unfortunately there are some schools where challenges to authority occur so often that the use of punishments is frequent and widespread. In such schools, teachers sometimes appear to be fighting a rear-guard action to maintain a satisfactory level of discipline, in circumstances where many pupils have become alienated and disaffected, and where frequent use of punishments fosters increasing resentment, truancy – and, in turn, suspensions (see for example, Galloway *et al*, 1982; Rutter *et al*, 1979).

As well as punishments given when the teacher is exerting authority, some punishments are given in order to encourage sound moral and social behaviour (eg for bullying, cheating, and lying) and acceptable study habits (eg for untidy work, and lack of effort). In such cases, the teacher's authority may not be challenged in any direct way, and the teacher's prime concern is to act in the pupils' best interests. A major danger here involves not identifying accurately the nature and cause of the problem; to punish lying when a pupil was simply too scared to tell the truth or to punish lack of effort which resulted from a learning difficulty, is not only inappropriate but may do immense harm. All punishments must be linked with a pastoral concern if their counter-productive consequences are to be minimised.

The main qualities which increase the effectiveness of punishments are described in Table 6. In addition, there are a number of pros and cons regarding the use of particular types of punishments:

Detention This is perhaps the most educationally sound of all the different punishments. Its main strengths are that it allows time for penance (both leading up to and during the detention), that its formal nature adds weight to its sense of being a form of justice administered by the school as a whole, and that it can be linked to record keeping concerning the pupil's conduct, thus involving pastoral concerns. Its main disadvantages are that it occurs some time after the incident (usually at least 24 hours if after school), it is time-consuming for the teacher (if the teacher giving the detention actually takes it), and it may precipitate further problems (eg if the pupil fails to attend or misbehaves during the detention). The content of the detention may vary: the pupil may simply be required to sit in silence, or he or she may write an essay on why the misbehaviour was reprehensible, write out lines, or do a piece of work. A particular problem is to ensure that the unpleasant nature of detention does not result in intense resentment which undermines the working relationship between teacher and pupil.

Table 6 Effective punishments

The following qualities increase the likelihood that a punishment will be effective in dealing with pupil misbehaviour; in addition the points made in relation to effective reprimands (in Table 5) also apply to effective punishments.

Judicious use Punishments should be used sparingly, and in the vast majority of cases only after other ways of dealing with the misbehaviour (such as changes in teaching strategies, counselling and reprimands) have been tried.

Timing Punishments should be given as soon after the offence as possible; if there is a long delay, the link should be re-established at the time given.

Tone Punishments should not be given as a result of a teacher losing his or her temper; rather, it should be an expression of just and severe disapproval of the misbehaviour, and given because it is in the interest of the pupil and the class as a whole.

Fit the crime The type and severity of the punishment should fit the offence.

Due process Fair warning and consistency must be applied; in addition, the pupil should be given an opportunity to defend his or her behaviour, and encouraged to understand and accept why the punishment is just, deserved and appropriate.

Relates to school policy The punishment must relate to the overall policy of the school towards discipline.

Aversiveness The punishment must actually be unpleasant for the pupil; some pupils may not mind in the least being sent out of the room, or may gain status in the eyes of the peers if given a detention; as such, the punishment should be given in a method, and be of a type, that ensures its aversiveness and minimises any possible factors which might weaken its effectiveness.

Extra work The main strength of this punishment is that it can take place in the pupil's own time; to ensure unpleasantness, teachers devise a number of mindless tasks from writing lines to crossing out all the vowels in a piece of text; its weakness lies in its inherent patronising quality and its demonstration of the teacher's authority in forcing a pupil to undertake a mindless task. It is important to note here that setting extra work *as a punishment* should not be confused with requiring that work missed or not completed in a lesson or for homework should be done. Normal coursework is not a punishment, and requiring coursework to be done must be justified to the pupil on different grounds.

Loss of privileges This can range from moving a noisy pupil to sit alone, so that he or she cannot talk to anyone, to preventing a pupil going on a school outing. The main advantage is that this can be quite upsetting to the pupil; the main disadvantage is that it can easily be seen as vindictive and unfair.

Exclusion from the class This emphasises a feeling that the misbehaviour is unacceptable to the society of the class, and is largely based on ostracism being unpleasant. Requiring a pupil to remain in the corridor may pose other problems (eg they disappear or keep looking through a window), and as a result in many schools misbehaving pupils are sent to a specific location where another teacher takes charge. A variation used in some primary schools is to exclude the pupil within the class, by making the pupil sit in the 'naughty chair' in the corner of the room. Its main disadvantage is that for some pupils such exclusion is not particularly unpleasant, although it may be demeaning and thereby may lead to resentment.

Informing significant others Informing or involving others, such as the headteacher or the pupil's parents is for most pupils very punishing; its main drawback is the danger of provoking alienation.

Verbal intimidation A really severe talking to, either by the teacher or by a senior colleague, can be considered a punishment rather than a reprimand if its essential aim is to be extremely unpleasant for the pupil. Its main strengths lie in its unpleasantness and the fact that it can be administered quickly (although this should be in private). Its main disadvantage is that it can easily provoke a confrontation which could become very bitter and serious in its consequences.

Symbolic punishments The most common example of this is the giving of bad conduct marks. These can be totalled up and a stated number automatically results in a detention, which may be recorded on school reports. This has the advantage of offering the teacher a somewhat mild punishment, although some systems can be administratively clumsy.

Physical punishment Formal physical punishment, such as caning, has a shock value which can be effective in inhibiting future misbehaviour; its main disadvantages lie in its dehumanising (and in a sense anti-educational) basis, and that it can provoke confrontations when pupils refuse to accept it. Most educationists now argue against the use of physical punishment (myself included); if 'adjusting' to school requires physical punishment, we need to look long and hard at why. Informal physical punishment must *never* be used.

Suspension from school This is the ultimate sanction, which may be the point of no return. Certain behaviours, such as violence and drug abuse, are so serious that the severest form of disapproval needs to be exercised, also taking into account the protection of other pupils. In other cases, the history of misbehaviour has been so extensive that suspension is the last resort, aimed to help the pupil to appreciate the gravity of the situation. For some, the return to school may be successful; for others it proves to be the point where disaffection and alienation are complete. In such cases, special support will be needed for the return to school, or some other provision should be made for the pupil to salvage some educational progress.

It will be clear from the consideration of the pros and cons of using the different types of punishments, that they offer no panacea for dealing with pupil misbehaviour, and if used unwisely can be counter-productive. By and large, pupils most likely to misbehave are those for whom punishments are least likely to be effective. In schools where misbehaviour is relatively infrequent the use of punishments such as extra work and detentions appears to have the required effect on those who misbehave. In schools where misbehaviour often occurs, the frequent use of punishments seems to have much less effect (see Rutter *et al*, 1979). Overall, the main message is that teachers should strive, as far as possible, to minimise the occurrence of circumstances where punishment is required as a last resort, and to ensure that other options are fully utilised first. Perhaps the single most important aspect of punishment, is that if it is threatened, then it must be applied. If pupils are made clear of the circumstances in which punishment will be applied, and that such application is sure and consistent, then the use of reprimands is much more likely to be sufficient.

Finally, two aspects of reprimands and punishments are of crucial importance; first, the need to avoid confrontations, and second their relationship to pastoral care and school policy towards discipline. These will now be considered.

Dealing with confrontations

One of the most unpleasant and distressing situations that can occur in the classroom is a heated and emotional confrontation between a teacher and pupil. The ability to avoid such confrontations or to deal with one which develops is crucial to the effective management of discipline (see Laslett and Smith, 1984). As was noted in the previous chapter, the effective exercise of authority involves the teacher being able to impose his or her will over pupils when such authority is challenged. In the vast majority of cases, this does not pose any problems. However, on some occasions the manner in which the authority is exercised, together with the psychological state of the pupil, leads to a confrontation. The most successful teachers seem to have a sixth sense that warns them early on in an exchange that a confrontation could develop. They are then able to use a variety of social skills and techniques, including humour, to alter the tone of the exchange and to give both the teacher and the pupil a face-saving solution to the incident.

Overall, there would appear to be four main aspects of the teacher's control style which may provoke a confrontation, and which therefore should be avoided. The first is physical or verbal intimidation, such as poking a finger into a pupil's chest, and making hostile remarks. The second is public embarrassment, which includes the use of sarcasm and ridicule, or attempting to make a pupil lose face in front of the class. The third is losing one's temper with a pupil. The fourth is behaving in a way which the pupil finds irritating. The first three aspects are to a large extent within the teacher's control, but the fourth can be very unpredictable, particularly as the teacher's behaviour may be quite innocuous in normal circumstances, and provokes the confrontation almost entirely because of the pupil's reactive psychological state. A teacher can often pick up subtle cues from a pupil's agitation that all is not well, but occasionally there are no warning signs. In such circumstances, the main danger is that the teacher will react inappropriately, perhaps in one of the three ways listed above (using intimidation, causing public embarrassment, and losing one's temper). Once a full-blown confrontation has begun, it is extremely difficult to regain control, particularly as the event may develop very quickly; the general air of nervousness and desperation can easily lead to further misunderstandings.

The first task in a confrontation is to remain calm. One way of doing this is to adopt a mental strategy: counting to ten, for example, or asking oneself why one feels so angry. If, in the midst of a heated exchange, the teacher can switch to a calm and relaxed tone, there is a good chance that the exchange can be toned down. The second task is to offer the pupil an escape route. Backing-off does not mean a loss of authority. The two main escape routes available are to defer action to the end of the lesson or to arrange immediate exclusion from the class (which may involve a colleague collecting the pupil).

It is certainly important to bear in mind that many pupils are emotionally immature and lack the social skills necessary to avoid a confrontation, thus it behoves teachers to use their maturity and skills to defuse such situations. It is all too easy to regard extreme challenges to authority as a personal attack, when they are really a reaction by the pupil to circumstances he or she is unable to cope with.

Studies of teacher–pupil confrontations (eg Pik, 1981) indicate that the key to a teacher's ability to deal with a confrontation lies in his or her interpersonal skills. Attempts to develop such abilities in teachers need to focus not so much on the actual discipline techniques they use, but rather on developing their power to recognise the nature of the confrontation they are engaged in and to be able to select the most appropriate course of action to resolve the confrontation satisfactorily rather than reacting in a stereotyped way.

Saunders (1979) has categorised the main strategies available to a teacher as 'avoidance', 'defusion' and 'confrontation'. Like many other authors, he highlights the importance of compromise and negotiation between teacher and pupil, so that both recognise each other's position and needs and can then adopt a course of action in which both sets of needs are accommodated in return for important concessions. While such compromise is a useful strategy, the ideal state is one in which the teacher and pupil are able to reach an understanding that enables both sets of needs to be fully met; not all conflicts actually require one party to make concessions but it may require some thought and attention to ascertain this. For effective teaching, the teacher needs to be able to match the strategy to the context; no one strategy will always be the best, and it is this sensitivity to the situation which is crucial to the teacher's ability to manage such conflicts successfully.

Pastoral care and school policy

Dealing with pupil misbehaviour is an important aspect of the classroom teacher's pastoral responsibility. A difficulty facing teachers in exercising discipline is that they sometimes have to decide between a course of action which will be effective in maintaining discipline for the class as a whole, and another course of action which more closely meets the misbehaving pupil's needs. This conflict of interests is particularly acute when the method of dealing with the misbehaviour is publicly visible, and a charge of unfair and inconsistent treatment can be levelled against a teacher if a special allowance appears to be made. In practice, however, this is not as problematic as one might expect, largely because both the offending pupil and the rest of the class are very much aware of such concerns, and are able to understand and tolerate a degree of differential treatment as long as it appears to be justified by the circumstances.

The teacher's pastoral responsibility places an emphasis on the need for the teacher to ascertain the reasons for a pupil's misbehaviour, and to come to some mutual understanding with the pupil with respect to its unacceptability in terms of the teacher's, the pupil's and the class' best interests. This goes beyond simply demarcating as clearly as possible what behaviour is unacceptable; it requires the teacher to help the pupil come to an informed understanding of the concern and an intention to behave as desired in future. Such counselling is of fundamental importance to dealing with misbehaviour; a teacher who relies simply on a mixture of reprimands and punishments is unlikely to establish this pastoral element in the pupil's educational development. Moreover, counselling enables the teacher to explore whether there are any problems facing the pupil (for example, particular learning difficulties or home circumstances) which require attention.

It is argued here that such counselling is generally more important and effective as a means of dealing with misbehaviour than recourse to punishments. This is certainly the case if the development of the pupil's ability to understand and accept responsibility for his or her behaviour is to be given priority. Punishment does have a role to play, but it is more effective if allied to counselling rather than applied as a further line of defence when reprimands have been insufficient. Athough in the infant school years pupils are clearly less able to reflect on their misbehaviour, it is still the case that such counselling provides an essential and complementary adjunct to the use of reprimands. Indeed, given the importance of the child's personal and social development in the early years of schooling, the case for counselling carries additional force.

A number of qualities and strategies may be adopted to increase the effectiveness of talking to a pupil (at the end of a lesson, or at some other time) about the misbehaviour that has occurred (see for example, Fontana, 1985; Robertson, 1981; Saunders, 1979). First, the conversation should take place in a context of trust, rapport and mutual respect. Second, it should take place in private. Third, the teacher should display a caring and concerned attitude towards the pupil (rather than a threatening and intimidating one). Fourth, the pupil should be encouraged to evaluate his or her misbehaviour and the undesirable consequences which may follow (including lack of educational progress and punishments); it is important here for the pupil to do most of the talking and not the teacher. Fifth, the pupil should agree to behave in a more desirable way in future.

This is not, of course, to argue that such counselling should constitute the teacher's response to every incident of misbehaviour, nor that recourse to punishments should not be made unless such counselling has occurred first. There are many occasions when the shared understanding and rapport between teacher and pupils makes such formalised counselling unnecessary and an inefficient use of the teacher's time. Furthermore as was noted earlier, talking to a pupil at the end of the lesson can also serve other purposes, such as giving a severe reprimand. What is being argued here however, is that on many occasions counselling is the more effective and appropriate course of action.

Nevertheless, two major problems need to be considered: that time pressures on teachers may lead to the exchange being superficial and cursory, and that the pupil may lack sincerity in cooperating with the teacher (by being ready to agree with whatever the teacher requires but with no intention to comply in practice, or by being entirely hostile to the exchange). Indeed, some pupils tend to see such a course of action by the teacher as a sign of weakness, particularly if, after the interview, they feel no concessions have been drawn from them. In such circumstances, it is important to call upon the support of colleagues, normally the pastoral staff, in order to formalise the school's concern. In doing so, it is important for all involved that this is not perceived as being the result of the teacher not being able to deal with the pupil; rather, it should reflect the need for a broader approach to consider that pupil's circumstances. The pastoral staff involved (including the form teacher and the head of house or year) should in the first instance support the teacher rather than be seen to take over. This is no mean task, as some teachers see the main role of the pastoral head as that of taking over and sorting out pupils who pose unacceptable problems; from the other perspective, there are times when it is evident to the pastoral head that part of the problem actually resides with the teaching. Nevertheless, in the wake of the 1981 Education Act and its requirement to meet children's special educational needs, the notion of partnership between classroom teacher and pastoral staff has become much more evident, and some of the best practice which already existed in schools has become more widespread.

Four school practices in particular appear to have increased markedly over the last few years. The first is the use of short-term formal monitoring of pupils in all their lessons. A pupil who appears to be having specific or wide-ranging problems is placed 'on report' for a period of about a week, during which each teacher who takes that pupil makes a comment about the pupil's behaviour after each lesson (in the secondary school) or at the end of each half-day or full-day (in the primary school). The pupil then discusses the report with the pastoral head at the end of the week. Such discussion can then be linked to evaluating whether the pupil has been able to behave better during the period of monitoring, and if not what further action is required. In many schools, monitoring is usefully coupled with involvement of the pupil's parents and soliciting their support. Placing pupils on report is now a very widespread practice, but its effectiveness is largely dependent on the counselling skills of the pastoral head together with the pastoral head's ability to alter the circumstances (ranging from classroom academic demands to drug abuse). This may often involve colleagues and those outside the school such as social workers, educational psychologists, and the pupil's parents.

A second major development has been a growing readiness to communicate with and involve parents when a pupil's behaviour is giving rise for serious concern. Good communication between the school and parents is essential if there is to be a sound partnership between the two, and the increasing involvement of parents in the school's concern has been a healthy and desirable trend. Nevertheless, many schools have an ambivalent attitude towards such involvement, in part because it may imply some failure in the school's ability to deal effectively with the pupil, and in part because the pupil can resent such an involvement. It is important for the teacher and pastoral staff to carefully prepare the ground so that when parents are involved, they can be given a full picture of the nature of the school's concern. In addition, it is desirable to indicate to the pupil why the parents are to be involved, to avoid possible resentment.

The third major development has been the use of 'contingency contracting' (see Laslett and Smith, 1984; Saunders, 1979), in which teacher and pupil agree to certain rewards which will follow if the pupil's behaviour improves over a given period. Such contracting is most effective when pupils are helped to appreciate that the improved behaviour required will be in their best interests and where the rewards are seen to assist the pupil to carry out an intention to behave as agreed (rather than acting as the sole motive for the improved behaviour). The use of a formal written contract signed by both parties has also proved to be helpful. The type of reward offered must be tailored to each individual pupil. Examples include arranging an extra swimming session, spending an afternoon in the art class, helping to run the school tuck shop, the award of a merit certificate for improved behaviour, or even being bought an ice cream after school. The effectiveness of contingency contracting depends on the quality of the teacher–pupil rapport; the clear and explicit selection of the appropriate target behaviour (which must take account of any underlying causes, particularly any learning difficulties); and being able to identify a suitable reward. Fontana (1985) has described an interesting variation of this approach in which the headteacher drafts a letter to the pupil's parent describing the misbehaviour causing concern, reads the letter to the pupil, and then agrees to file the letter for a specified period during which the pupil is required to improve the behaviour in return for the letter being destroyed. Such a strategy appears to be somewhat dubious; it could easily be seen by the pupil (and the parents) as unfair duress, appears to go against the notion of school–parent partnership, and may encourage the pupil to play the system. Generally, however, contingency contracting seems to have been quite effective in dealing with a whole range of pupil misbehaviour.

The fourth major development has been the growth in the establish-ment of on-site centres within the school for dealing with disruptive pupils, as was noted earlier in this chapter. Studies of their effectiveness (see Docking, 1980; Galloway *et al,* 1982; Mortimore *et al,* 1984) indicate that while the pupils appear to adjust quite well to placement in such a centre, as indicated by reduced levels of truancy and a healthy rapport with the teachers in charge of the centre, there is little evidence of a successful return to mainstream schooling, or of substantial academic progress. The marked increase in such centres sadly appears to reflect a need to withdraw disruptive pupils from mainstream schooling, rather than evidence of their success in achieving educational progress.

The central point of this discussion of pastoral care and school policy in relation to dealing with misbehaviour is that the classroom teacher's effectiveness in dealing with misbehaviour cannot be considered separately from the strategies and policy adopted in the school as a whole. Studies which have sought to compare the effectiveness of different schools in dealing with misbehaviour have employed a range of outcome measures, including misbehaviour in the classroom, truancy, and juvenile delin-quency (eg Rutter *et al,* 1979). Such studies are notoriously difficult to conduct, particularly because of the need to take account of many diverse factors such as the intake characteristics of pupils into the school (social class, ethnic composition, previous history of misbehaviour etc). Never-theless, the quality of the pastoral care offered in the school appears to be an important factor in explaining the relative effectiveness of some schools over others with a similar intake or when intake differences have been allowed for (see for example, Galloway *et al,* 1982; HMI, 1979; Reynolds, 1985; Rutter *et al,* 1979). Perhaps the single most important factor, largely undiscussed in such studies, is the status given within the school to the views of the pastoral head. Pastoral care aims not only to help the pupil adjust to the demands of the school, but also to adapt, where possible, the school's demands (including in particular the cur-riculum experiences offered) to meet the pupil's needs. Thus the status and influence of the pastoral head (or other senior staff acting in a pastoral role) seems to be crucial.

Behaviour modification

Behaviour modification refers to the use of principles derived from behavioural psychology to bring about improved behaviour in the classroom. In its purest form, behaviour modification draws upon the principles of operant conditioning as outlined by Skinner (see chapter 3). This is based on the notion that behaviour which is followed by reward is reinforced and as such is more likely to occur in the same circumstances in future, while behaviour which is *not* rewarded (ie is ignored or punished) is less likely to occur. A number of writers have outlined how such principles may be used in the classroom (eg Fontana, 1985; Laslett and Smith, 1984; Wheldall, 1983), and it is interesting to note that terms such as 'positive teaching' and 'the behavioural approach' seem to have been adopted recently to combat some of the prejudice attached to the term 'behaviour modification'.

The use of behaviour modification in the classroom usually involves a period in which the level of some desirable and undesirable behaviour is recorded (amount of time spent out of seat, amount of time spent working, number of times pupil hits another pupil . . .). A treatment phase is then implemented, in which instances of the desirable behaviour by the target pupil are systematically rewarded (eg use of praise, award of tokens to be redeemed for sweets, or other rewards) and in which instances of undesirable behaviour are ignored (ignoring is generally used rather than any form of punishment). Once behaviour has improved, the level and frequency of the rewards is gradually reduced. Finally, a post-treatment phase is used to monitor the level of the desirable and undesirable behaviour and the level of reward to be employed in future. The key to behaviour modification in the classroom lies in following these phases rigorously: carefully monitoring the target pupil's behaviour and systematically and consistently applying the treatment.

The use of behaviour modification contrasts with most teachers' approach to discipline, by adopting the strategy of rewarding desirable behaviour and ignoring undesirable behaviour. Most teachers appear to accept that they should more frequently reward desirable behaviour, but find the idea of ignoring undesirable behaviour somewhat suspect.

A large number of schemes employing behaviour modification in the classroom have been reported (see Fontana, 1985; Merrett, 1981). They are more common during the primary school years (both in ordinary and in special schools) than in the secondary school years, and have been particularly successful in dealing with misbehaviour which appears to be mainly attention seeking, and with disturbed pupils whose misbehaviour (in the form of being aggressive) or lack of participation in the lesson (being extremely withdrawn) is primarily a reaction to being unable to cope with the demands made upon them. The lower number of schemes reported in secondary schools appears to be largely a reflection of the greater organisational difficulties which arise there together with a more restricted availability of effective rewards. Nevertheless, many successes are reported in secondary schools too.

Three examples will serve to illustrate the diversity of approaches that have been reported. Merrett and Wheldall (1978) reported a scheme based on a junior school class which adopted the *good behaviour game* approach. This involved awarding housepoints to all the pupils sitting at a table if, when the teacher looked at the table, the pupils were following three classroom rules: 'we stay in our seats whilst working', 'we get on quietly with our work', and 'we try not to interrupt'. Merrett and Blundell (1982) reported two studies conducted in the remedial department of a secondary school, in which pupils used a self-recording schedule to monitor their own behaviour and where improved behaviour resulted in a reward. The first study was based on a single pupil and the reward was allowing the pupil to colour in a doodle art picture; the second study was based on a class of 16 pupils (the nature of the reward was not reported). Finally, Harrop and McCann (1983) reported a study based on a first-year mixed ability class in a comprehensive school where the reward was a favourable report home for those pupils who made progress in reading.

The purest form of behaviour modification involves simply controlling the rewards following behaviour. It is evident from the schemes reported that there has been an increasing involvement of pupils in discussing the desired and undesired behaviour and in agreeing on the nature of the rewards to follow the desired behaviour. Many schemes are, in essence, a form of contingency contracting (as outlined earlier) linked with a systematic recording and rewarding of the desirable behaviour. This is a far cry from the strict operant conditioning notion of behaviour modification, which now seems to be largely restricted to use in special schools for pupils with particularly severe problems.

Criticism of the use of behaviour modification can be categorised in five main areas. The first is that it is very time-consuming to apply, so it tends to be used in cases where there is a favourable teacher–pupil ratio or where the teacher's concern is so great that the effort involved is worthwhile. The second criticism is that the strategy of ignoring misbehaviour to promote its extinction can pose very real problems; it may involve the disruption of other pupils, and it may create some ambiguity in the classroom regarding the normal expectations for behaviour. The third criticism is that the 'shaping' of pupils' behaviour is in a sense anti-educational. The essence of discipline involves educating pupils to accept responsibility for their actions and to freely accept the teacher's authority as legitimate. It can be argued that such self-control needs to be based on rational understanding and not inculcated as a habit. While this criticism has some force, and reflects a commonly held view among teachers, the current move towards the use of contingency contracting together with pastoral counselling has enabled behaviour modification schemes to take on a more explicit educational role. The fourth criticism is that behaviour modification focuses exclusively on the pupils' misbehaviour and neglects to assess its underlying causes. Although in principle this is the case, in practice almost all teachers will attempt to examine the causes of the misbehaviour, whether it lies in the curriculum experiences offered or in factors external to the classroom. In such cases, behaviour modification is employed as part of a total package of action intended to facilitate educational adjustment, and not as an isolated activity narrowly utilised. The fifth, and final criticism is that the systematic use of rewards (including praise) is somewhat cold-blooded and insincere, and as such is not compatible with establishing discipline based on mutual respect and rapport. In many ways this is perhaps the strongest criticism. While the use of behaviour modification need not undermine mutual respect and rapport, the importance of a sound teacher–pupil relationship cannot be overestimated. If such a relationship does not exist, behaviour modification schemes may have only limited success. Such mutual respect and rapport demand that teachers act with sensitivity and intuition in their dealing with pupils, and this may well be the reason for many teachers feeling uncomfortable when operating a behaviour modification scheme, despite acknowledging the scheme's effectiveness in promoting the desired behaviour.

The behaviour modification perspective explicitly requires the teacher to consider the desired behaviour which is to be fostered and the undesired behaviour which is to be extinguished, and in doing this to consider how the consequences for the pupil of behaving in these ways may increase or decrease the occurrence of such behaviour. Such analysis enables the teacher to consider a number of aspects of how discipline and authority are exercised in the classroom, and to identify a strategy which will more effectively bring about the intended changes in pupil behaviour. In general, teachers have not widely adopted behaviour modification strategies; nevertheless, many do operate such schemes, and many more have adapted some of the principles underlying behaviour modification in their own practice. Given the five main criticisms described above, it is unlikely that the use of behaviour modification will ever be employed by the majority of teachers in the classroom, and the case for its more widespread use still needs to be made. The strategies outlined in the other sections of this chapter are the ones primarily advocated by the author, but there is, nevertheless, a role for behaviour modification schemes for some pupils, with some teachers, in particular circumstances.

Conclusions

It will be evident from the discussion of dealing with pupil misbehaviour that the key task facing teachers is to minimise its occurrence in the first place. Once pupil misbehaviour has occurred, the teacher's recourse to reprimands, punishments and counselling must involve the careful and sensitive selection of an appropriate course of action which maximises the chance that future misbehaviour will not occur, but at the same time attempts to ensure that this course of action does not undermine the mutual respect and rapport upon which a sound working relationship needs to be based. The emphasis in this chapter has been on the use of pre-empting skills and the use of reprimands, together with the judicious use of punishments and the appropriate use of counselling. There are no panaceas here, and each method of dealing with pupil misbehaviour has its strengths and weaknesses. An attempt has been made to indicate those qualities which will increase the likelihood of a course of action being effective, but in the final analysis most seems to depend on the quality of the teacher–pupil relationship as discussed in the previous chapter and as indicated where appropriate in this chapter. Of paramount importance in such a relationship is that teachers convey that they genuinely care about pupils' educational progress and adjustment. It is for this reason that the teacher's pastoral care role has been considered in both this and the previous chapter.

9 Three professional concerns

This chapter addresses the three most pressing professional concerns challenging teachers. The first is the need to develop the school curriculum so that it meets as fully as possible the educational aspirations held for it. The second is to develop systems of teacher appraisal which will foster more effective in-service professional development. The third is to develop ways in which the levels of stress experienced by teachers can be reduced.

The curriculum

The broadest definition of the curriculum is that it covers all the learning experiences set up by a school to achieve specified educational objectives. An analysis of the school curriculum thus needs to explore its educational aims, the content and processes involved in the learning experiences, and the assessment and examination practices adopted. As was noted in chapter 3, this must include both the formal curriculum (embodied primarily in the subjects and topics taught) and the hidden curriculum based on the less overt messages conveyed to pupils from their experiences of schooling).

It is sometimes argued that discussion of effective teaching too readily accepts the current school curriculum as its starting point, focusing on how teachers can be as effective as possible *within* the school's curriculum and thereby failing to address how pupils' educational progress can be better fostered by certain curriculum changes. In recent years, however, it has been increasingly recognised that discussion of effective teaching must extend to all aspects of the school curriculum.

Since the mid-1970s, the debate about the school curriculum has been fierce. It can be traced back to the 'Great Debate' concerning the school curriculum launched by the Labour Government in 1976, which, through a series of regional conferences, addressed four main topics: the curriculum, the assessment of standards, the education and training of teachers, and the school and working life (DES, 1977). The debate about the curriculum was further developed by HMI's survey of primary and secondary schools (HMI, 1978, 1979) and a variety of DES and HMI discussion papers, including the influential *A View of the Curriculum* (HMI, 1980) and culminating more recently in *The Curriculum from 5 to 16* (HMI, 1985a). During this period, a number of critics (eg Hargreaves,

1982; Walker, 1983) have pointed to the need for changes in aspects of the school curriculum. As a result of such intense discussion and debate, together with a recent concern regarding the economic health of the nation, the school curriculum in the 1980s has been, and will continue to be, a period of unparalleled development in aspects of both the formal curriculum and the hidden curriculum.

Clearly a discussion of the school curriculum is too vast an enterprise to cover in depth here, given the large number of issues and developments involved (see Ball, 1984; Bennett *et al*, 1984; Broadfoot, 1984). A very well-informed attempt to take stock of current developments and to propose a way forward formed the basis of two reports commissioned by the ILEA, *Improving Primary Schools* (Thomas Report, 1985) and *Improving Secondary Schools* (Hargreaves Report, 1984). In the context of this book, however, attention will be paid to the developments taking place which have the most important implications for effective teaching; indeed, many of these have already been noted and discussed where appropriate in previous chapters.

The DES' view of the curriculum is clearly the most influential one, and the DES has largely set the agenda for the debate. Its view, reiterated in *Better Schools* (DES, 1985b), lists the purposes of learning at school as:

1   To help pupils develop lively, enquiring minds, the ability to question and argue rationally and to apply themselves to tasks, and physical skills.
2   To help pupils to acquire understanding, knowledge and skills relevant to adult life and employment in a fast-changing world.
3   To help pupils to use language and number effectively.
4   To help pupils to develop personal moral values, respect for religious values, and tolerance of other races, religions, and ways of life.
5   To help pupils to understand the world in which they live, and the inter-dependence of individuals, groups and nations.
6   To help pupils to appreciate human achievements and aspirations.

The verb 'to help' used at the start of each statement is significant; it reflects a trend towards seeing the teacher's role as one of setting up learning experiences for pupils, as opposed to the more directive tone of the verb 'to teach'; this shift in emphasis is probably the single most important trend in the curriculum, and we shall return to it later. Also of particular significance is the emphasis given to the preparation for adult life and employment (statement 2 above). This will be a second major issue to which we shall return later.

In its discussion of curriculum design, HMI (1985a) make a distinction between *areas of learning and experience,* which are listed as aesthetic and creative, human and social, linguistic and literary, mathematical, moral, physical, scientific, spiritual, and technological, and *elements of learning,* namely knowledge, concepts, skills, and attitudes. In addition, HMI list a number of essential issues which are not necessarily contained within subjects, but which need to be included in the curriculum: environmental education, health education, information technology, political education, and education in economic understanding. HMI also advocate that the curriculum should possess four key characteristics:

- *breadth*: it should engage pupils adequately in all nine areas of learning and experience and with the four elements of learning associated with them;
- *balance*: each area of learning and experience and each element of learning should be given appropriate attention in relation to each other and to the whole curriculum;
- *relevance*: the curriculum must be perceived by pupils to meet their present and future needs; what is taught and learnt should be worth learning;
- *differentiation*: the curriculum must allow for differences between pupils in their abilities and other characteristics.

In the final analysis, effective teaching is not simply a matter of the teacher attaining his or her intended learning outcomes, since these intended outcomes need to be in line with the school's overall policy, which in turn needs to reflect LEA and DES policies. In view of the rapid curriculum development currently taking place, it is not surprising to find increasing demands being made on teachers. Perhaps the greatest professional challenge facing teachers is to keep abreast of such changes, to be able to accommodate those trends which appear to be educationally justifiable, and to then implement learning experiences which are effective (in terms of sustaining attentiveness, receptiveness and appropriateness) in accordance with the outcomes desired. To help teachers meet this challenge, the degree of support in terms of information availability, in-service courses, and resources, must be adequate, since teachers are able to change their practice only as far as support provision allows.

Since 1982, I have acted as the Research Director for the *Centre for the Study of Comprehensive Schools* (CSCS), based at the University of York. CSCS, through its computerised databank, now provides inquirers with much needed information about current curriculum developments in comprehensive schools, and enables schools to share their experience. The pressing need for information about curriculum developments has led to many such databanks being set up by other organisations, covering both primary and secondary schools, and a whole range of curriculum initiatives. My involvement with CSCS, together with my work in the Department of Education at York, has given me an impression of the massive scale of current curriculum developments in schools, but also a sense of the desperate need for more support and resources to enable such initiatives to be successful.

Overall, I would single out four major curriculum challenges as worthy of particular attention, as described below.

1 Improving the learning process

As noted earlier, the most significant change in schools over the last few years, has been a shift towards seeing the teacher's role as one of setting up learning experiences in which pupils are active and have a marked degree of control over the work they undertake. This change can be characterised as a move away from a passive acquisition of knowledge (based on teacher presentation, exposition and demonstration) towards activities which enable pupils to develop intellectual and social skills involved in learning, and which thereby foster greater self-confidence across the full ability range, and the development of skills which will be useful beyond the subject matter in hand.

The best argument for the approach is that of the *Education for Capability* movement (see Burgess, 1986; CSCS, 1986) based at the Royal Society of Arts, which outlines the changes for pupils thus:

- *active learning*: they will learn through the practical activity of doing and through applying to their own experiences their knowledge and skills;
- *problem solving*: they will be encouraged to identify problems and find their own solutions to them;
- *creativity*: they will discover and develop their creative abilities by doing, making and organising;
- *communication*: they will be encouraged to share with others their work, ideas and problems;
- *co-operation*: they will learn to get on with others by working in groups and teams of different sizes;
- *negotiation*: they will negotiate their work programme with teachers to meet their personal learning needs;
- *assessment*: they will receive frequent and appropriate recognition of their achievements and experiences as recorded and assessed by themselves and others.

Developments along these lines have occurred within the traditional curriculum subjects as well as through cross-curricular, inter-disciplinary and extra-curricular activities.

The challenge of improving the learning process is an on-going one: views of the learning processes which are of the greatest educational value will continue to be redefined in the light of how our understanding of the processes themselves develops, and in the light of changing educational priorities. In the context of effective teaching, maintaining attentiveness, receptiveness and appropriateness is likely to be facilitated if the learning processes involved enable pupils to be more active in the learning experience. As such, the current shift appears to make good psychological as well as good educational sense.

2 Getting the curriculum right

All schools need to make a decision about the formal content of the curriculum as embodied in the school timetable, together with the content to be covered within each element of the timetable. In recent years, the debate about curriculum content has been wide-ranging: no subject or topic appears to be sacrosanct. In particular, there has been a move towards more centralised control (through the DES) of the school curriculum to ensure greater uniformity of educational experience between schools and also to ensure that each child has an education which covers some defined core of experiences. Thus far, no clear consensus has emerged from the discussion of such a 'core curriculum' although the DES' (1985b) views are likely to be gradually implemented in schools, whether a consensus is established or not. This is demonstrated in the area of vocationalism, discussed below.

In the context of effective teaching, two major factors relating to the curriculum are relevant. First, the content should be meaningful to pupils, both in terms of their current understanding and interest, and in terms of their educational needs (that is, the quest for personal development and understanding). Second, the content should be appropriate for achieving the desired outcomes of education. This is based on a number of value judgements about the aims of education; effective teaching requires that the content matches these aims.

The majority of developments in the school curriculum – ranging from topic work in the primary school to life and social skills courses in the secondary school – are advocated primarily in terms of the learning processes involved, rather than a knowledge content to be covered. Indeed, even those new subject areas which do introduce a new content area, such as World Studies (Whitaker, 1984), on close inspection appear to be advocated as much if not more because of the new approaches to teaching and learning they embody than because of their content. Similarly, developments in teaching traditional curriculum subjects such as history and geography, are characterised more by shifts in learning processes geared to the acquisition of intellectual skills than by changes in content areas. Nevertheless, there have been shifts in content towards reflecting wider concerns which increase the relevance of the subject to everyday life, and to meet the problems of stereotyping and bias linked to gender, class and race.

A further very important aspect of getting the curriculum right involves coordination across different subjects and topics and across the years. Pupils' experience of schooling from five to 16 must make sense as a programme, so that each experience relates to, builds upon, or prepares for, other experiences. This degree of coordination is most vulnerable at the point of transfer between primary and secondary schools, as has been noted by HMI (1985a). They maintain that primary and secondary schools should each appreciate what the other is aiming to achieve, both in general terms and in specific areas of the curriculum. A number of secondary schools and their feeding primary schools have collaborated in just such a way, although the time and effort involved should not be underestimated, given the complexity and logistical difficulties involved.

Finally, the importance of utilising pupils' interests and giving them more control over their curriculum can be expressed by offering pupils more choice regarding courses they follow or topics they cover. Whilst some degree of choice is already available, for example, over optional subjects taken at the age of 14, it is surprising that more schools have not been able to implement modular courses, where a number of discrete units can be selected and combined to form a programme of learning. Hargreaves (1982) advocated such an approach in his proposed second ary school curriculum and increasing choice and the development o modular courses may well become a major trend in the near future.

3 Preparing pupils for adult and working life

The most radical development in the school curriculum in recent years has been the increasing emphasis in secondary schools on courses explicitly aimed to prepare pupils for adult and working lives. Under this umbrella can be included courses of social and personal education, development, understanding of society and the world of work, vocational and pre-vocational courses. This emphasis may be contrasted with the traditional liberal/humanist emphasis on cognitive and intellectual understanding which dominated the grammar school curriculum of the 1950s and 1960s.

There is little doubt that much of the impetus for this development stems from social and economic concerns: on the one hand, the implications of high levels of youth unemployment, and on the other hand, demands from employers (particularly in industry and commerce) for school leavers to possess the types of knowledge, skills and attitudes they require. These changes have been most marked in the area of 'vocationalism', with courses, aimed to prepare 14 to 18-year-old pupils for working life, spear-headed by the *Technical and Vocational Education Initiative* (TVEI) funded by the Manpower Services Commission (MSC, 1983).

Whatever the arguments for and against vocationalism, the development has been noteworthy in generating a number of changes in curriculum practices in terms of the learning processes and assessment procedures employed, which include pupil profiling, experiential learning (especially work experience), curriculum negotiation, and the use of learning modules (CSCS, 1984; Wallace, 1985). The influence of vocationalism in general, and TVEI in particular, has gone well beyond its own domain, and has had a major impact on the whole school curriculum. In addition, many of the school–industry links established have led to a whole range of benefits for schools, across the curriculum and beyond, particularly in terms of in-service training for teachers and school managerial and organisational development (CSCS, 1985; Everard, 1984; Jamieson, 1985; RSA, 1985).

Developing new forms of assessment

Changes in the school curriculum need to go hand in hand with changes in assessment practices if such developments are to be successful. Indeed, implementing new assessment practices often acts as a useful device for producing changes in teaching and learning.

One of the most significant developments in assessment has been the introduction of pupil profiling and records of achievement, as discussed in chapter 6. The DES (1985b) has recently established as a policy objective that by 1990 all pupils leaving school should be provided with such a record of their achievements. An example of a major development along these lines is the *Oxford Certificate of Educational Achievement* (OCEA) which will include three components in a final leaving certificate: a personal record of achievement; criterion-referenced statements regarding English, science, mathematics and modern languages; and the results of public examinations (Wakefield, 1986).

If curriculum changes are to have currency for pupils on leaving school, they must generate associated accreditation in line with the new content area, learning processes, or skills, which the change has aimed to develop. In the area of vocationalism, for example, a major development has been the *Certificate of Pre-Vocational Education* (CPVE) based on courses taken for one year after the end of compulsory education. CPVE courses are intended to combine core areas (eg industrial, social and economic studies; information technology; creative development; social skills; numeracy; practical skills) with vocational studies (including work experience) in one or more of five areas, and additional studies designed to complete an appropriate individualised programme. CPVE will thus require important changes in schools' and teachers' methods of working (DES, 1985d).

Without doubt, the major examination development of the 1980s is the introduction of the *General Certificate of Secondary Education* (GCSE) to replace GCE 'O' level and CSE (DES, 1985b, 1985d). The GCSE has important implications for effective teaching. First, it attempts to overcome the problem of demotivation among pupils who in the past took a relatively low status examination (the CSE as opposed to 'O' level) or no examination at all. Second, it introduces national criteria aimed at achieving a common content and assessment procedure for each subject syllabus, as far as possible. Third, it places greater emphasis on oral and practical skills, coursework, reasoning and application. Fourth, through the use of carefully differentiated papers or questions, it aims to enable pupils to display and be assessed on what they know, understand and can do, rather than on what they do not know or cannot understand; thus teachers should be able to more fairly assess, motivate and offer appropriate challenge to each level of ability.

Whilst the GCSE has a major impact in fostering a number of changes which will aid effective teaching, there is a real danger that the need for assessment during coursework will place such undue demands on teachers that it may actually undermine the quality of their teaching. It may take quite some time for teachers to develop the necessary skills to formally assess pupils for GCSE whilst simultaneously organising and sustaining their learning (see Torrance, 1986).

Teacher appraisal

One of the most significant developments in schools in recent years has been the introduction of formal and systematic schemes of teacher appraisal.

Self-appraisal and critical reflection by teachers on their own teaching is an important aspect of their ability to continue to improve and develop the quality of their teaching. Whilst this is often done on a somewhat informal and intuitive basis, a number of attempts have been made to utilise self-evaluation pro-forma or checklists either adopted by a teacher on his or her own initiative, or introduced as part of a whole school self-evaluation programme. A typical example of the latter is contained in the ILEA's (1977) whole school self-appraisal booklet, which contains such questions for the teacher as: Do I prepare properly? Am I evaluating my lessons? Do I 'label' pupils prematurely? Am I aware of pupils with particular problems? (see also Heywood, 1982). In addition, many teachers have evaluated their own teaching by collecting research data on their own performance, a move that was stimulated by some curriculum development programmes (eg Elliot and Adelman, 1975) and which formed the basis of what has now been termed 'teacher action research' (Nixon, 1981).

The debate about standards in schools, noted earlier in this chapter, has led, under the direction of the DES to a move to ensure that all teachers are formally and systematically appraised. In part, this move stemmed from a dissatisfaction with the impact of whole school self-evaluation schemes, and in part from a belief that such appraisal will contribute to more effective teaching. This move was embodied in *Teaching Quality* (DES, 1983) and more recently in *Better Schools* (DES, 1985b):

The Government holds to the view expressed in 'Teaching Quality' that the regular and formal appraisal of the performance of all teachers is necessary if LEAs are to have the reliable, comprehensive and up-to-date information necessary for the systematic and effective provision of professional support and development and the deployment of staff to best advantage. Only if this information relates to performance in post can LEA management make decisions affecting the career development of its teachers fairly and consistently. Taken together, these decisions should result in improved deployment and distribution of the talent within the teaching force, with all teachers being helped to respond to changing demands and to realise their full professional potential by developing their strengths and improving upon their weaknesses; with the most promising and effective being identified for timely promotion; with those encountering professional difficulties being promptly identified for appropriate counselling, guidance and support; and, where such assistance does not restore performance to a satisfactory level, with the teachers concerned being considered for early retirement or dismissal. (p. 55)

The debate about teacher appraisal has been intense. The two main concerns are that such appraisal may be expected to fulfil a variety of functions which may, in some cases, be incompatible, and that the actual method of appraisal may not be fair or just (Stenning and Stenning, 1984; Suffolk Education Department, 1985). Overall, there seem to be three major purposes advocated for teacher appraisal.

1 Managerial

It is argued that regular teacher appraisal enables the headteacher to monitor more effectively the extent to which teachers are carrying out their professional duties (teaching, administrative, and other), to identify any problems which have managerial implications, and to consider the potential role of particular teachers in any future developments within the school.

2 Public accountability

This aspect of teacher appraisal focuses on establishing a means by which the DES and LEA can satisfy themselves that teachers are effectively carrying out their duties. Much of the impetus here stems from a belief in some quarters that there are teachers who are unacceptably ineffective and who will be more likely to be improved or removed if a formal system of appraisal is in operation.

3 Professional development

Professional development involves two main strands. The first concerns the use of appraisal as a means by which teachers can improve and develop their skills in order to meet more effectively their current duties and take on any further duties or responsibilities. The second concerns fostering career development which will enhance promotion opportunities. Whilst these two strands are often complementary, they need not necessarily be so.

Teacher appraisal schemes are already in use in a number of countries. A consideration of such schemes in the United States in particular has highlighted the problems and issues involved (eg Peaker, 1986; Suffolk Education Department, 1985). First, there is a real tension between using a scheme to enhance professional development and using it, however rarely, to formally evaluate the teacher's competence with a view to possible dismissal. Second, the use of an observation checklist to evaluate classroom teaching tends to encourage safe (often exposition-dominated) teaching at the expense of interactive approaches. Third, where appraisal is used as a basis for dismissal, it has become embroiled in legal issues regarding fair and natural justice and due process: a problem which has also arisen in relation to the use of written teacher competency tests (Lines, 1985). Fourth, the attempt to link teacher performance with merit pay or some other form of reward for outstanding work has been largely unsuccessful and in many cases harmful and divisive in its effects (Murnane and Cohen, 1986). Fifth, the operation of a scheme may be so time consuming that it has a dysfunctional effect on the school.

A fully fledged teacher appraisal scheme would be compulsory for all teachers and comprise four main stages:

1 *A pre-appraisal stage* in which the teacher is asked to reflect on his or her own performance. This would normally be in response to a pro-forma ideally developed and established for use in the school, and which will produce a written response that the teacher submits to the appraiser.

2 *Classroom observation* of either one lesson or a series of lessons. Ideally this would include a pre-lesson discussion of the aims of the lesson and an immediate post-lesson discussion of its apparent success. An observation pro-forma completed by the appraiser would enable a written record of the appraiser's observations to be given.

3 *An appraisal interview* in which the teacher's all round contribution to the school and his or her future professional development is discussed. In particular, targets or objectives will be set which will contribute to the teacher's improved effectiveness and foster professional development.

4 *A follow-up stage* in which the appraiser formally monitors and evaluates whether any issues or problems highlighted have been satisfactorily dealt with and whether the targets or objectives set have been achieved.

Studies of teacher appraisal schemes in the United Kingdom have indicated that such fully fledged schemes are few and far between (DES,

1985c; James and Newman, 1985; Metcalfe, 1985; Turner and Clift, 1985). The majority of schemes emphasise professional development in the sense of fostering teacher improvement (ie a *formative* assessment) rather than as a means of making explicit decisions about pay, promotion or competence (ie a *summative* assessment). This emphasis on formative assessment is very much in line with the views advocated by teacher unions (AMMA, 1985; NUT, 1985). The main method of appraisal used is the appraisal interview; few schemes employ regular and systematic classroom observation, but a sizeable minority employ classroom observation to some extent. About half of the schemes are voluntary, or compulsory only for probationary or other new teachers. While a few schemes owe their origin to a whole school self-evaluation initiative (usually LEA inspired), the vast majority are very recent in origin and were initiated by the headteacher alone or together with deputy heads. It is clear from these studies that most of the schemes currently in operation (emphasising formative assessment, being voluntary in nature, and involving no classroom observation) would not meet the guidelines for teacher appraisal advanced by the DES.

Of particular interest has been the type of model adopted for these schemes. Two main models have been employed. The first simply involves the headteacher – alone or together with deputy heads – as the appraiser. The second involves a hierarchical structure where members of staff are appraised by their immediate superior (teacher, head of department, deputy head, headteacher, etc); this model can include some interesting variations, such as when the headteacher's teaching is appraised by the head of the department in the subject area concerned. Interestingly, very few schemes involve appraisal by peers or subordinates, although some examples have been reported (see Bunnell and Stephens, 1984). Few schemes involve appraisal of the headteacher (in relation to that role), although many headteachers claim that the appraisal interview of staff provides appropriate feedback to do this; those schemes which do, utilise either deputy heads, the LEA, or a self-appraisal which may make use of a questionnaire to staff.

Enough information has been gained from the schemes in operation to identify a number of aspects of both good and bad practice, and to identify some of the central issues and problems involved. Not surprisingly perhaps, the main problem has arisen over time and resources; indeed, this has been the most frequent reason given for not implementing or for discontinuing a scheme (eg James and Newman, 1985). A second major problem has been the level of teacher suspicion and hostility regarding teacher appraisal, stemming from concerns about the fairness and validity of using such schemes to make summative assessments. A third major problem has been the disaffection that has resulted from teachers having false hopes raised (regarding, for example, promotion prospects, or in-service opportunities) or feeling that the appraisal did not offer them a fair opportunity to put their case or display their capabilities.

With regard to the appraisal interview, teachers have commonly reported three main benefits. The first is that it offered an opportunity for the headteacher (or other appraiser) to express gratitude to staff for their hard work and commitment; for many teachers this was the first time they had received a personal commendation of this type, and it was much appreciated. Second, it offered an opportunity to receive realistic advice and guidance; even when some critical feedback was received, many teachers appreciated learning this sooner rather than later (eg when they were applying for promotion). Third, it offered an opportunity to have a two-way professional dialogue on matters of concern which often resulted in a clarification of job descriptions and expectations (although this can sometimes lead to recognition of a problem which might have been better left unaired). Nevertheless, conducting a successful appraisal interview requires sound planning and preparation as well as the appropriate social skills; in addition, there are often potential problems regarding, for example, how to deal with comments made about colleagues given in confidence or how to ensure honesty if teachers' honest comments may be to their disadvantage.

In the context of effective teaching, it is the appraisal of classroom teaching that is of the greatest interest. Such appraisal involves a number of issues and problems which are difficult to resolve. First, is it possible to adopt a scheme which will enable both formative and summative assessments to be made? Experience to date indicates that if both are attempted simultaneously the quality of the formative assessment is markedly reduced, to the extent that it will foster little if any useful feedback to the teacher. In addition, summative assessments tend to promote procedures aimed to protect teachers which can become bureaucratic and which undermine the opportunity to develop a professional dialogue between the teacher and the appraiser. As such, quite separate observations may need to be made for formative and summative assessments, each with its own set of ground rules and agreed procedures; this type of clear separation is common in the United States.

A second major issue is whether the appraiser should be a school colleague and/or a subject specialist. The appraiser must be able to make allowance for the school and class circumstances (eg level of resources available, ability of the pupils) and must have the appropriate professional expertise and credibility for the assessment to be valid and useful.

A third major issue is the type and nature of the feedback to be given. In general, such feedback should constitute a professional dialogue rather than instruction. Written comments are also very helpful, and in many schemes, schools have devised their own pro-forma for these. It is important to remember that much appraisal takes place between teachers who are equal regarding professional competence. Indeed, it would not be unusual for an appraiser to be appraising a teacher who is generally more competent. Appraisers may have much to learn from observing a colleague – often as much, if not more, than they themselves can offer. It is for this reason that schemes which encourage all teachers to act as appraisers are likely to have the greatest benefits for improving the quality of teaching, for it is in observing others that one is best able to reflect on one's own practice.

A much neglected aspect of appraisal feedback is the difficulty, in part for social reasons, of giving critical feedback to a colleague. This demands great social skills if it is to be constructive and helpful; as such, some prior staff discussion aimed to facilitate a non-threatening climate for feedback will go some way to increasing its success. At the same time, it must be recognised that some appraisers may be too blunt, and the organiser of the appraisal scheme will need to ensure that such teachers are helped to develop their feedback skills as part of their own staff development programme.

Schemes currently involving the appraisal of classroom teaching have displayed much diversity of practice regarding the degree of pre-lesson appraiser preparation (eg whether the aims of the lesson are discussed), the method of observation (eg whether completely unstructured, or guided by a list of prompting questions, or using a rating of designated qualities), the method of feedback given (eg whether spoken, or written), and the criteria adopted (eg whether open, explicit, or based on other evidence such as pupils' written work). Most schemes seem to focus on whether the lesson was successful in terms of general teaching tasks (see also chapter 6). Turner (1985) for example, has listed the following prompting questions as typical:

- Did the lesson begin well?
- Was there any delay in getting started?
- Were the children interested and attentive?
- Were the materials appropriate to the tasks involved?
- Were the tasks appropriate to the aims and objectives of the lesson?
- Were pupils of above and below average ability adequately catered for?
- Did the teacher attempt to involve all pupils?
- Were a variety of methods used?
- Was the teacher able to maintain interest for the whole of the lesson?
- Was the lesson understood by all pupils?
- Were there any significant discipline problems?
- What use was made of audio-visual aids?
- How did the teacher conclude the lesson?

While such prompting questions may provide a useful agenda for classroom observations, the quality of the appraisal feedback clearly depends on the appraiser's views of how the teaching observed could be improved. At face value these questions are no more sophisticated than those typically used for student teachers. They are certainly not appraiser-proof (in the sense of ensuring that appraisal feedback will be helpful regardless of the appraiser's skills or views). The main challenge facing those concerned with effectiveness is to help teachers develop teaching methods and activities which offer learning experiences that are effective in their own right, and in line with curriculum developments (eg use of group work, experiential learning techniques, emphasis on communication skills). At its best, appraisal feedback will promote professional development in teaching through stimulating such ideas; this would constitute good formative assessment practices. The danger is that if the appraiser is not versed in the appropriate curriculum developments, the appraisal feedback will tend to become a superficial summative assessment checklist resulting in little if any such development.

HMI's study of teacher appraisal (DES, 1985c) was based on visits by HMIs to 37 primary, 7 middle and 35 secondary schools. Its conclusions highlighted three major issues of concern. The first was that if a scheme involved passing information to external agencies (such as the LEA) concerning the appraisal of teachers, a number of problems were involved. In particular, HMI were concerned with the variability of criteria employed by different schools and by different appraisers in the same school. In addition, such transfer of information must not transgress individuals' rights to access of information held about themselves. The second major issue was the importance of staff goodwill towards the scheme, which in part depended on good management–staff rapport and in part on the participatory nature of a scheme's initial development and adoption. An important implication is that if a scheme is seen by staff to be imposed upon them with little prior consultation and if there is a context of poor rapport, the implementation of the scheme is unlikely to have a beneficial effect on the school and could in some cases be harmful to staff morale. The third major issue is the need for extensive inservice training and education to accompany this development in order to ensure that appraisers are adequately trained for their tasks and that those appraised have their professional needs met.

Many people involved in staff appraisal in commerce, industry and public services find it hard to understand why similar appraisal does not occur in schools, and indeed many such schemes have much to offer (see Everard, 1986). Nevertheless, it is becoming apparent that unless good sense prevails, the implementation of some formal and systematic schemes has as much potential for harm as good; it would be a tragedy if some of the political considerations involved in this development served to undermine the potential benefits in improving the quality of education offered in schools.

Teacher stress

Occupational stress among schoolteachers (teacher stress) has over the last decade become an area of increasing discussion and concern (Dunham, 1984; Kyriacou, 1986b). Teacher stress may be defined as the experience by a teacher of unpleasant emotions such as tension, frustration, anxiety, anger and depression, resulting from aspects of his or her work as a teacher. The increasing awareness of teacher stress stems in part from a more general concern to increase the quality of teachers' working lives, in part from the mounting evidence that prolonged occupational stress can precipitate both mental and physical ill-health, and in part because of indications that such stress may well undermine teachers' classroom effectiveness.

In addressing the question of why teachers experience stress, Kyriacou and Sutcliffe (1978b) argued that the key element was teachers' perception of threat based on three aspects of their perception of their circumstances:

1   that demands were being made upon them;
2   that they were unable to meet, or had difficulty in meeting, these demands;
3   that failure to meet these demands threatened their mental or physical well-being.

The experience of stress is largely dependent on how teachers perceive their circumstances. There are three important factors which seem to make teachers more prone to stress:

- a feeling that they are required to meet a high level of demands (either from significant others such as the headteacher, or because of self-imposed standards);
- a feeling that they are unable to meet these demands (either because they lack the appropriate skills and ability or because to do so is not within their control, for other reasons);
- as a result of the above, a feeling of being threatened (perhaps arising from fear of losing face in their own eyes or those of colleagues, or of reduced promotion prospects – even actual dismissal).

Teachers who experience all of the above are more susceptible to stress than are colleagues for whom one or more of these elements is not a problem. This is not to argue that the teacher's actual circumstances are unimportant in accounting for the experience of stress. Clearly, most teachers in circumstances which can be objectively judged as 'difficult' will experience stress. However, this analysis does offer an explanation of why some teachers appear to experience more stress than others in what at face value seem to be very similar circumstances, by focusing on the underlying differences which exist in the teachers' perceptions.

A number of authors have explored whether there are personality traits which may make some teachers more prone to stress than others (Kyriacou, 1980a). Of these studies, the most interesting trait linked to stress appears to be that which characterises differences between those individuals who believe that things in their lives are generally within their control (a belief in 'internal control') and those who tend to believe such things are generally outside their control – attributable primarily to luck, fate, powerful others, or essentially unpredictable (a belief in 'external control'). There is evidence to indicate that teachers with a belief in external control are more stress-prone (Kyriacou, 1980b, 1986b). Such findings are particularly interesting in view of the widely accepted observation that individuals' perceived lack of control over a potentially threatening situation markedly increases the likelihood that they will experience stress. This observation has importance for exploring how teachers can best deal with stress.

Studies exploring the extent of teacher stress have tended to rely heavily on questionnaire surveys using a self-report measure of the experience of stress. My own research over the last decade is typical of this approach. In a series of studies involving teachers in comprehensive schools, I employed a questionnaire that contained the following question: 'In general, how stressful do you find being a teacher?', which was linked to a five-point response scale of 'not at all stressful', 'mildly stressful', 'moderately stressful', 'very stressful' and 'extremely stressful'. Of the 714 respondents, 24 per cent used the categories 'very' and 'extremely' stressful (Kyriacou, 1980a, 1980b). Studies of teacher stress in both primary and secondary schools indicate that teachers commonly report high levels of stress, and compared with other professions report one of the highest if not the highest levels of stress. Despite this, there is little evidence of teachers having a higher than average level of stress-related physical or mental ill-health, a finding which may be largely attributable to the influence of school holidays in mitigating the effects of stress on health (Kyriacou, 1980c; Kyriacou and Pratt, 1985).

Over the last decade a large number of studies have identified the main sources of stress facing teachers. Overall, these may be grouped into four main areas:
- pupils' poor attitudes and misbehaviour
- conflicts with colleagues
- time pressures and general work overload
- poor working conditions.

For example, in a study of 124 primary school teachers, Pratt (1978) reported the following sources of stress in order of the ten most severe:
- the weather made the children restless
- some children did not do as they were told straight away
- a child did not do as I told him to
- there was one difficult child in my class

- the children did not listen to what was said
- children had difficulties in learning/understanding
- I was interrupted by other people/events
- I found it difficult to reach the standard I wanted during this session
- extra-curricular activity was an additional strain
- a child deliberately defied me.

In a study of 257 comprehensive school teachers, Kyriacou and Sutcliffe (1978a) reported the following 'top ten':

- pupils' poor attitudes to work
- trying to uphold/maintain values and standards
- poorly motivated pupils
- covering lessons for absent teachers
- too much work to do
- lack of time to spend with individual pupils
- individual pupils who continually misbehave
- pupils who show a lack of interest
- not enough time to do the work
- lack of time for marking

Frequent discussion of teacher stress in the context of pupil indiscipline (eg Galloway *et al*, 1982; Laslett and Smith, 1984) tends to imply that directly disruptive pupil behaviour is the major source of stress. Careful reading of the two lists above, however, indicates that it is pupils' poor attitudes, low motivation and general uncooperativeness which teachers report as the most serious. In effect, it is the less intense (when compared with pupil disruption) but more insidious and day-to-day nature of such attitudes that in the long run appears to give the greatest concern: a finding observed in a number of studies (Kyriacou, 1986b). This may primarily reflect the high degree of mental effort, alertness and vigilance that teachers need to maintain throughout a typical school day – leading to a level of nervous and emotional exhaustion which, in turn, makes them more vulnerable to other sources of stress.

In considering sources of teacher stress, two important points need to be borne in mind. First, that individual teachers will differ markedly in what for them is their own major source of stress. For one teacher it may be poor promotion prospects, for another friction with the head of department, and for yet another difficulty in mastering the subject content area satisfactorily. Such individual profiles will also vary throughout the teacher's career. For example, there is a tendency for junior and less experienced teachers to be more concerned with problems of pupil misbehaviour compared with their more experienced senior colleagues who are likely to be more concerned with administrative work and managerial issues (Dunham, 1984; Kyriacou and Sutcliffe, 1978a).

The second point is that teachers may well tend to identify as sources of stress the more salient aspects of their circumstances (eg pupil misbehaviour, lack of resources). It is important, however, to take account of the prevailing climate in schools as a whole; it would appear that if individuals feel they are doing work that is well-rewarded (in terms of salary), is regarded as worthwhile, and is respected by the community, this can mitigate the experience of stress. When teachers perceive this is not the case, as was to some extent evident during the pay disputes of the mid-1980s, morale in schools tends to drop and in consequence stress is likely to increase.

In recent years, increasing attention has focused on how teachers can best cope with stress as well as what schools can do, through their organisational and managerial practices, to reduce stress (Dunham, 1984). Coping actions used to deal with stress can usefully be grouped into two main categories. The first is *direct-action techniques,* which consist of those actions aimed at dealing with a situation that is potentially stressful. For example, if a teacher feels that a particular pupil is being disruptive on a number of occasions, an intervention strategy is used (eg a severe reprimand, exploratory counselling, seating the pupil at the front of the classroom); if the teacher feels unable to keep up with deadlines for marking work, more time at home is devoted to this; if a teacher feels that the level of resources is inadequate, a strong case is made to improve these. If such actions are successful, the source of stress is removed. At the same time, it is worth noting that such actions may well in themselves cause stress, which partly explains why some teachers are reluctant to do anything despite the fact that if the source of stress is left unchallenged it may well become more serious. In addition, some direct action techniques are based on simple avoidance such as arranging for a difficult pupil to be transferred to another class or even taking a day off when a particularly difficult class is timetabled; such actions may in the short-term enable the teacher to deal with the source of stress, but they do not offer an effective long-term solution and may well cause problems for colleagues.

The second main category of coping actions can be termed *palliative techniques.* These do not deal with the source of stress itself, but rather aim at reducing the individual's subjective emotional experience of stress. Palliative techniques can be mental or physical in nature. The former involve strategies which try to help the teacher perceive the stressful circumstances in a different way, thus reducing the level of perceived threat (the key element in experiencing stress, as noted earlier). Such strategies may be conscious, such as deliberately trying to see the humorous side of a pupil's insolence, or stepping back and distancing oneself emotionally from a situation; they may also be partly unconscious, for example, refusing to admit to oneself that important demands are not being met. Physical techniques involve behaviours aimed directly at reducing the emotional state (eg tension, anxiety, frustration) and include taking deep breaths to try and relax, smoking tobacco and drinking alcohol, and playing squash or jogging. The main aim of such techniques is to dissipate the build up of tension.

In general, direct-action techniques are best in dealing with a source of stress if such techniques can be realistically and effectively employed. However, many sources of stress are not amenable to direct-action techniques, and in such cases, palliative techniques need to be used. All teachers need to develop their own individual combination of direct-action and palliative techniques tailored to their own profile of sources of stress and taking account of their own abilities, preferences and personality characteristics.

In a study of coping actions, Kyriacou (1980d) explored the frequency with which a sample of 42 comprehensive school teachers reported using a list of 33 such actions. The following ten actions were the most frequently reported:

- try to keep things in perspective
- try to avoid confrontations
- try to relax after work
- try to take some immediate action on the basis of your present understanding of the situation
- think objectively about the situation and keep your feelings under control
- stand back and rationalise the situation
- try to nip potential sources of stress in the bud
- try to reassure yourself everything is going to work out all right
- don't let the problem go until you have solved it or reconciled it satisfactorily
- make sure people are aware you are doing your best.

An analysis of these responses indicated that the coping actions formed three main groups: the first involved actions based on expressing feelings to others and seeking their social support, the second involved careful consideration of the situation followed by taking appropriate action, and the third involved actions based on thinking about pleasurable activities in the future.

While some coping actions involve the teacher acting alone and in isolation, it appears that the majority rely on social support from colleagues or others. Indeed, Kyriacou (1981) has argued that the degree of social support available in a school is a crucial factor in mitigating the level of stress. Such support may be direct, in terms of colleagues positively supporting or assisting those having difficulties, and monitoring the school's organisational and management practices accordingly, or indirect, through, for example, good staffroom facilities and communication channels which facilitate friendly social relations and exchanges. In this respect, Kyriacou (1981) has explicitly called for senior management in schools to review ways in which the school's climate and practices can reduce teacher stress.

In recent years there have been a vast number of in-service courses for teachers dealing with teacher stress, ranging from one-off speaker sessions to short courses and residential workshops. Woodhouse *et al* (1985), reported an evaluation of a six-day course in human relations for teachers based on experiential learning sessions. 90 teachers completed a pre-course diary which detailed incidents experienced as stressful. Of the 327 incidents recorded, 187 concerned pupils and 140 concerned other staff members. The authors argued that the reports indicated that teachers' habitual responses to stressful situations tend to be ineffective, unplanned and potentially damaging to personal relationships. Of particular concern was the tendency to try to re-assert control over disruptive pupils by recourse to punishment, which they saw as an inefficient tactic that often resulted in pupil anxiety, alienation and suffering. The course attempted to help teachers to respond in stressful situations in a more creative (and less habitual) way, thereby increasing their effectiveness in dealing with potentially stressful demands made upon them. Post-course interviews indicated that most course members had taken responsibility for changing their behaviour at work in ways that reduced stress.

In the context of effective teaching, teacher stress raises a number of concerns and issues. First, it needs to be borne in mind that many teachers who experience high levels of stress are also very effective as teachers in the classroom. Indeed, it is sometimes their high standards and commitment that make them vulnerable to stress. This raises a dilemma, in that it may seem to imply that for the teacher's own health it may be advisable to be less effective. In part, this is probably the case. All teachers should attempt to be as effective as possible, but if the standards they set for themselves are excessively high, there is a real danger that over a long period they may succumb to stress related ill-health, or a general state of exhaustion, widely termed as 'burnout' (see Kyriacou, 1986b). To prevent this, teachers need to either moderate their standards to a more realistically achievable level or to ensure that they are utilising an effective set of coping actions (most notably, that they do not become easily upset when their aims are thwarted, but are able to put things in perspective and maintain a healthy and well-balanced emotional state).

In addition, for some teachers the experience of stress does indeed undermine their effectiveness. This may occur directly, in that the experience of stress in the classroom impairs the quality of their teaching, such as when they are unable to think coherently about their lesson organisation or instructions; it may also occur indirectly, through a reduction in their general morale and commitment towards teaching, resulting in less well planned lessons and less enthusiasm being displayed while teaching. It is imperative for such teachers to be helped to diagnose the nature of their problems, and to receive appropriate support and guidance to enable them to regain and sustain their effectiveness.

Finally, it needs to be borne in mind that teaching is a demanding profession, and if teachers are to be helped to give of their best, they will need the appropriate level of support to do so. This support includes both professional development and school resources. In the light of the two professional concerns outlined earlier in this chapter, it is clear that the next decade offers major challenges to the teaching profession; if this period is not to be unnecessarily stressful, these changes will require sensible planning and support.

Conclusions

It is evident from the three professional concerns discussed in this chapter that teachers face a number of important challenges, which they must meet if they are to sustain the effectiveness of their teaching. It is also clear that teachers cannot do this successfully if they act as isolated individuals, relying only on their own personal resources and professional commitment. Rather, what is required is teamwork, involving all aspects of the educational service, which will foster, facilitate and support the activity of teaching. Such effective teamwork requires an appropriate ethos and infrastructure, both at a micro-level (in terms of the school's internal organisational and managerial practices) and at a macro-level (in terms of the partnership between teachers, parents, the LEA and the DES). Great strides have been made over the last decade in increasing the quality of learning experiences offered to pupils. If effective teamwork can be established and maintained in the face of the challenges which now need to be met, then such progress will continue. Therein lies the major challenge and hope facing effective teaching for the future.

10 Conclusions

Having completed our analysis of effective teaching, what conclusions can we draw? First, that in discussing effective teaching, we need to be clear about what type of educational outcomes the teacher is trying to foster, and how far the learning experience set up to achieve these outcomes takes account of the context for that learning experience. Setting up an effective learning experience to foster recall of a poem for eight-year-olds may be very different in kind from setting up one to foster hypothesis forming in a science lesson for 15-year-olds.

Our second conclusion is that a consideration of the psychological basis of pupil learning provides a very helpful focal point in order to explore the effectiveness of a learning experience. In essence, it draws attention to the importance of eliciting and maintaining the pupil's *attentiveness* (ensuring that the pupil is attending to the learning experience); of sustaining the pupil's *receptiveness* (making sure that the pupil is motivated and willing to learn and respond to the experience), and of achieving *appropriateness* (setting up an experience that is appropriate for the desired outcomes). Consideration of these three aspects of pupil learning forces one to see the learning experience from the pupil's perspective in exploring how to maximise its likely effectiveness.

Third, there are many different types of learning experiences, and there is now a recognition of the importance of making greater use of those experiences which involve pupils being more actively involved and having greater control. In part, this is a reflection of the greater emphasis now placed on those skills which are fostered in pupils when involved in more active learning experiences (such as developing communication skills, and the skills involved in setting up learning tasks and organising one's own work or collaborating with others).

Fourth, despite the complexity of teaching (when one takes account of the nature of pupil learning, the different types of learning activities, and the range of pupil differences) an agenda of important teaching qualities can be drawn up. These qualities, and the related division of teaching tasks need to be considered and discussed. Doing so will enable us to separate out the holistic and complex nature of teaching into its constituent elements, and to consider the ways in which effective teaching can be fostered and maintained.

Fifth, that effective teaching is bound up with (rather than separate from) sound relationships with pupils, which includes the strategies used to minimise and deal with pupil misbehaviour. More than any other, the notion of mutual respect and rapport between teacher and pupils serves to illustrate the important interplay between the cognitive and affective aspects of learning experiences.

In fostering effective teaching in schools there is a need to recognise the challenges now facing teachers. Without doubt the last decade has witnessed a marked shift in emphasis regarding the types of learning experiences offered and of educational outcomes being encouraged. Such a shift is likely to continue and even accelerate in the wake of current developments and re-evaluation of educational priorities. Such a period of rapid change, however, requires proper resources and support for teachers. This involves the necessary physical resources in terms of equipment and materials and the necessary education and training through in-service courses and support activities. However, more than these, it requires time; the time for teachers to engage in the necessary planning and preparation, including collaboration with colleagues, and the time for reflection and appraisal concerning the development in hand. This may mean having to create an infra-structure within the school system which will enable such time to be made available.

Effective teaching also requires teacher commitment towards being effective. All professionals who do their work well have a commitment towards doing so, and take a personal pride in the quality of their work. This degree of commitment tends to call for an effort over and above that strictly required by the call of duty. To foster such commitment in schools, two conditions need to be met. First, teachers need to feel that their work is worthwhile and that it is respected, valued and appreciated. by the school itself (experienced through feedback from others such as the headteacher or head of department) as well as by the community as a whole (as manifested by the attitudes of parents, the DES, and the media towards teachers). Second, teachers need to feel part of a professional community in which the quality of their work is allied to the support necessary for professional development and enhancement. While many teachers already possess levels of commitment above and beyond the call of duty, if these two conditions can be more fully met, it would make a significant contribution to fostering more effective teaching.

Finally, the challenges and developments involving schools, make this a very exciting time to be a teacher. Many of these changes involve long overdue steps towards increasing the educational benefits to pupils of learning experiences which are educative in the most worthwhile and broadest sense; they aim at the development of autonomous learners who value and can apply their education in their adult lives. If all those concerned with education (pupils, teachers, parents, the LEA and the DES) can establish a mutually supportive sense of teamwork and cooperation, the learning experiences which we set up for pupils will truly live up to the name of education.

Bibliography

Aitkin, M., Bennett, S. N. and Hesketh, J. (1981) 'Teaching styles and pupil progress: a re-analysis' *British Journal of Educational Psychology*, 51, 170–186.

Allen, V. L. (ed.) (1976) *Children as Teachers: Theory and Research on Tutoring* New York: Academic Press.

AMMA (1985) *Appraisal: Trick or Treat?* (An AMMA discussion document). London: Assistant Masters and Mistresses Association.

Anderson, L. M., Evertson, C. M. and Emmer, E. T. (1980) 'Dimensions in classroom management derived from recent research' *Journal of Curriculum Studies*, 12, 343–356.

Anderson, L. W. (ed.) (1984) *Time and School Learning* London: Croom Helm.

Anderson, L. W. and Scott, C. C. (1978) 'The relationship among teaching methods, student characteristics, and student involvement in learning' *Journal of Teacher Education*, 29(3), 52–57.

Archer, J. and Lloyd, B. (1982) *Sex and Gender* Harmondsworth: Penguin.

Ausubel, D. P. (1968) *Educational Psychology: A Cognitive View* New York: Holt, Rinehart and Winston.

Bailey, B. and Lienard, B. (1984) *Making Numbers Make Sense* (A set of six computer programs) London: Hodder and Stoughton.

Baldwin, J. and Wells, H. (eds) (1979, 1980, 1981) *Active Tutorial Work, Books 1 to 5* (first year to fifth year) Oxford: Blackwell.

Ball, S. J. (1980) 'Initial encounters in the classroom and the process of establishment' In Woods, P. (ed.) *Pupil Strategies* London: Croom Helm.

Ball, S. J. (1981) *Beachside Comprehensive* Cambridge: Cambridge University Press.

Ball, S. J. (ed.) (1984) *Comprehensive Schooling: A Reader* Lewes: Falmer Press.

Barnes, D. (1969) 'Language in the secondary classroom' In Barnes, D., Britton, J., Rosen, H. and the LATE (eds) *Language, the Learner and the School* Harmondsworth: Penguin.

Barnes, D. (1976) *From Communication to Curriculum* Harmondsworth: Penguin.

Barnes, D., Britton, J., Rosen, H. and the LATE (eds) (1969) *Language, the Learner and the School* Harmondsworth: Penguin.

Barnes, D. and Todd, F. (1977) *Communication and Learning in Small Groups* London: Routledge and Kegan Paul.

Beaumont, J. R. and Williams, S. W. (1983) *Project Work in the Geography Curriculum* London: Croom Helm.

Bell, A. W., Costello, J. and Küchemann, D. (1983) *A Review of Research in Mathematical Education, Part A: Research on Learning and Teaching* Windsor: NFER-Nelson.

Bennett, S. N. (1976) *Teaching Styles and Pupil Progress* London: Open Books.

Bennett, S. N. (1978) 'Recent research on teaching: a dream, a belief, and a model' *British Journal of Educational Psychology*, 48, 127–147.

Bennett, S. N., Desforges, C., Cockburn, A. and Wilkinson, B. (1984) *The Quality of Pupil Learning Experiences* London: Lawrence Erlbaum Associates.

Berlyne, D. E. (1960) *Conflict, Arousal and Curiosity* New York: McGraw-Hill.

Bernstein, B. (1970) A critique of the concept of 'compensatory education'. In Rubinstein, D. and Stonemen, C. (eds) *Education for Democracy* Harmondsworth: Penguin.

Bernstein, B. (ed.) (1971) *Class, Codes and Control, Volume 1: Theoretical Studies towards a Sociology of Language* London: Routledge and Kegan Paul.

Best, R., Jarvis, C. and Ribbins, P. (eds) (1980) *Perspectives on Pastoral Care* London: Heinemann.

Bird, C. (1980) 'Deviant labelling in school: the pupils' perspective' In Woods, P. (ed.) *Pupil Strategies* London: Croom Helm.

Bloom, B. S., Engelhart, M., Furst, E., Hill, W. and Krathwohl, D. (1956) *Taxonomy of Educational Objectives: the Classification of Educational Goals, Handbook 1: Cognitive Domain* New York: Longmans Green.

Broadfoot, P. (ed.) (1984) *Selection, Certification and Control* Lewes: Falmer Press.

Brown, G. (1983) 'The development of thinking' In Wheldall, K. and Riding, R. (eds) *Psychological Aspects of Learning and Teaching* London: Croom Helm.

Brown, G. A. and Armstrong, S. (1984) 'Explaining and explanations' In Wragg, E. C. (ed.) *Classroom Teaching Skills* London: Croom Helm.

Brown, G. A. and Edmondson, R. (1984) 'Asking questions' In Wragg, E. C. (ed.) *Classroom Teaching Skills* London: Croom Helm.

Brown, J. M. and Armstrong, R. (1982) 'The structure of pupils' worries during transition from junior to secondary school' *British Educational Research Journal*, 8, 123–131.

Bruner, J. S. (1960) *The Process of Education* Cambridge, Mass: Harvard University Press.

Bruner, J. S. (1966) *Toward a Theory of Instruction* Cambridge, Mass: Harvard University Press.

Bryant, P. E. (1974) *Perception and Understanding in Young Children* London: Methuen.

Buckby, M., Bull, P., Fletcher, R., Green, P., Page, B. and Roger, D. (1981) *Graded Objectives and Tests for Modern Languages: An Evaluation*. London: Schools Council.

Buckley, J. (1980) 'The care of learning: some implications for school organisation' In Best, R., Jarvis, C. and Ribbins, P. (eds) *Perspectives on Pastoral Care* London: Heinemann.

Bullock Report (1975) *A Language for Life* London: HMSO.

Bunnell, S. and Stephens, E. (1984) 'Teacher appraisal: a democratic approach' *School Organization*, 4, 291–302.

Burgess, T. (ed.) (1986) *Education for Capability* Windsor: NFER-Nelson.

Burns, R. B. (1982) *Self-Concept Development and Education* London: Holt, Rinehart and Winston.

Calderhead, J. (1984) *Teachers' Classroom Decision-Making* London: Holt, Rinehart and Winston.

Cattell, R. B. (1931) 'The assessment of teaching ability' *British Journal of Educational Psychology*, 1, 48–72.

Centra, J. A. and Potter, D. A. (1980) 'School and teacher effects: an interrelational model' *Review of Educational Research*, 50, 273–291.

Chapman, B. L. M. (1979) 'Schools do make a difference' *British Educational Research Journal*, 5, 115–124.

Chazan, M. and Williams, P. (1978) *Deprivation and the Infant School* Oxford: Blackwell.

Child, D. (1986) *Applications of Psychology for the Teacher* London: Holt, Rinehart and Winston.

Clark, M. M. (1983) 'Language, communication and learning in the classroom' In Wheldall, K. and Riding, R. (eds) *Psychological Aspects of Learning and Teaching* London: Croom Helm.

Claxton, G. (1985) 'Experiential learning and education' In Entwistle, N. (ed.) *New Directions in Educational Psychology 1: Learning and Teaching* Lewes: Falmer Press.

Cockcroft Report (1982) *Mathematics Counts* London: HMSO.

Cohen, L. and Manion, L. (1981) *Perspectives on Classrooms and Schools* London: Holt, Rinehart and Winston.

Corno, L. (1979) 'Classroom instruction and the matter of time' In Duke, D. L. (ed.) *Classroom Management* (78th yearbook of the National Society for the Study of Education) Chicago: NSSE.

Craft, M., Raynor, J. and Cohen, L. (eds) (1980) *Linking Home and School: A New Review* (3rd edition) London: Harper and Row.

CSCS (1984) *TVEI: An Observer's Guide* (Broadsheet No 4) Centre for the Study of Comprehensive Schools, University of York, York.

CSCS (1985) *Helping Firms to Work with Schools* (Broadsheet No 8) York: CSCS.

CSCS (1986) *Education for Capability* (Broadsheet No 9) York: CSCS.

Cuttance, P. (1980) 'Do schools consistently influence the performance of their students?' *Educational Review*, 32, 267–280.

Davie, R. (1979) 'The home and the school' In Coleman, J. (ed.) *The School Years* London: Methuen.

Davies, B. and Evans, J. (1984) 'Mixed ability and the comprehensive school' In Ball, S. J. (ed.) *Comprehensive Schooling: A Reader* Lewes: Falmer Press.

Davies, L. (1984) 'Gender and comprehensive schooling' In Ball, S. J. (ed.) *Comprehensive Schooling: A Reader* Lewes: Falmer Press.

de Bono, E. (1976) *Teaching Thinking* Harmondsworth: Penguin.

de Bono, E. (1982) *de Bono's Thinking Course* London: British Broadcasting Corporation (BBC).

Deem, R. (ed.) (1984) *Co-education Reconsidered* Milton Keynes: Open University Press.

Demaine, J. (1980) 'Compensatory education and social policy' In Craft, M., Raynor, J. and Cohen, L. (eds) *Linking Home and School: A New Review* (3rd edition) London: Harper and Row.

Denscombe, M. (1980) 'Keeping 'em quiet: the significance of noise for the practical activity of teaching' In Woods, P. (ed.) *Teacher Strategies* London: Croom Helm.

Denscombe, M. (1984) 'Control, controversy and the comprehensive school' In Ball, S. J. (ed.) *Comprehensive Schooling: A Reader* Lewes: Falmer Press.

Denton, C. and Postlethwaite, K. (1985) *Able Children: Identifying them in the Classroom* Windsor: NFER-Nelson.

DES (1977) *Educating our Children: Four Subjects for Debate* London: DES.

DES (1983) *Teaching Quality* (Government White Paper, cmnd no. 8836) London: HMSO.

DES (1985a) *Science 5–16: A Statement of Policy* London: HMSO.

DES (1985b) *Better Schools* (Government White Paper, cmnd no. 9469) London: HMSO.

DES (1985c) *Quality in Schools: Evaluation and Appraisal* London: HMSO.

DES (1985d) *General Certificate of Secondary Education: A General Introduction* London: HMSO.

Dickson, L., Brown, M. and Gibson, O. (1984) *Children Learning Mathematics* London: Holt, Rinehart and Winston.

Docking, J. W. (1980) *Control and Discipline in Schools* London: Harper and Row.

Donaldson, M. (1978) *Children's Minds* London: Fontana.

Doyle, W. (1983) 'Academic work' *Review of Educational Research*, 53, 159–199.

Doyle, W. (1984) 'How order is achieved in classrooms: an interim report' *Journal of Curriculum Studies*, 16, 259–277.

Driver, R. (1983) *The Pupil as Scientist?* Milton Keynes: Open University Press.

Dulay, H., Burt, M. and Krashen, S. (1982) *Language Two* New York: Oxford University Press.

Dunham, J. (1984) *Stress in Teaching* London: Croom Helm.

Eggleston, J. F., Galton, M. J. and Jones, M. E. (1976) *Processes and Products of Science Teaching* London: Macmillan.

Elliot, J. and Adelman, C. (1975) 'Teacher education for curriculum reform: an interim report on the work of the Ford Teaching Project' *British Journal of Teacher Education* 1, 105–114.

Entwistle, N. (1981) *Styles of Learning and Teaching* Chichester: Wiley.

Everard, K. B. (1984) *Management in Comprehensive Schools – What can be Learned from Industry?* (2nd edition) Centre for the Study of Comprehensive Schools, University of York.

Everard, K. B. (1986) 'Staff appraisal: lessons from industry' *Combe Lodge Reports*, 18, 393–401.

Evertson, C. M. and Emmer, E. T. (1982) 'Effective management at the beginning of the school year in junior high classes' *Journal of Educational Psychology*, 74, 485–498.

Fitz-Gibbon, C. T. and Clark, K. S. (1982) 'Time variables in classroom research: a study of eight urban secondary school mathematics classes.' *British Journal of Educational Psychology*, 52, 301–316.

Floyd, A. (ed.) (1979) *Cognitive Development in the School Years* London: Croom Helm.

Fontana, D. (1981) 'Educational guidance and counselling' In Fontana, D. (ed.) *Psychology for Teachers* London: British Psychological Society and Macmillan.

Fontana, D. (1985) *Classroom Control* London: British Psychological Society and Methuen.

Foxman, D., Joffe, L. and Ruddock, G. (1984) 'Problem solving: the APU approach' *Mathematics in School*, 13(3), 28–32.

Freiberg, H. J. (1983) 'Consistency: the key to classroom management' *Journal of Education for Teaching*, 9, 1–15.

Fyfe, R. and Mitchell, E. (1985) *Reading Strategies and their Assessment* Windsor: NFER-Nelson.

Gagné, R. M. (1985) *The Conditions of Learning and Theory of Instruction* (4th edition) New York: Holt, Rinehart and Winston.

Galloway, D. (1985) *Schools, Pupils and Special Educational Needs* London: Croom Helm.

Galloway, D., Ball, T., Blomfield, D. and Seyd, R. (1982) *Schools and Disruptive Pupils* London: Longman.

Gammage, P. (1982) *Children and Schooling: Issues in Childhood Socialisation* London: George Allen and Unwin.

Good, T. L. and Brophy, J. E. (1980) *Educational Psychology:*

A Realistic Approach (2nd edition) New York: Holt, Rinehart and Winston.

Good, T. L., Ebmeier, H. and Beckerman, T. (1978) 'Teaching mathematics in high and low SES classrooms: an empirical comparison' *Journal of Teacher Education*, 29(5), 85–90.

Goodlad, S. (1979) *Learning by Teaching: An Introduction to Tutoring* London: Community Service Volunteers.

Grace, G. (1984) 'Headteachers' judgements of teacher competence: principles and procedures in ten inner-city schools'. In Broadfoot, P. (ed.) *Selection, Certification and Control* Lewes: Falmer Press.

Gray, J. (1981) 'School effectiveness research: key issues' *Educational Research*, 24, 49–54.

Gray, J. and Satterly, D. (1981) 'Formal or informal? A reassessment of the British evidence' *British Journal of Educational Psychology*, 51, 187–196.

Gruber, H. E. and Vonèche, J. J. (ed.) (1977) *The Essential Piaget* London: Routledge and Kegan Paul.

Gulliford, R. (1985) *Teaching Children with Learning Difficulties* Windsor: NFER-Nelson.

Gunning, S., Gunning, D. and Wilson, J. (1981) *Topic Teaching in the Primary School* London: Croom Helm.

Haertel, G. D., Walberg, H. J. and Weinstein, T. (1983) 'Psychological models of educational performance: a theoretical synthesis of constructs' *Review of Educational Research*, 53, 75–91.

Hallam, R. (1969) 'Piaget and the teaching of history' *Educational Research*, 12, 3–12.

Hamblin, D. H. (1981) *Teaching Study Skills* Oxford: Blackwell.

Hargreaves, D. H. (1967) *Social Relations in a Secondary School* London: Routledge and Kegan Paul.

Hargreaves, D. H. (1975) *Interpersonal Relations and Education* (student edition) London: Routledge and Kegan Paul.

Hargreaves, D. H. (1982) *The Challenge for the Comprehensive School: Culture, Curriculum and Community* London: Routledge and Kegan Paul.

Hargreaves, D. H. (1984) 'Teachers' questions: open, closed and half-open' *Educational Research*, 26, 46–51.

Hargreaves Report (1984) *Improving Secondary Schools* London: ILEA.

Harrop, A. and McCann, C. (1983) 'Behaviour modification and reading attainment in the comprehensive school' *Educational Research* 25, 191–195.

Hart, K. (ed.) (1981) *Children's Understanding of Mathematics 11–16.* London: Murray.

Harter, S. (1981) 'A new self-report scale of instrinsic versus extrinsic orientation in the classroom: motivational and informational components *Developmental Psychology*, 17, 300–312.

Hartley, R. (1985) 'Using the computer for learning and teaching' In Entwistle, N. (ed.) *New Directions in Educational Psychology 1: Learning and Teaching* Lewes: Falmer Press.

Heywood, J. (1982) *Pitfalls and Planning in Student Teaching* London: Kogan Page.

HMI (1978) *Primary Education in England: A Survey by HM Inspectors of Schools* London: HMSO.

HMI (1979) *Aspects of Secondary Education in England: A Survey by HM Inspectors of Schools* London: HMSO.

HMI (1980) *A View of the Curriculum* (HMI Series: Matters for Discussion, no. 11) London: HMSO.

HMI (1982) *The New Teacher in School* (HMI Series: Matters for Discussion, no. 15) London: HMSO.

HMI (1984) *Education Observed 2: A Review of Published Reports by HM Inspectors on Primary Schools and 11–16 and 12–16 Comprehensive Schools* London: DES.

HMI (1985a) *The Curriculum from 5 to 16* (HMI Series: Curriculum Matters, no. 2) London: HMSO.

HMI (1985b) *Education Observed 3: Good Teachers* London: DES.

Holmes, R. H. (1984) *The Experience of Work: An Industrial Simulation* Report for the Diploma in Applied Educational Studies, University of York.

Holt, J. (1969) *How Children Fail* Harmondsworth: Penguin.

Hopson, B. and Scally, M. (1981) *Lifeskills Teaching* London: McGraw-Hill.

Howarth, C. I. and Gillham, W. E. C. (eds) (1981) *The Structure of Psychology* London: George Allen and Unwin.

Howe, M. J. A. (1984) *A Teachers' Guide to the Psychology of Learning* Oxford: Blackwell.

Hull, R. (1985) *The Language Gap: How Classroom Dialogue Fails.* London: Methuen.

ILEA (1977) *Keeping the School under Review* London: ILEA.

James, C. R. and Newman, J. C. (1985) 'Staff appraisal schemes in comprehensive schools: a regional survey of current practice in the South Midlands and the South West of England' *Educational Management and Administration*, 13, 155–164.

Jamieson, I. (ed.) (1985) *Industry in Education* London: Longman.

Jeffcoate, R. (1984) *Ethnic Minorities and Education* London: Harper and Row.

Jersild, A. T. (1940) 'Characteristics of teachers who are "liked best" and "disliked most"' *Journal of Experimental Education*, 9, 139–151.

Kent, D. (1979) 'More about the processes through which mathematics is lost' *Educational Research*, 22, 22–31.

Kerry, T. (1982) *Effective Questioning: A Teaching Skills Workbook* London: Macmillan.

Kerry, T. (1984) 'Analysing the cognitive demand made by classroom tasks in mixed-ability classes' In Wragg, E. C. (ed.) *Classroom Teaching Skills* London: Croom Helm.

Kerry, T. and Sands, M. K. (1984) 'Classroom organisation and learning' in Wragg, E. C. (ed.) *Classroom Teaching Skills* London: Croom Helm.

Kirby, J. R. (ed.) (1984) *Cognitive Strategies and Educational Performance* London: Academic Press.

Klauer, K. J. (1985) 'Framework for a theory of teaching' *Teaching and Teacher Education*, 1, 5–17.

Kounin, J. S. (1970) *Discipline and Group Management in Classrooms* New York: Holt, Rinehart and Winston.

Kyriacou, C. (1980a) 'Sources of stress among British teachers: the contribution of job factors and personality factors' In Cooper, C. L. and Marshall, J. (eds) *White Collar and Professional Stress* Chichester: Wiley.

Kyriacou, C. (1980b) 'Occupational stress among schoolteachers: a research report' *CORE*, 4, No. 3.

Kyriacou, C. (1980c) 'Stress, health and schoolteachers: a comparison with other professions' *Cambridge Journal of Education*, 10, 154–159.

Kyriacou, C. (1980d) 'Coping actions and occupational stress among schoolteachers' *Research in Education*, No. 24, 57–61.

Kyriacou, C. (1981) 'Social support and occupational stress among schoolteachers *Educational Studies*, 7, 55–60.

Kyriacou, C. (1982) 'Heads of departments' perceptions of the effective teacher at O-level' *CORE*, 6, no. 3.

Kyriacou, C. (1983) 'Research on teacher effectiveness in British secondary schools' *British Educational Research Journal*, 9, 71–80.

Kyriacou, C. (1985) 'Conceptualising research on effective teaching *British Journal of Educational Psychology*, 55, 148–155.

Kyriacou, C. (1986a) 'Sixth-formers' perceptions of the effective teacher of mathematics at 'O' level, *British Educational Research Journal*, 12, 137–144.

Kyriacou, C. (1986b) 'Teacher stress and burnout' Invited address delivered at the first international meeting on psychological teacher education held at the University of Minho, Braga, Portugal.

Kyriacou, C. and McKelvey, J. (1985a) 'An exploration of individual differences in "effective" teaching' *Educational Review*, 37, 13–17.

Kyriacou, C. and McKelvey, J. (1985b) 'Individual differences in "effective" teaching behaviour among secondary school teachers' (ESRC research grant report, grant ref: HR 8791). *CORE*, 9, no. 1.

Kyriacou, C. and Newson, G. (1982) 'Teacher effectiveness: a consideration of research problems' *Educational Review*, 34, 3–12.

Kyriacou, C. and Pratt, J. (1985) 'Teacher stress and psychoneurotic symptoms' *British Journal of Educational Psychology*, 55, 61–64.

Kyriacou, C. and Sutcliffe, J. (1978a) 'Teacher stress: prevalence, sources and symptoms' *British Journal of Educational Psychology*, 48, 159–167

Kyriacou, C. and Sutcliffe, J. (1978b) 'A model of teacher stress' *Educational Studies*, 4, 1–6.

Lang, P. and Marland, M. (eds) (1985) *New Directions in Pastoral Care* Oxford: Blackwell.

Laslett, R. and Smith, C. (1984) *Effective Classroom Management* London: Croom Helm.

Laszlo, J. I. and Bairstow, P. J. (1985) *Perceptual-Motor Behaviour Developmental Assessment and Therapy* London: Holt, Rinehart and Winston.

Law, B. (1984) *Uses and Abuses of Profiling* London: Harper and Row.

Lawrence, J., Steed, D. and Young, P. (1984) *Disruptive Children Disruptive Schools?* London: Croom Helm.

Lewis, R. and Lovegrove, M. N. (1984) 'Teachers' classroom contro procedures: are students' preferences being met?' *Journal of Education for Teaching*, 10, 97–105.

Lindsay, G. (ed.) (1983) *Problems of Adolescence in the Secondary School* London: Croom Helm.

Lines, P. M. (1985) 'Testing the teacher: are there legal pitfalls?' *Phi Delta Kappan*, 66, 618–622.

Lovell, K. (1979) 'Some aspects of the work of Piaget in perspective' In Floyd, A. (ed.) *Cognitive Development in the School Years*. London: Croom Helm.

Maccoby, E. E. (1980) *Social Development: Psychological Growth and the Parent–Child Relationship* New York: Harcourt Brace Jovanovich.

Marland, M. (1975) *The Craft of the Classroom: A Survival Guide*. London: Heinemann.

Marland, M. (ed.) (1977) *Language Across the Curriculum* London: Heinemann.

Marsh, P., Rosser, E. and Harré, R. (1978) *The Rules of Disorder* London: Routledge and Kegan Paul.

Maslow, A. H. (1968) 'Some educational implications of the humanistic psychologies' *Harvard Educational Review*, 38, 685–696.

Maslow, A. H. (1970) *Motivation and Personality* (2nd edition) New York: Harper and Row.

McDonough, S. H. (1981) *Psychology in Foreign Language Teaching* London: George Allen and Unwin.

McKelvey, J. and Kyriacou, C. (1985) 'Research on pupils as teacher evaluators' *Educational Studies*, 11, 25–31.

McNamara, D. R. (1980) 'The outsider's arrogance: the failure of participant observers to understand classroom events' *British Educational Research Journal*, 6, 113–125.

McNamara, D. R. (1981) 'Teaching skill: the question of questioning' *Educational Research*, 23, 104–109.

McNamara, D. R. (1986) 'The personal qualities of the teacher and educational policy: a critique' *British Educational Research Journal*, 12, 29–36.

Measor, L. and Woods, P. (1984) *Changing Schools* Milton Keynes: Open University Press.

Merrett, F. E. (1981) 'Studies in behaviour modification in British educational settings' *Educational Psychology*, 1, 13–38.

Merrett, F. E. and Blundell, D. (1982) 'Self-recording as a means of improving classroom behaviour in the secondary school' *Educational Psychology*, 2, 147–157.

Merrett, F. E. and Wheldall, K. (1978) 'Playing the game: a behavioural approach to classroom management in the junior school' *Educational Review*, 30, 41–50.

Metcalfe, C. K. (1985) 'Appraising appraisal: an examination of some of the issues involved in staff appraisal in secondary schools' *British Journal of In-Service Education*, 11, 91–95.

Moore, M. and Crisp, J. (1984) *Developing Communication Skills through the Medium of a School Based Business* (A CSCS project report). Centre for the Study of Comprehensive Schools, University of York.

Morgan, M. and Foot, H. C. (1985) 'The understanding of learning difficulties: implications for peer-tutoring' *Education Section Review* (British Psychological Society), 9, 7–11.

Mortimore, J. and Blackstone, T. (1982) *Disadvantage and Education* London: Heinemann.

Mortimore, P., Davies, J., West, A. and Varlaam, A. (1984) *Behaviour Problems in Schools: An Evaluation of Support Centres* London: Croom Helm.

MSC (1983) *TVEI* London: Manpower Services Commission.

Murnane, R. J. and Cohen, D. K. (1986) 'Merit pay and the evaluation problem: why most merit pay plans fail and a few survive' *Harvard Educational Review*, 56, 1–17.

Newson, J. and Newson, E. (1977) *Perspectives on School at Seven Years Old* London: George Allen and Unwin.

Nisbet, J. and Watt, J. (1984) *Educational Disadvantage: Ten Years On* Edinburgh: HMSO.

Nixon, J. (ed.) (1981) *A Teachers' Guide to Action Research* London: Grant McIntyre.

Norris, R. (1975) 'An examination of schedules of criteria related to teacher competence' *British Journal of Teacher Education*, 1, 87–95.

NUT (undated: c. 1980) *Teaching Practice* London: National Union of Teachers.

NUT (1985) *Teacher Appraisal and Teaching Quality* (An NUT policy statement) London: National Union of Teachers.

O'Hagan, F. J. and Edmunds, G. (1982) 'Pupils' attitudes towards teachers' strategies for controlling disruptive behaviour' *British Journal of Educational Psychology*, 52, 331–340.

Partington, J. (1981) 'Teachers' strategies in the foreign language classroom' *British Educational Research Journal*, 7, 71–78.

Pavlov, I. P. (1927) *Conditioned Reflexes* New York: Oxford University Press.

Peaker, G. (1986) 'Teacher management and appraisal in two school systems in the Southern USA' *Journal of Education for Teaching*, 12, 77–83.

Perrott, E. (1982) *Effective Teaching: A Practical Guide to Improving your Teaching* London: Longman.

Peterson, P. L. and Walberg, H. J. (eds) (1979) *Research on Teaching* Berkeley: McCutchan.

Piaget, J. (1972) *Psychology and Epistemology* Harmondsworth: Penguin.

Piaget, J. (1976) 'Piaget's theory' In Neubauer, P. B. (ed.) *The Process of Child Development* New York: Meridian.

Piaget, J. and Inhelder, B. (1969) *The Psychology of the Child* London: Routledge and Kegan Paul.

Pik, R. (1981) 'Confrontation situations and teacher support systems' In Gillham, B. (ed.) *Problem Behaviour in the Secondary School* London: Croom Helm.

Plowden Report (1967) *Children and their Primary Schools, Volume 1: Report* London: HMSO.

Pollard, A. (1980) 'Teacher interests and changing situations of survival threat in primary school classrooms' In Woods, P. (ed.) *Teacher Strategies* London: Croom Helm.

Povey, R. M. (1975) 'A comparison of three methods of evaluating teaching performance in a college of education' *British Journal of Educational Psychology*, 45, 279–285.

Povey, R. M. (ed.) (1980) *Educating the Gifted Child* London: Harper and Row.

Pratt, J. (1978) 'Perceived stress among teachers: the effects of age and background of children taught' *Educational Review*, 30, 3–14.

Reynolds, D. (ed.) (1985) *Studying School Effectiveness* Lewes: Falmer Press.

Riding, R. J. (1983) 'Adapting instruction for the learner' In Wheldall, K. and Riding, R. (eds) *Psychological Aspects of Learning and Teaching* London: Croom Helm.

Roberts, K. (1980) 'Schools, parents and social class' In Craft, M., Raynor, J. and Cohen, L. (eds) *Linking Home and School: A New Review* (3rd edition) London: Harper and Row.

Robertson, J. (1981) *Effective Classroom Control* London: Hodder and Stoughton.

Rogers, C. (1982) *A Social Psychology of Schooling* London: Routledge and Kegan Paul.

Rogers, C. R. (1983) *Freedom to Learn for the 80s* Columbus, Ohio: Merrill.

Rosenshine, B. (1971) *Teaching Behaviours and Student Achievement* Slough: NFER.

Rosenthal, R. and Jacobson, L. (1968) *Pygmalion in the Classroom* New York: Holt, Rinehart and Winston.

RSA (1985) *Education and Industry* (A series of folders for Industry Year 1986) London: Royal Society of Arts.

Rutter, M. (1978) 'Family, area and school influences in the genesis of conduct disorders' In Hersov, L. A., Berger, M. and Shaffer, D. (eds) *Aggression and Anti-social Behaviour in Childhood and Adolescence* Oxford: Pergamon.

Rutter, M., Maughan, B., Mortimore, P. and Ouston, J. (1979) *Fifteen Thousand Hours: Secondary Schools and their Effects on Children* London: Open Books.

Ryan, D. W. and Butler, L. F. (1982) Effectiveness of teaching: the Canadian experience *Studies in Educational Evaluation, 7, 247–262.*

Salmon, P. and Claire, H. (1984) *Classroom Collaboration* London: Routledge and Kegan Paul.

Salzberger-Wittenberg, I., Henry, G. and Osborne, E. (1983) *The Emotional Experience of Learning and Teaching* London: Routledge and Kegan Paul.

Saunders, M. (1979) *Class Control and Behaviour Problems* London: McGraw-Hill.

Shaw, B. (1981) *Educational Practice and Sociology* Oxford: Martin Robertson.

Shayer, M. (1978) 'The analysis of science curricula for Piagetian level of demand' *Studies in Science Education, 5, 115–130.*

Shayer, M. and Wylam, H. (1978) 'The distribution of Piagetian stages of thinking in British middle and secondary school children II: 14–16 year olds and sex differentials' *British Journal of Educational Psychology, 48, 62–70.*

Shemilt, D. (1980) *History 13–16: Evaluation Study* Edinburgh: Holmes McDougall.

Skinner, B. F. (1968) *The Technology of Teaching* New York: Appleton Century Crofts.

Start, K. B. and Laundy, S. (1973) Successful teachers in the secondary school *Research in Education, No. 9, 1–15.*

Steedman, J. (1980) *Progress in Secondary Schools* London: National Children's Bureau.

Stenning, W. I. and Stenning, R. (1984) 'The assessment of teacher's performance: some practical considerations' *School Organisation and Management Abstracts, 3, 77–90.*

Stones, E. (1979) *Psychopedagogy: Psychological Theory and the Practice of Teaching* London: Methuen.

Stones, E. and Morris, S. (eds) (1972) *Teaching Practice: Problems and Perspectives* London: Methuen.

Stott, D. (1982) *Helping the Maladjusted Child* Milton Keynes: Open University Press.

Strivens, J. (1985) 'School climate: a review of a problematic concept' In Reynolds, D. (ed.) *Studying School Effectiveness* Lewes: Falmer Press.

Stubbs, M. (1983) *Language, Schools and Classrooms* (2nd edition London: Methuen.

Suffolk Education Department (1985) *Those Having Torches . . . Teacher Appraisal: A Study* Ipswich: Suffolk Education Department.

Swann Report (1985) *Education for All* London: HMSO.

Tansley, P. and Panckhurst, J. (1981) *Children with Specific Learning Difficulties* Windsor: NFER-Nelson.

Taylor, P. H. (1962) 'Children's evaluations of the characteristics of the good teacher' *British Journal of Educational Psychology, 32, 258–266.*

Thomas Report (1985) *Improving Primary Schools* London: ILEA.

Tomlinson, P. (1981) *Understanding Teaching: Interactive Educationa. Psychology* London: McGraw-Hill.

Topping, K. and Wolfendale, S. (ed.) (1986) *Parental Involvement in Children's Reading* London: Croom Helm.

Torrance, H. (1986) 'Expanding school-based assessment: issues, problems and future possibilities' *Research Papers in Education, 1, 48–59.*

Turner, G. (1984) 'Assessment in the comprehensive school: what criteria count?' In Broadfoot, P. (ed.) *Selection, Certification and Control* Lewes: Falmer Press.

Turner, G. (1985) 'Nascent schemes for teacher appraisal' *School Organization, 5, 155–161.*

Turner, G. and Clift, P. (1985) *A First Review and Register of School and College Based Teacher Appraisal Schemes* Milton Keynes: Open University.

Wakefield, A. (1986) *School as a Learning Community: The Challenge of OCEA* (A CSCS project report) Centre for the Study of Comprehensive Schools, University of York.

Walker, G. (1983) *Comprehensive Themes* Centre for the Study of Comprehensive Schools, University of York.

Wallace, B. (1983) *Teaching the Very Able Child* London: Ward Lock.

Wallace, R. G. (ed.) (1985) *Introducing Technical and Vocational Education* London: Macmillan.

Warnock Report (1978) *Special Educational Needs* London: HMSO.

Waterhouse, P. (1983) *Managing the Learning Process* London: McGraw-Hill.

Watson, F. R. (1976) *Developments in Mathematics Teaching* London: Open Books.

Webb, P. K. (1980) 'Piaget: implications for teaching' *Theory into Practice, 19, 93–97.*

Weiner, B. (1980) *Human Motivation* New York: Holt, Rinehart and Winston.

Wellington, J. J. (ed.) (1985) *Children, Computers and the Curriculum* London: Harper and Row.

Wheldall, K. (1983) 'A positive approach to classroom discipline' In Wheldall, K. and Riding, R. (eds) *Psychological Aspects of Learning and Teaching* London: Croom Helm.

Wheldall, K. and Mettem, P. (1985) 'Behavioural peer tutoring: training 6-year-old tutors to employ "pause, prompt and praise" method with 2-year-old remedial readers' *Educational Psychology*, 5, 27–44.

Whitaker, P. (1984) *World Studies and the Learning Process. World Studies Journal*, 5, No. 2.

White, R. (1959) 'Motivation reconsidered: the concept of competence' *Psychological Review*, 66, 297–333.

Whyld, J. (ed.) (1983) *Sexism in the Secondary Curriculum* London: Harper and Row.

Whyte, J. (1986) *Girls into Science and Technology* London: Routledge and Kegan Paul.

Willey, R. (1984) *Race, Equality and Schools* London: Methuen.

Williamson, D. (1980) ' "Pastoral care" or "pastoralization"?' In Best, R., Jarvis, C. and Ribbins, P. (eds) *Perspectives on Pastoral Care* London: Heinemann.

Winne, P. H. and Marx, R. W. (1977) Reconceptualizing research on teaching *Journal of Educational Psychology*, 69, 668–678.

Woodhouse, D. A., Hall, E. and Wooster, A. D. (1985) Taking control of stress in teaching *British Journal of Educational Psychology*, 55, 119–123.

Woods, P. (1979) *The Divided School* London: Routledge and Kegan Paul.

✳ Woods, P. (ed.) (1980a) *Teacher Strategies* London: Croom Helm.

✳ Woods, P. (ed.) (1980b) *Pupil Strategies* London: Croom Helm.

Wragg, E. C. (ed.) (1984) *Classroom Teaching Skills* London: Croom Helm.

Wragg, E. C. and Dooley, P. A. (1984) 'Class management during teaching practice' In Wragg, E. C. (ed.) *Classroom Teaching Skills* London: Croom Helm.

Wragg, E. C. and Wood, E. K. (1984a) 'Pupil appraisals of teaching' In Wragg, E. C. (ed.) *Classroom Teaching Skills* London: Croom Helm.

Wragg, E. C. and Wood, E. K. (1984b) 'Teachers' first encounters with their classes' In Wragg, E. C. (ed.) *Classroom Teaching Skills* London: Croom Helm.

Author Index

Subject Index